W9-AHW-036

WILLIAM G. MILLIKEN

AUTHOR'S NOTE

William and Helen Milliken cooperated in the research and writing of this biography, and have generously supplied photographs from their personal collection. They reviewed drafts of the text for factual errors. The observations and conclusions drawn about the lives and work of the Millikens are the author's own. No approval by the Millikens was sought or given for the text.

WILLIAM G. MILLIKEN

Michigan's Passionate Moderate

DAVE DEMPSEY

THE UNIVERSITY OF MICHIGAN PRESS
Ann Arbor

Copyright © 2006 by the Michigan Environmental Council
All rights reserved
Published in the United States of America by
The University of Michigan Press
Manufactured in the United States of America
⊛ Printed on acid-free paper

2009   2008   2007   2006   4   3   2   1

A CIP catalog record for this book is available from the British Library.

Library of Congress Cataloging-in-Publication Data

Dempsey, Dave, 1957–
    William G. Milliken : Michigan's passionate moderate / Dave
Dempsey.
        p.   cm.
    Includes bibliographical references and index.
    ISBN-13: 978-0-472-11545-7 (cloth : alk. paper)
    ISBN-10: 0-472-11545-6 (cloth : alk. paper)
    1. Milliken, William G., 1922–   2. Governors—Michigan—Biography.
3. Michigan—Politics and government—1951–   4. Michigan—Social policy.
5. Environmentalism—Michigan.   6. Michigan—Environmental conditions.
7. Milliken, Helen, 1922–   8. Governors' spouses—Michigan—Biography.   I. Title.

F570.25.M55D46   2006
977.4'043092—dc22   2005029462

TO JENNIFER
_____

An unparalleled teacher

FOREWORD

WHY WOULD A nonprofit environmental organization use its scarce resources to ensure that the historical record of a governor—now more than two decades into retirement—be brought to life in a frank and factual biography? The answer lies in our interest in discovering how the web of politics and cultural values determines the way societies choose to interact with their environments.

By reviewing Michigan's past through a biography of Michigan's longest-serving governor, we hope to find answers to questions that directly impact Michigan's environmental future. For instance, is a rise in environmentalism mainly a willingness to invest in long-term public needs in contrast to letting short-term private interests dominate? If so, what drives the oscillations that sometimes make Michigan a progressive leader in everything from higher education to environmental protection and at other times reflect values commonly associated with penurious conservatism? How much of this is a reflection of differences among the governors who have led Michigan or the times in which they have governed?

These are some of the knotty issues author Dave Dempsey illuminates as he takes us through the life of William G. Milliken, a man who has come to be revered across the country and, in more recent times, ignored by his party. In *William G. Milliken, Michigan's Passionate Moderate,* Dempsey has written an insightful biography that dives right into the rough-and-tumble political world in which Milliken operated. Rich with anecdotes and insights into Milliken's childhood, family, staff, and service under fire in World War II, as well as his campaigns and toughest legislative fights, Dempsey rises above the temptation to simply extol the nice-guy virtues for which Milliken is known.

Dempsey introduces us to a quiet man who does not easily give up his private thoughts even as he pursues a career that puts him under the white heat of politics. But, more than the personal story of a man born to privilege who sacrifices his yearning for privacy to his political impulses, this biography offers essential insights into the long-running battle for the soul of the Republican Party.

With a reminder of the party's nineteenth-century roots in Jackson, Michigan, Dempsey leads his readers through a quick review of the GOP's schizophrenic development. We learn it's not inconsequential that Milliken, like his father before him, identified with the Republican reformists led by President Theodore Roosevelt and Wisconsin senator Robert M. La Follette. William Milliken believes that the benefits of free market capitalism must be balanced by investments in public institutions and natural resources and restrained by some regulatory controls. This philosophy and his unapologetic defense of well-delivered government services propelled him into a lifelong battle with the right wing of his party.

While Milliken never seems to drop his reserve completely, he's not above disparaging his Republican opponents as "entrenched politicians practically married to lobbyists." Milliken, it seems, never went looking for a fight, except when he broke into politics by beating a right-wing incumbent, redefined his party's program as a freshman legislator, or defended a cherished government program or principle in countless battles against the conservative wing of his party. Readers who think the fight between Republican moderates and their party's right wing is a recent phenomenon will come away with a new perspective on an old battleground.

During the Milliken years, Michigan enjoyed advantages since lost. As a progressive state with decades of exceptional investment in its extraordinary, independent, higher education system, Milliken could tap that excellence before other states had begun to compete or catch up. He rode the national wave of social reforms and environmentalism of the 1970s to boldly place Michigan in the forefront of everything from open housing to a ban on the pesticide DDT. In addition, Milliken served before term limits precluded the building of trusting relationships across party lines, before highly funded conservative think tanks had more than three decades in which to erode public confidence in public services, and before the religious right and neoconservatives came to dominate his party.

But the good old days weren't easy, and Milliken lost his share of battles. Detroit, Grand Rapids, and Flint were already bleeding their more affluent populations to the suburbs. Prescient enough to know that sprawl posed a growing threat to both urban and rural Michigan, Milliken recognized that his failure to pass land use reform legislation would cost the state dearly in decades to come. Today that loss means that older communities are fighting decay while productive farmland is being converted to big-box stores, suburban estates, and see-through commercial buildings. The fact that he's still actively fighting these battles reflects Milliken's love of Michigan's landscape and his bulldog capacity to hang on to an issue for half a century.

We're living today in a more competitive world. Michigan no longer controls the manufacturing capacity for the world's cars and furniture. Its largest industry has been slow to embrace essential changes. But it's not just economic loss that makes us yearn for Milliken-style leadership. Michigan needs a leader who has the ability to bring divergent sides together to work for the whole state. Since Milliken left office, Michigan has had no governor who's had the political will to stand up and unapologetically call for adequate investments in public goods. To varying degrees, we've had a quarter century of an every man for himself model, in which the political outcomes mean that cutting taxes is deemed of higher value than educational excellence and profit margins for power companies trump the protection of children from mercury poisoning.

Bill Milliken believes in the power and importance of a government that doesn't apologize for protecting the common good. That is the principal lesson of this biography and the reason why the Michigan Environmental Council is proud to be associated with this man and his story.

Lana Pollack
Michigan Environmental Council

PREFACE AND ACKNOWLEDGMENTS

I WANT TO MAKE it clear at the outset that this work is not and does not attempt to be the complete story of the lives of William and Helen Milliken. It concentrates on their impact on the public life of Michigan and the reasons for that impact, ranging from the natural and human history of the Traverse City region to their temperaments, upbringing, and self-discovery and self-expression. In an epoch of vicious, personalized politics, it is particularly important to recognize how and why Bill and Helen Milliken articulated a different approach to public life and governance.

It is critical not to idealize the Millikens. Doing so puts them behind glass and could prevent future public servants from believing they can approach public life in a similarly constructive way.

On the other hand, as I came to know the Millikens better in the course of writing this book, I also came to realize that many of their most fervent admirers and longtime associates saw in them the expression of their own finest qualities and ideals. To some extent, this means the Millikens were symbols as well as human beings. That does not diminish their characters or contributions, but it underscores the ways in which their natural civility and love of privacy helped them reflect back the best that many had to offer. In a time when we reflexively suspect the worst of many politicians, it is useful to remember an age in which the Millikens inspired many to believe the best of them.

No one, including the Millikens, can survive the expectation of perfection, and I have tried in the course of this book to pinpoint mistakes of judgment, character flaws, and other blemishes on the public records of two Michigan leaders. But I did not attempt to probe deeply into their private lives except to the extent that events in those lives influenced the public people the Millikens became.

Every author owes thanks to hundreds of helpful friends and sources. In this case, the thanks are especially abundant in light of the subject matter—for Bill and Helen Milliken have accumulated scores of thoughtful and helpful friends through the years—and the process by which the book came to be.

I want to begin by thanking Lana Pollack, president of the Michigan Environmental Council (MEC), for supporting this book from day one. While working tirelessly to make MEC a major-league environmental organization visible on the national landscape, she has also been an effective advocate for clean air and water policies, a skillful and supportive boss, a loyal and loving friend, and an invaluable critic. She keenly grasps the relationship between the story of the Millikens and the character of Michigan that MEC and so many others work to protect.

I also want to honor the memory of my late father, who worked for the former governor for 13 years. He instilled in my siblings and me an appreciation for the joys and sacrifices of public service and an understanding of the unique humaneness of the governor he served.

The Millikens are to be thanked not just for their contributions to the welfare of Michigan but also for cooperating with this project, literally throwing open their doors for the inspection of lives well lived. They were candid, reflective, wry, and willing to risk an independent judgment of their mistakes as well as their achievements in this book. They have not approved and did not attempt to censor a word of it.

Many family members, friends, and former aides responded quickly and repeatedly to requests for information and opinions about the Millikens' lives. Joyce Braithwaite-Brickley and George Weeks both provided the behind-the-scenes narrative that only two of the former governor's closest advisers and friends could and screened the manuscript for errors, exaggerations, and misinterpretations. They were unflagging in their patience with my questions and scrupulous in their honesty about the good and bad of the Milliken years. I appreciate the courtesy of William Milliken's brother and sister, John and Ruth, in meeting with me to discuss memories of a childhood spent in Traverse City. William Milliken Jr. was also forthcoming in an interview about the blessings and burdens of being a prominent politician's son.

Other Milliken associates who generously answered every question put to them—and went far beyond in explaining their work—include Charlie Greenleaf, Billie Harrison, Richard Helmbrecht, and James Phelps. Governor Jennifer M. Granholm graciously took time from her punishing schedule to offer thoughts on how the Milliken style and values affect her work. I also want to thank Jack Bails, Dennis Cawthorne, Nancy Dockter, Phyllis Dell, Peter Ellsworth, Don Gordon, Fred Grasman, Gus Harrison, Paul Hillegonds, Christine Hollister, Noble Kheder, Richard McLellan, Keith Molin, Frank Ochberg, Maurice Reizen, Bill Rustem, Craig Ruff, Tim Skubick, and Howard Tanner for taking the time to meet with me and answer numerous questions.

A number of people stepped forward to pick up the research slack for this book. Stephanie Burns was unselfish and helpful in tracking down information about the work of the Millikens. Margie Cooke provided an astonishing collection of newspaper articles and other information about the role of Helen Milliken and women's issues in the 1982 gubernatorial campaign. Special thanks to Dennis Cawthorne for reviewing the manuscript and correcting a number of factual and typographical errors.

Critical support for the book came from the Lloyd and Mabel Johnson Foundation. My wholehearted thanks to Gordon Kummer and the foundation for assuring that the story of the Millikens and their legacy could be told.

Many friends have encouraged and tolerated me over the years, and they deserve recognition, too, for birthing the book. These include Kathleen Aterno, Tom Baldini, Doug Bauer, Sharon Bothwell, Leslie Brogan, Lois Debacker, Sandy DiCesare, Patrick Diehl, Tracy Dobson, Marlene Fluharty, Libby Harris, Carol Misseldine, Lisa Reed, Derwin Rushing, Margaret Schulte, Tom Vance, Lisa Wyatt Knowlton, Louise Wirbel, and Joe VanderMeulen.

As years pass, the importance of family ties becomes more apparent to me. My mother, Barbara, brothers Jack and Tom, sister-in-law Suzzanne, niece Anna, and nephew Michael are remarkably kind and generous people, and I appreciate them deeply.

Several of the environmental organizations for which I've worked deserve note; they have enabled me to find a home and do meaningful work while exercising remarkable restraint about my frailties and providing generous support for the job of recording environmental and political history. Besides the Michigan Environmental Council, I want to acknowledge Clean Water Action, one of the nation's oldest and best environmental advocacy organizations with a strong record of mobilizing people to support clean water, and the Ecology Center, a group based in Ann Arbor that has scored enormous environmental health victories even during the hard times of the 1990s and the early twenty-first century. Those who follow us will benefit greatly from the pollution these groups have prevented and the places they have protected for all time.

During the writing of this book, one of Michigan's most formidable and unforgettable advocates and spirits, Mary Beth Doyle, tragically lost her life. In her absence, many have come to appreciate even more than before her role as a source of inspiration, insight, and strategic thinking and as a conscience for Michigan's environmental movement. Her work and great love of life continue to send ripples outward. Like many, I miss her. The spirit of public service illustrated by the lives of the Millikens is consistent with Mary Beth's belief in a more compassionate, humane, and sustainable society. In a small way, this book is a tribute to her.

CONTENTS

PROLOGUE

As WINTER SEIZED control of Michigan in December 1981, a season of cold and above-average snowfall was forecast. But more than the weather gave the season solemnity. Michigan was still struggling with its worst economic conditions since the Great Depression. The state's employment agency announced in early December that the state had suffered a 12.5 percent unemployment rate the previous month, culminating the second straight year of double-digit unemployment.[1] That was actually mildly good news; a year previously the state's unemployment rate had hit 13.5 percent. About 200,000 workers were on indefinite layoffs from manufacturing jobs, 40 percent of them in the auto industry. "So many people have been out of work for so long that the numbers of those who exhaust their state and federal unemployment benefits are actually declining," reported a Lansing newspaper.[2] On December 5, the *Detroit Free Press* ran a front-page article headlined "Job Outlook Bleak." It added that Michigan continued to lead the 10 most industrialized states in unemployment.[3] As Democratic gubernatorial candidate James Blanchard would repeatedly point out in 1982, Michigan had more unemployed workers than some states had people.

Based in the fading manufacturing city of Lansing, 90 miles northwest of Detroit, the Michigan state government was coping with declining tax revenues and increased outlays resulting from recession and unemployment. State officials projected a deficit of over $1 billion, a hefty proportion of its $4.4 billion general fund budget. Another round of steep budget cuts in everything from police patrols to welfare payments loomed. Michigan State University, located just east of the capital in East Lansing, announced that it would terminate almost 20 degree programs, among 45 being dismantled by the state's colleges and universities as aid declined.[4]

To combat the image of Michigan as a state unfriendly to business, Governor William G. Milliken spent much of the month fighting for passage of legislation reforming the state's workers' compensation system. Hoping to reduce the system's more than $1 billion annual cost to business, Milliken and Democratic legislators, who controlled the House and Senate, had an unusually bitter battle. But on December 15 and 16, lawmakers sent for the governor's signature a dozen bills that reduced benefits to employees who sustained injuries or contracted illness in the workplace.[5]

The Capitol press corps covered these stories in depth, but as the month advanced reporters squirreled away in their spartan press quarters in the Capitol obsessed about another topic. Would the 59-year-old Milliken, who had been the state's chief executive for nearly 13 years, seek a fourth full term in 1982, run for the U.S. Senate, or retire? Many of the reporters had covered Milliken's entire career as governor, and some had never covered anyone else who held the job. Having served longer as governor than Franklin Delano Roosevelt had served as president of the United States, Milliken had cast a similarly long shadow over Michigan politics, shaping the tone and content of the state's political discourse in a way no other governor of the state had done.

Usually accessible to reporters and direct in his response to their questions, Milliken kept silent on the subject of his future, which only fueled reporters' speculations.

"Milliken sure can keep a good secret," ran the headline in an article in the governor's hometown newspaper, the *Traverse City Record-Eagle*.[6] "It's really a very personal and closely held decision," George Weeks, Milliken's chief of staff, told the paper. "At this point, I can't really say who knows what about anything."

Milliken's potential rivals in the 1982 gubernatorial race had their own thoughts. "I think 13 years in that job has to take its wear and tear on the man," said Oakland County Prosecutor L. Brooks Patterson.[7] "I think he senses what I sense . . . that it's time for a change."

The even more conservative Jack Welborn, a state senator, predicted that Milliken would try for another term. "I really think I'll be running against him. And if it isn't him it's going to be [Lieutenant Governor James] Brickley and he's Milliken's clone."[8]

Early in the month, Milliken's wife Helen told *Detroit News* reporter Joanna Firestone, "Basically, he's made his decision." She added that the decision was two-thirds his and one-third hers. She declined to say what the decision was. Firestone wrote, "Many of his potential opponents and confidants, although professing to have no inside information, cautiously wager there will be a campaign in Milliken's future. The odds timidly favor a fourth bid for governor over a challenge to incumbent Democrat Donald W. Riegle Jr. for the U.S. Senate."[9]

Gannett Newspapers' Lansing bureau chief, Jerry Moskal, reported on December 17 that "a source close to the governor said Milliken would 'hang it up'" the next day. He didn't. But he pledged to make and announce his decision before Christmas.

Milliken's deliberations drew some national attention. The *Washington Post* observed, "Republican Gov. William G. Milliken of Michigan says he will announce his future plans this week and, as always, is keeping them to himself . . . For what it's worth, the Lansing press corps polled itself on Milliken's plans. The result: 11 predicted he'd run for re-election, 9 predicted retirement, 1 thought he'd run for the Senate."[10]

A local Republican official reflected the ambivalence of many in the increasingly conservative party who distrusted the longtime governor's frequent alliances with Democrats. The opposition party had largely controlled the legislature during Milliken's reign. In the eyes of the conservatives, Milliken was more liberal than Republican—though still the party's most reliable vote getter. "I would be happier with another Republican, a more conservative Republican," said Houghton County Republican chairperson Tony Pizzi. "But he is the strongest candidate we could have."[11]

When Milliken's executive assistant, Bob Berg, announced that the chief executive would make a statement about his political future on December 22, the speculation reached a crescendo. At a time when state politics was front-page news around Michigan, the fate of the governor took on a dramatic tone.

So when Milliken entered the small, cluttered news media area just outside his personal office in the Capitol accompanied by his wife,

Helen, on the morning of December 22, TV cameras, photographers, and reporters packed the room. Some of them, taking note of Helen's presence—and remembering that she had been said to yearn for a return to private life—thought they knew what was coming. "Milliken always made himself available, but I cannot recall any previous news conference that had such a feeling of electricity and anticipation," said Tim Jones, a reporter for WJR Radio in Detroit.[12]

Milliken, dressed in a dark blue three-piece suit with a tie of thin red stripes on a blue background, slender in build, his still largely dark hair carefully combed back, strode to a podium covered with a dozen microphones. He spoke clearly, with the measured tones and reasoned words that contributed to what one Capitol reporter called his "quiet, yet warm manner." Even as he delivered his verdict on another term or a Senate candidacy, reporter Chris Parks of United Press International "shuffled out quickly" to file the first story and TV reporter Tim Skubick used a phone on a desk nearby to call in the news to his station.

Milliken said:

> Nineteen eighty-one has demonstrated just how vulnerable Michigan is to economic factors beyond its control, and how vulnerable it is to the partisan conflict and confrontation that all too often allow special interests to thwart the public interest.
>
> Nineteen eighty-two can be a year of economic resurgence for Michigan. But Michigan will need two things above all else:
>
> It will need an unprecedented degree of bipartisan cooperation and achievement between Republicans and Democrats—between the Legislature and the Governor.
>
> And it will need a full-time Governor—a Governor who does his job and is not diverted by trying to keep his job.

He added:

> I do not intend to campaign for Governor. I do not intend to campaign for the U.S. Senate. I intend to campaign for Michigan—to devote my final year in office to promoting the interests of the state I love—a state I am proud to have served longer than any other Governor.[13]

WILLIAM G. MILLIKEN

Coming from another politician of a different background—perhaps almost any other Michigan politician of the day—such words might have inspired skepticism for their high-mindedness, the cloaking of personal motives in the garb of public responsibility. But Milliken was different, as even the most hard-boiled of the reporters agreed. "I don't think reporters necessarily agreed with him on everything, but there was sort of a universal respect and affection there," said Malcolm "Kim" Johnson of the Associated Press.[14]

Skubick, a Capitol correspondent and host of the weekly public television show *Off the Record,* which had won a reputation for its cynical tone toward the adventures of state political figures, would later say, "I think [Milliken] tried to do the right thing and didn't base his actions on reelection." As he watched and heard Milliken's announcement of his imminent retirement from politics, Skubick, who had covered the Capitol beat almost as long as Milliken had been governor, grew teary.

A few minutes after the press conference ended, Skubick got a call from Joyce Braithwaite, Milliken's appointments director and chief liaison to the state Republican Party. Noted for her political smarts but also possessing a reputation as a fierce Milliken loyalist and stern protector of the governor's interests, she told Skubick, "I want you to come down here." Not sure whether he was to be chided, Skubick made his way to Braithwaite's office on the second floor of the Capitol, which overlooked the lawn and Michigan Avenue to the east. Braithwaite closed the door.

"We both bawled, she and I," said Skubick. "She said through her tears, 'I didn't know you had it in you.'"[15] Their laughter concealed their melancholy over the end of the Milliken era in state politics.

The end of an era: that was the way the state's newspapers reported it. The suspense leading up to the announcement—it turned out that only Helen Milliken, daughter Elaine, son William Jr., and a few others knew about his decision before that morning—intensified the reaction.

One reporter found out who had received a phone call from Milliken before he began reading his statement at the news conference: Democratic mayor Coleman A. Young of Detroit. Young's friendship with Milliken spanned not just parties but personality types: an African American and outspoken civil rights and labor activist before becoming a state legislator and then Detroit mayor, Young was adored by his largely African American constituency but was the regular target of suburban and outstate white politicians because of his sometimes coarse and invariably pro-Detroit rhetoric.

Asked what he thought of Milliken the day after the announcement, Young said that he would "probably go down as one of the great governors."[16] He cited Milliken's leadership on state aid to Detroit, including a so-called equity package that shipped state grant money to the city in recognition and support of institutions that benefited the entire state such as the Detroit Institute of Arts. Young hailed Milliken's recognition of "the importance of the city's stability to the state's stability."

The *Michigan Chronicle* newspaper, which was Detroit based and African American owned, also offered unusual praise to the Republican politician. Beside a political cartoon and column condemning Republican president Ronald Reagan, the *Chronicle* called Milliken "one of the great political figures of our era," citing his support of Detroit, his appointments of African Americans to his cabinet, his education reforms, and his commitment to civil rights. The paper added:

> Although we have not been pleased with every one of his actions, as we judge his overall performance, there are many more positives than negatives—so much so that we consider him a "Grand Statesman" . . . His accomplishments over the past 13 years are many. They are actions which might be expected from a person raised in an urban environment like Detroit but certainly not expected from a middle class Republican born in the northern part of the state.[17]

Even newspapers that had often criticized Milliken found reasons to mark his departure with respect. The conservative *Detroit News,* while arguing that Milliken had "allowed himself to be identified more with the interests of the poor than with the aspirations of the middle class," added that the governor "fought a thousand battles with uncommon integrity and grace. We wish him well."[18] The *Marquette Mining Journal* said, "We have not always agreed with the governor's proposals and we have at times questioned motives behind his actions, but the sum of the past 12 years adds up to an individual who has served Michigan unselfishly and unfailingly during some very difficult periods."[19]

Editorial reactions from newspapers across the state that had long admired Milliken signaled that a divide had been crossed in the state's history. "The polltakers indicate that the luster has gone off the Milliken charm," said the *Grand Rapids Press*. "Possibly, but as time goes by, don't be surprised if his successors are ultimately measured by Milliken honesty, decency and his unerring non-partisan sense of right and wrong."[20] The *Detroit Free Press* suggested that it was "difficult to imagine Lansing without William Milliken in the governor's chair" and said that his decision to retire "surely marks a watershed in Michigan politics." Then the newspaper put its finger on the pulse of the winning formula for the Republican Milliken.

> The key to the success of the Milliken governorship lies almost equally in that unique political coalition—a union of moderate Republicans and progressive Democrats, of outstate and urban interests—and in the personality of the governor himself . . . His reputation for decency is reflected in the goodwill with which even his political enemies tend to regard him . . . a political balance that has endured for years is severely shaken, and perhaps upset forever.[21]

It turned out that Milliken's decision had come at a typical moment—while he was walking alone on December 12, dressed in corduroy slacks, a sweater, and a windbreaker on a beach trail near the Old Mission Lighthouse on the tip of the peninsula of the same name, a finger of land poking directly northward into and dividing Grand Traverse Bay. Milliken's chief of staff, George Weeks, described it as "sort of a traditional walk he takes out on the Peninsula. It was the same place he walked in 1978 before deciding to run for a third term. The call of the north runs deep in the Milliken family. It always has. Grand Traverse Bay is a fountain of energy to him."[22]

Whoever would follow Milliken as governor, it was clear that for many things wouldn't be the same. Interviewing him the summer following his departure from office, writer Deborah Wyatt observed, "I was 12 years old when William Milliken was first elected Governor. I voted for him in a mock seventh grade election, primarily because my parents were voting for him, and I saw his office in 10th grade on the standard government tour of the Capitol. I studied his policies toward labor relations as a college freshman and ranted over his education cuts in Sociology 403. And when I began to pay taxes, I complained along with everyone else. Until last November, Governor Milliken was the only Governor I'd ever known."[23]

At the end of her interview with Milliken, Wyatt added, "In an era of seemingly endless political ego, it was heartening to spend time with one politician who truly seems to take his commitment to our state and our country as seriously as the originators meant it to be."

The reaction of a western Michigan Republican to Milliken's retirement announcement, however, suggested that the conservatives, who had chafed at the long-serving governor's partnerships with urban and Democratic interests, would make a move to recapture the party. Calling Milliken's departure "semi-sad," Republican national committeeman Peter Secchia of Grand Rapids criticized the governor for paying insufficient attention to western Michigan needs and especially for his accommodation of the Democrats. "I was never anti-Milliken," Secchia said, as would many who challenged the Milliken legacy within the Republican Party in the next two decades. "I just thought there was too much compromise . . . I think it probably bodes well for the party in the sense that he was a governor of all the people, and it was difficult for him to be a partisan leader. I happen to believe in partisan politics."[24]

Milliken had struck a lot of observers, friends, and even many political enemies that way. Even when they disagreed with his positions, they rarely disliked him. But would likability be his chief legacy? Only the passage of time would answer that question—a passage even longer than the journey of a Traverse City boy from a small town to Yale University to a foreign war and finally to the top office in Michigan government.

Meanwhile, as Michigan floundered in hard times, there was work to be done—one more year at the helm of a state battered by global and national economic gales. And Milliken prepared for it. The political climate, as much because of as in spite of his retirement, would also be stormy. Nine Democrats had already announced their candidacy for governor, and four Republicans, including three conservatives seeking to recapture their party from the Milliken wing represented by candidate and lieutenant governor James H. Brickley, would soon be publicly quarreling over the meaning of the Milliken legacy.

There would be more surprises—many more than Milliken expected—on the way to retirement in 1982. It would not be a typical year in Michigan politics. But then very few of Milliken's years in office had been.

I

A SIMPLE CHILDHOOD

THE TRAVERSE CITY in which William G. Milliken was born on March 26, 1922, was emblematic of small-town northern Michigan. Traverse City liked to think of itself as reflecting the traditional American values of industry, piety, and civility. Yet it was the product of the hungry frontier impulses of the mid–nineteenth century, which by the time of Milliken's birth had long since depleted the native timber of northern Michigan and forced the local economy into fruit growing, light manufacturing, and tourism. Perhaps this memory of a squandered heritage—though somewhat belied by the continuing beauty of the twin bays the city straddled—contributed to the Milliken attitude of moderation.

In Traverse City, a city then of approximately 11,000 residents tucked against the underside of the West Arm of Grand Traverse Bay, the weeks surrounding Bill Milliken's birth were remarkable only for their normalcy. The *Traverse City Record-Eagle* reported that W. W. Parr, president of Brown Lumber Company, had unveiled plans to expand its manufacturing operation in town. At the same time, "this city was assured of hearing the string quartet of the Detroit symphony orchestra" that summer when a telegram confirmed the engagement. Grand Traverse County paid $138.10 in bounties to rat catchers that month for their haul of 1,381 rats. Men's Easter hats were for sale at the Hamilton Clothing Company for prices between $2.50 and $7.00.

"Clothesline thieves are Traverse City's most recent criminal acquisition," the newspaper reported, writing of several "successful raids" of women's and children's clothing conducted in broad daylight, at least one by a woman.

There were other criminals afoot. Police chief John Blacken reported three automobile parts thefts: one of two new tires, another of 30 gallons of gasoline, and a third of a car battery. "This is the start of an epidemic of car-stealing that Traverse City has been forced to suffer the past two years," the *Traverse City Record-Eagle* predicted, and "The police believe the same gang is responsible for the deals."[1]

But there was bigger news. On March 29, the newspaper breathlessly told of an attempt on the life of A. W. Wiedoft "when what was apparently a homemade bomb" exploded in his car as he was driving home near the corner of Jefferson and Monroe Streets around midnight. The *Record-Eagle* observed that Wiedoft had earlier been in a local poolroom and "had an altercation" with a high school boy, who denied he was a student and barred from playing. The bomb, with an oil base confined in a bottle, sprayed glass but did not succeed in killing Wiedoft.[2]

Equally bold headlines announced on April 7 that the city's drinking water supply was contaminated. A state sanitary engineer had ordered the city to add four to five pounds of chlorine per million gallons to the supply to disinfect it, but the city's chlorine machine was malfunctioning. "Traverse City is faced by a certain epidemic if proper caution is not taken immediately, and by every man, woman and child who drinks city water," warned acting health officer H. B. Kyselka.[3] The next day the newspaper editorialized, "We have known in the back of our heads for thirty years that such a situation would arise. We knew it was impossible and unreasonable to believe that we could pour a solid stream of sewage into the Grand Traverse Bay for several decades and then believe the water supply was pure for drinking purposes."[4]

A sign of growing interest in the rehabilitation of the logged-over wastelands of the country surrounding Traverse City was the front-page coverage on April 10 of a new novel, *Timber*, by area writer Harold Titus. "Between the covers of 'Timber,' Harold Titus' latest novel, lies the economic salvation of not only Michigan, but every other cut-over state, just as surely as the religious salvation of the soul rests between the covers of the Bible," gushed reviewer Jay P. Smith. "It is not too late. Too late, perhaps, for you and me to see the pine back in merchantable condition, but not too late for our children and the coming generation to see Traverse City again as a 'pine town.'"[5] A half century later, William G. Milliken would play a significant role in helping clean up the contamination that had fouled the state's waters, and he would join with his wife Helen to press for protection of some of the most spectacular of the rehabilitated forest lands.

The Milliken family had arrived in the area with the second generation of settlers. Born on May 20, 1848, in Denmark, Maine, one of four children of Mary Ann and Joseph Milliken, the future governor's grandfather, James W. Milliken, traveled to Traverse City at approximately the age of 19 after the Civil War.[6] The young man, according to one account, had been afforded "very little chance" to secure an education yet "never let an opportunity for bettering himself pass without improving it."[7] Working in a dry goods store in Saco, Maine, the young Milliken and another store clerk named Frank Hamilton were recommended to Smith Barnes, manager of the mercantile business of Hannah, Lay and Company. Barnes "enquired for a couple of bright young men to work in the general store at Traverse City."[8] In June 1868, Milliken and Hamilton made the journey to Traverse City. William G. Milliken recalled the family lore concerning their arrival this way.

> My grandfather came to this part of Michigan in his late teens with a friend of the same age. The talk of new opportunities in the west drew them from their native Maine to Chicago, where they heard of even greater promise in a place called Traverse City. They crossed Lake Michigan and arrived in Grand Traverse Bay as dark was falling one Saturday night . . . On Sunday morning they rowed ashore and landed at what is now Clinch Park.
>
> Setting off to explore the wonders of their new home, they sank into the wallow of mudholes that served as Traverse City's main street. Here and there a wooden plank fought to stay on top of the mire, but for the most part, mud prevailed. A brief walk through the raw settlement was enough. They returned to the boat where my grandfather recorded the impact of the visit in his diary (I have it still)—"And so we saw Traverse City, Michigan. The less said about it, the better."[9]

Although its conclusion was inauspicious, the voyage of Milliken and Hamilton proved successful within a short time. Hannah, Lay and Company was already a dominant business. Perry Hannah, dubbed the "Father of Traverse City," was "arguably the closest thing to a great man that this city ever had."[10] Hannah was the state representative for the backwoods district in 1856, built the first local railroad in 1872, and opened a bank at about the same time. He served as president of the village of Traverse City from 1881 to 1895. Despite his popularity, he was called "a man with a cool eye," who presided over "an empire of lumbering, shipping, milling, banking, merchandising and real estate."[11]

After five years with Hannah, Lay, the two Maine émigrés opened their own business, Hamilton, Milliken and Company, in partnership with their former employer and Smith Barnes. Five years later Hamilton and Milliken bought out their partners and began independent operations. In 1889, they constructed a "brick block" on Front Street, the western half devoted to Milliken's dry goods and the eastern to Hamilton's clothing department. After almost 20 years as Hamilton, Milliken and Company, in February 1893 the one firm became two, "Mr. Milliken taking the dry goods and Mr. Hamilton the clothing stock."[12] Apparently the separation was amicable. Said the *Michigan Tradesman* after James Milliken's passing in 1908, "The stores are joined by archways and they are still as closely connected as two stores can possibly be and contain stocks owned by two different men."[13]

Well before the division of the business, Milliken had found another partner. On June 8, 1881, he married 23-year-old Callie Thacker, who had been born in Ohio and moved to Traverse City as a young child. They would have only one child, James Thacker Milliken, born August 20, 1882.

The Millikens' home life, it was said, was tranquil. Described as "a lover of his home," the father, James W. Milliken, would retreat there as soon as the day's work was done, "visit for a while, read the local paper and then retire, being a man, no matter how tired or how much energy he had expended during the day, who could throw aside his business cares."[14]

Milliken was active in the First Congregational Church, becoming its first Sunday school superintendent in 1877. He served in the post for more than 30 years.

The Sunday school was Mr. Milliken's pride. He knew its short-comings and imperfections. While he sought to remedy these, he did not dwell upon them. It was a good school. He was pleased to see the attendance kept up year after year, and the interest always manifest.[15]

Business, however thriving, was not enough to keep the elder Milliken occupied. "Early in life Mr. Milliken cast his lot with the Republican party, and had been a staunch republican ever since," an obituary would report. In 1888, he was chairman of the Grand Traverse County Republican Party and was credited with contributing to its success at the polls. Ten years later, he began a family tradition by winning election to the local state Senate seat in a district that reached from Benzie County on the southwest to Charlevoix County on the northeast. In the heavily Republican district, Milliken won in a landslide, more than doubling Herman B. Sturtevant's 3,256 votes.[16] He served one two-year term.

A major figure in a growing community whose population jumped from 2,663 in 1880 to 9,407 in 1900, Milliken had interests outside of politics. He was associated with the Traverse City Potato Implement Company and a large holder of real estate, including resort properties.

In any enterprise that stood for the betterment of Traverse City Mr. Milliken was always counted on to support it. When the Grand Traverse Region Fair association was organized, Mr. Milliken was selected as chairman of several important committees . . . In everything that came up in a public way, Mr. Milliken was one of the first to put his shoulder to the wheel.[17]

The good community works of the elder Milliken came to a sudden, tragic end. En route by train to his son James T. Milliken's graduation from Yale College on June 19, 1908, he suffered a heart attack and died at the age of 60. "In his usual good health when he left Traverse City" for the ceremony, the elder Milliken was taken ill at about midnight on a New York Central train and five critical hours passed before the train reached Albany and medical care could be summoned. He passed away two hours before the train reached its destination, New York City. "An attempt was made to notify friends in New York," an obituary reported, "but the message was not delivered until after the train had arrived. James T. Milliken, the son, was there at the station, expecting to meet his father and mother well and happy."[18]

The impact of Milliken's death on the community was significant. The *Bay City Times* reported that the Sunday after his death he was marked "present" in his Sunday school at the First Congregational Church. "He was present—not in the flesh, but in the spirit. He will live as long as the present generation of Traverse City lives. And when a new generation arises Mr. Milliken will still live. Such men never die."[19]

Although there is no clear record of how James T. Milliken responded to his father's death, the church bulletin that summarized the outpouring of sadness at the passing included one tribute from "a Yale friend" of the younger man: "The thing that you must think of most is that your father lived just the kind of life that you felt like accepting as a pattern for your own. I think that is the greatest inheritance that any father can leave a son."[20]

In many ways, the younger Milliken did follow the pattern of the father. Assuming control of the family business, he would also go on to become a community leader and serve in the state Senate. But his political career stumbled at first; he finished third in a three-way Republican primary for the local Senate seat in 1926. A 1938 appointment by Democratic governor Frank Murphy to the Commission on Reform and Modernization of Government preceded his successful Senate candidacy in 1940. He served for 10 years in the Senate.

Long before his rise to political prominence, James T. Milliken and the woman he married in June 1912, Hildegarde Grawn, established a household their children would remember fondly. Balancing their father's reserve and formality, Hildegarde was more sensitive and doted on the children, especially her second son, William Grawn.

Grawn is a Swedish word meaning "pine tree," an appropriate name for a family lineage that would lead to a governor of the state whose official state tree is the primeval white pine. The mother's family traditions also included public service. Her father, Charles T. Grawn, served as president of Central Michigan State Normal School, later Central Michigan University, from 1900 to 1918. An authority on Swedish literature and the Swedish education system, he also served on corporate boards, was president of the Michigan State Teachers Association, and received an honorary master of arts degree from the University of Michigan in 1906. After retiring from Central, he founded the Grawn Realty Company and the Charlesworth Apartments Company before his death in 1942. Hildegarde was one of two children. Grawn, a village southwest of Traverse City, was platted by James R. Blackwood, Hildegarde's uncle.

By most accounts, the home life of Hildegarde and James T. Milliken was serene and rich with the stimulation of divergent parental interests. Concentrating on business and community affairs, Bill Milliken's father reinforced the Milliken heritage of public service. A 1906 graduate of the University of Michigan, his mother "was a totally different person than my father. She was very well educated, she had great sensitivities. She was involved in the drama club, she loved gardening and reading, she loved poetry . . . She had outstanding taste in dress and in her home."[21] She also played the piano and was a member of the art committee at Interlochen, a nearby school for budding musical talents.

But, unusual for a woman of her day, Hildegarde Milliken did not confine her interests to the home. A member of the International Women's League for Peace and Freedom, she was strongly opposed to war and politically active. For a short time, she also operated an antique shop near the family's summer home, Green Gables, on the eastern shore of the East Arm of Grand Traverse Bay near Acme. "In some ways, my father and mother perhaps did not belong together," William Milliken reflected in 2003. "They were different in many ways . . . I think their children, and their love for their children, bonded them together."[22]

Both parents conveyed a sense of compassion and responsibility, daughter Ruth recalled. "During the Depression years, Father and Mother were adamant about how you had to share. If you were going to the movies, you had to take someone with you."[23] Unlike his father, James T. Milliken was not formally religious, a trait that his second son would evidence in adulthood. Ruth remembered her father saying, "I go to church every two years, just before the election."

At the summer home, Bill Milliken began to appreciate the wonders of the natural world. A stream, Acme Creek, reached its outlet in the bay after passing through the Millikens' cottage land.

"I spent many wonderful summer days and nights there," he

recalled. "You could paddle right up the stream in a canoe. We fished for trout, never with very much success. I learned every part of that shoreline."[24] Eighty years later, the peaceful setting the Millikens had known was splattered with a shotgun burst of motels, cottages, gas stations, convenience stores, resorts and large retailers.[25]

Bill Milliken also learned the art of fly-fishing from his father. In addition to fishing on the cottage land, James T. Milliken showed his sons John and Bill the beauty of the Manistee and Pere Marquette Rivers, south of Traverse City. Never an enthusiastic angler himself, William Milliken remembered something even more important as his father's heritage.

> My father set such an example for me of personal integrity and honesty. It was inconceivable to him to be dishonest in any of his dealings or public life. He was so open, so candid, so frank in what he said. His sense of fairness has been a great influence all of my life. It provided an example for me. It made doing the right thing easy for me.[26]

He also remembered that his father was "least of all a vindictive person." He did not bear grudges—with one vivid exception. The family dog, Gyp, got loose one day and wandered through the neighborhood around the Millikens' Washington Street home. The sheriff shot the dog. "My father never forgave him for that," William Milliken said. "We were young children at the time, and it broke our hearts. My father forever considered him an enemy."[27]

His mother, however, may have been an even bigger influence on the young Bill. Describing her decades later as "very nervous and high strung," he admitted he sought to comfort her. Ads for the beverage Ovaltine suggested it would provide a restful sleep if taken before bed. He went to the store, purchased a jar of Ovaltine, took it home, mixed it up, and took it to his mother in her bedroom. Although she was gracious about it, "I'm not sure it made much difference."

The devotion was returned. Bill was her mother's favorite child. "That may have been good for me, and it may have been bad for me," he said. "It may have been bad for my siblings. She didn't conceal her feelings for me from them. Maybe I received more attention than was good for me."[28]

The combination of an innately benign temperament and his mother's high regard appears to have combined to shape a political personality that would be remembered by staff and allies with some reverence. "I would say that his mother held up a mirror to Bill and said, 'You're wonderful,'" said psychiatrist Dr. Frank Ochberg, who served as director of mental health in Milliken's cabinet. "You take someone who by nature is sunny, smiling, and happily disposed and provide that kind of reflection and you produce a secure, stable, and generous adult."[29]

As a student, Bill made more of an impression with his character than with his scholastic achievements. His second-semester report card for ninth grade is undistinguished academically, with B-minus grades in algebra, science, and Latin, an A-minus in English, and a C-plus in gym. But he earned superior marks for citizenship and checkmarks for the "desirable qualities" of being "courteous," "thoughtful of others," "loyal," and "dependable." He also possessed "initiative." He won the comment "very commendable attitude" for the third six weeks of the semester from an unnamed teacher.[30]

By the same ninth-grade year, Bill later remembered, he knew he wanted to serve in public office "and start laying the groundwork by reading books on politics."[31] Bill suggested to his brother, who was two years older, that he should consider running for "governor" of Traverse City High School. The new position, equivalent to a supreme class president over all high school class chiefs, was the first electoral success of the newest Milliken generation. The primary benefit of the job—the freedom to avoid study hall—may have persuaded Bill to run and win the same office when his turn came.[32] The early competition for stature between the two boys set the pattern for a subtle rivalry that continued into adulthood. John made his life in Traverse City and opened a medical clinic bearing the family name, while his brother took on the family business and ultimately won statewide notice.

As governor of the high school in 1939, Bill vowed to "strive to the utmost to make our student government as effective and helpful to every student as possible" and called for tennis courts and an "active, efficient police force and student court."[33] A biography of Milliken published in 1970 during his first gubernatorial campaign listed other activities of the high school governor: "Under his auspices, the [student] council raised a $50 scholarship fund, passed and enforced traffic rules, eliminated all student automobiles from 7th and 8th Streets during school hours, revised, printed and distributed the school constitution, and began the task of paving Pine Street. Young Milliken had gone before the City Commission personally to promote the road paving project."[34]

Remembering his adolescence when he was the lieutenant governor of Michigan 30 years later, Bill talked of Friday night school dances as the main social events. Under a strict weekend curfew—and a parental policy that forbade him to go out on weeknights–he said he chafed. "I thought of all the other kids who could stay out later than I and who had more freedom than I did."[35]

Bill was particularly close to his younger sister, Ruth, who had been born two years after him. An early memory of both is connecting their toes with string from one bedroom to another on Christmas Eve so that the first one to wake up the next morning would rouse the other for the joy of opening their gifts. Ruth remembered young Bill as "extremely impish, full of the devil . . . but he protected me . . . Bill looked at me as a gift to him personally."[36]

If the Milliken childhood involved any serious misbehavior, there is no evidence of it. William Milliken remembered at least considering taking grapes from the land of a farmer near the Acme summer home. "There was another farmer who had pigs," he said. "I was all for going out after dark and letting the pigs out. I think I did it once."[37] When there was any youthful disobedience, James Milliken met it with disapproval rather than corporal punishment. Both parents set standards, their second son said, and their expectations alone were enough to prompt appropriate behavior.

The most memorable trauma in the life of young Bill occurred when he was approximately 12 years old.

> We had a large basement, and we had made sort of a small basketball court. It had a wooden floor. The space was also used as a laundry room. One day I was home playing basketball with a friend. He had to leave and either deliberately or accidentally locked the door on his way out. I was trapped in the basement. I figured the best way to get out was to climb out the window, which was high on the wall. I wasn't tall enough, so I stood on the basketball. There was a great big hook on the wall to hang the clothesline and as I reached

up, I hooked my right hand. I could feel the hook going through my hand. Obviously I made a ruckus about it.[38]

The reaction of his parents was immediate and sympathetic. Upstairs at the time of the accident, his mother came running and called her husband. But neither parent could release Bill from the hook. Instead, his mother called a plumber with "great big cutters" and Bill was taken down. "You didn't go to the hospital in those days," he remembered. "I went to the doctor's office, and about an hour and a half later, he got the hook out."[39] Bandaged for weeks, his hand still bears a scar from the incident.

During the Depression, the family fared relatively well. Throughout most of Bill's childhood, the family employed maids. But despite the family's ample means, the result of the profitability of the family store, Bill was expected to earn money himself. In junior high school, he served as a packer and floor sweeper at Milliken's. In his high school years, he spent 50 hours a week during summer vacations pumping gas at a Sinclair station for eight dollars, according to one account.[40]

Generous helpings of politics were served along with food at the family dinner table. Brother John Milliken recalled that "we always talked politics at the dinner table, and Bill always listened the most carefully." When Bill expressed the desire to be a politician someday, his mother said, "I hope you'll be a statesman rather than a politician."[41]

Having served as mayor of Traverse City for six years, the elder Milliken was a champion of public service. One priority after he left office was the construction of a sewage treatment plant to improve sanitation and help clean up Grand Traverse Bay. This and other costly initiatives did not win him universal popularity. His son John remembers seeing a newspaper advertisement during the campaign, which read:

IF YOU VOTE 'YES'
It Means
MORE MILLIKENISM,
MORE DEBTS . . .
. . . and . . .
VOLUNTARY
BANKRUPTCY.

"That makes a big impression on you when you're in fifth grade," said John Milliken.[42] But the voters sided with James Milliken's position, rejecting a proposal to let a private corporation operate the sewage plant by a margin of 1,699 to 212 and authorizing a bond issue to pay for a public plant.[43] And it didn't deter Bill, the younger son, from pursuing a political life.

Bill's high school political success had something to do with the untroubled temperament that won him raves as a practicing politician later in life, an unusual combination of approachability, geniality, and privacy. "His disposition then is what it's like now," a childhood acquaintance recalled in 1982. "He got everything he wanted without throwing a tantrum or using his fists. He dated a lot of girls and was considered popular, but he never had cohorts or buddies—I mean the type of people you pour your heart out to. If he had any troubles, I don't think anybody knew about them."[44]

As a member of the school's basketball team in 1940, Bill participated in its Class B state championship. Admitting that he was "not a star," Milliken was described as "fast and a reasonably accurate shooter." A teammate, Jack Bensley, said, "Bill was the fastest dribbler on the team. But sometimes the ball didn't keep up with him."[45] In that low-scoring era, Bill's Traverse City team defeated Detroit St. Theresa 26 to 23 for the school's first state basketball title.

Already, though, Bill's thoughts were on college. Family tradition—and the family's position in the upper middle class—ruled out local options and dictated the choice of an eastern school. His brother John suggested that Bill join him at Amherst, but Bill toured Yale, Dartmouth, and Princeton as well. Yale was his choice. His application for admission, dated February 21, 1940, made no bones of his lack of interest in science and mathematics. Indeed, it was candid about his true desire.

> I believe I can say without hesitation, however, that of all the extracurricular activities that I have participated in during my last four years in school, none has given me more satisfaction or enjoyment than work with the student council and student government . . . [A]s governor I have gained a great deal of experience in public speaking. Last year I was chosen as representative of the school in extemporaneous speaking.

WILLIAM G. MILLIKEN

Ever since I can remember I have had a great interest in Politics and Government, and I have done considerable reading along this line. If I am admitted to Yale, I would like to specialize in Government, Economics and History in preparation for a political career or for the diplomatic service.[46]

Claiming no pressure from his father, the Yale alumnus, Bill ultimately enrolled at Yale in the fall of 1940, just months before his father won election as Traverse City's state senator and began earning the Lansing nickname of Gentleman Jim. Soon the attentions of both father and son would be turned elsewhere, toward a looming conflict across both the Pacific and Atlantic Oceans.

2

FACING WAR AND MORTALITY

ENTERING YALE ON September 21, 1940, as a freshman in the class of 1944, Bill Milliken was unsure how long he would remain on campus. War had already broken out in Europe and menaced the Pacific. Professor Robert Dudley French told the entering students that "the majority of those seated here now [will] not finish their course of study in 1944" because of likely U.S. involvement in a war.

It was also an election year. Milliken remembers the Republican presidential nominee, Wendell Willkie, campaigning at Yale that fall. Aviator and isolationist Charles Lindbergh spoke against U.S. involvement in the European war from Yale's Woolsey Hall. The campus was bristling with debate and speculation about the trajectory of global affairs.

But the preoccupations of young male college students also included more typical fare. In a 1970 gubernatorial campaign biography, *William G. Milliken: A Touch of Steel,* author Dan Angel recounted memories of Milliken's freshman roommate, Richard A. Smith: "One girl was so popular that Bill used a casual, disinterested approach to her. He reasoned she didn't respect the guys who fell all over her. His hard-to-get tactics were eventually successful. Perhaps this was his first 'political' campaign."

Angel also interviewed Milliken's sophomore roommate, John Clement, who saw the sensitive side of the future governor. Traveling to Michigan during the summer to spend time with his roommate, Clement ran out of money and gasoline 75 miles south of Traverse City. He called Bill. Along with his parents, Bill traveled to retrieve Clement, impressing his roommate.

Another Yale friend who remained so more than 60 years later, Conley Brooks, said, "My first impression was, 'What a nice guy' . . . He was one of those people whom everyone liked; he was humble, had a marvelous sense of humor, and had appeal to his peers."[1]

Despite the battles raging overseas, Milliken's generation was not expecting the nation to go to war as soon as it would. On December 7, 1941, when the Japanese attacked Pearl Harbor, Milliken was returning from a weekend with friends at Vermont's Bennington College. Hearing the "shocking news," Milliken said he recognized at that moment "the inevitability of my later involvement in what was to be a declaration of war. And I knew, along with all of my other friends, that our lives would never again be the same."[2]

Milliken became active in the Undergraduate War Council on campus, which organized students to participate in civil defense activities. In September 1942—two years after entering Yale and already halfway through his junior year because of summer school—Milliken enlisted in the Army Reserve Corps. In February 1943, hoping that volunteering would improve his chances of selecting his branch of service, he signed up for duty in the Army Air Corps. He had finished his third year of college and along with 30 of his classmates was called to report for active duty at Fort Devens, Massachusetts.

Having grown up in comfortable surroundings, Milliken was now rooming with between 60 and 80 other men in a barracks.

> The day I reported for duty at Fort Devens, Massachusetts, was the grimmest, bleakest day of my life. The weather was cold, gray and miserable. I went there with about thirty other classmates so at least we had that opportunity to be together as we began doing K.P. duty at 4 a.m.[3]

It was a harsh awakening in more ways than one. "I remember the Master Sergeant on the first morning," Bill said. "The outside door opened and cold air blew in and he shouted, 'All right, you men, drop your cocks and grab your socks.'"[4]

The joke going around among the new recruits, Milliken said, was that the best way to avoid trouble was, "If it moves, salute it; if it doesn't move, pick it up; if you can't pick it up, paint it."

Soon the Yale classmates dispersed, and Milliken for the first time in his life formed lasting friendships with men of "totally different backgrounds," as he described it. Some of these friendships would last into and beyond his time in public office.

In the late spring of 1943, Milliken was selected to become a B–24 waist gunner. He would train at Lowry Field near Denver, Colorado. Milliken had signed up for officers' training school, but gunners were in demand. Among other things, he learned to take down a 50-caliber machine gun and reassemble it blindfolded. He told Dan Angel, "That was the greatest achievement I had in the Army."

But more than military service was soon on his mind. A former Yale roommate, Eaton H. Magoon Jr., who had attended a private school in Colorado Springs, organized a social gathering of his service friends and some female friends from Denver. One of the latter was Helen Wallbank, the daughter of a prominent area attorney. About 10 couples met and attended a dance. Although Helen had been attending Smith College in Northampton, Massachusetts, only 80 miles from Yale, the two had never crossed paths until the dance, as at the moment she was home between her freshman and sophomore years.[5]

Helen Wallbank's family was politically conservative. Her father, Stanley T. Wallbank, a postman's son who had worked his way to success, "used to excoriate FDR," she remembered. He was also driven, she recalled, focusing on his work. He sent Helen and her two sisters to a private college-preparatory school, the Kent School for Girls, beginning in the ninth grade. "He was always in motion," she said of her father. He was a perfectionist who expected top school performance from his children. This was "sometimes hard for kids," especially since Helen was a B student.[6]

The family, which included three daughters and a son, was a loving one. Stanley Wallbank passed along to his offspring an interest that Helen would later express as first lady of Michigan: an appreciation of growing things expressed as a love of gardening. "He liked to plan the garden, and he expected all of the family to work in it. All of us became gardeners and took it into adulthood," she said.[7]

The influence of her mother, Nellie Wallbank, a former beauty queen from the University of Colorado, was warm and traditional. Although as Helen Milliken she would become well-known for her advocacy of women's rights, the young Helen Wallbank grew up in a household with conventional gender roles. "My mother pretty much went along with Dad," Helen said. "She was of her generation. Many, if not most, women then followed along with their husbands."[8]

The young Helen's first impression at the dance where they met was that Bill Milliken was "very personable but probably too short for me. I was as tall as he was, and at that time that seemed to be a consideration. After we got married, he said, 'Why do you always wear flat heels?' I said, 'because I don't want to be taller than you.'" Bill Milliken, she remembers, was also "a marvelous dancer."[9]

The couple dated throughout the summer of 1943 as Milliken's training continued. In October, he left to attend gunnery school at Harlingen Field, Texas, graduating with a pair of aerial gunner's wings. Just before leaving for combat in June 1944, Bill and Helen rendezvoused in Topeka, Kansas, and reached an understanding that they would marry after the war. For more than a year, they sustained their relationship via the mail.

Milliken's air crew had been assembled in April 1944. The 10 men—who had never met before—hailed from across the United States. In Topeka, they took over a brand new B–24 heavy bomber, flew it to Bangor, Maine, then to Gander, Newfoundland, and finally to the Azores, getting temporarily lost before landing there. After a stop in Tunisia, the crew and the plane were assigned to the Fifteenth Air Force, 721st Squadron, Forty-second Wing, 450th Bombardment Group in Italy.

Four days after arriving in Italy, Milliken's crew was divided among experienced crews for a bombing mission over the oil fields of Polesti, Romania, which was considered a dangerous target. It was Milliken's first experience with the seemingly innocuous phenomenon of flak—the black puffs of smoke resulting from the explosion of aerial shells. Because the smoke looked "far away and harmless," Milliken was puzzled at first by the reaction of the experienced crew. Then flak struck the B–24 next to his. "I watched as the plane turned on its side, with smoke and fire coming from one of the engines. It began an erratic downward plunge." The crewmen bailed out over enemy territory. Milliken counted five parachutes—meaning five men on the plane didn't escape.[10]

In the 10 months during which Bill was assigned to bombing missions with the Army Air Force out of Italy, he flew 50 missions and confronted his mortality almost daily. Never religious in a formal sense, he had earlier received a pocket Bible from his mother—who was active in the Congregational Church—and carried it on bombing runs. He often read the Twenty-third Psalm and sometimes found great comfort in it. He developed "a religious feeling in a much larger sense, believing in a divine presence, realizing that there was a Creator of this world, that I was only a small part of something much larger."[11] But even when he was in harm's way he never attended services, believing firmly that religion for him was "much more private, much more personal."

On October 7, 1944, while on his twenty-fifth bombing mission, whose target was a marshaling yard used for enemy supplies outside of Vienna, Milliken came close to disaster. The B–24 had dropped its bombs on the target and begun to return to base when it encountered a storm of flak, which knocked out an engine. Unable to keep pace with its squadron, the bomber tried to fly below the flak. But enemy radar tracked the aircraft and ground fire again began to reach the B–24.

> They got our range and were tracking us. I was standing in the waist where it was my duty to protect the aircraft from attack, and shells were exploding all around us. The anti-aircraft shells make big puffs of smoke two or three times the size of a man. From a distance they look harmless, but as they explode they can be lethal.[12]

A shell burst through the fuselage of the plane, piercing Milliken's flak suit, wounding him in the stomach, and knocking him to the floor of the plane. "It wasn't serious," he told Dan Angel in 1970. Nevertheless, Milliken was hospitalized for four days at the Thirty-fifth Field Hospital before returning to duty two weeks after he was wounded.[13] Although he was the first of his crew to be wounded, four others would be injured at various times by flak. All 10 crew members survived the war.

On the second flight after returning to service, again flying over

Vienna, Milliken's plane took intense flak. Turning to the radio operator, Milliken remembers seeing a sudden look of shock in the man's eyes. "I knew instantly that there was something wrong. Then I looked down at his shoulder. He had been hit by flak and blood was gushing out."[14] The crewman fell to the floor of the plane, where Milliken stanched the flow of blood. Trying to give the wounded man a shot of morphine, Milliken broke the needle, but on a second try, with the help of the navigator, he was able to administer the medicine. After a three-hour flight back to base, the plane fired a flare on approach to signal that it had wounded aboard. The critically wounded man recovered, but he never flew again with that crew.

There were other narrow escapes. "We were taking off one time on a mission that was considered a milk run," Milliken said. "No sooner had we gotten into the air than one of the engines started throwing oil. We landed immediately and were met by the base commander, who said, 'I've got another plane for you.' That plane had been checked out, warmed up and loaded with bombs. But it was a battle-weary plane. We took off again down the runway, hoping to catch up with our formation already in the air, but as we got within 20 seconds of liftoff the right landing gear collapsed." As the right wing dropped down onto the runway, the number four engine was torn off. Carrying 2,200 gallons of high-octane fuel, the plane spilled its bombs over the pavement. "I will never forget the sound of metal on concrete as the plane skidded along the runway," Milliken said. The previous week, a similar incident at the base had resulted in the explosion of a plane, killing all crewmen aboard. The entire crew had the memory of that disaster in mind as the plane foundered.

Some of the crewmen sought to escape through the opening at Milliken's waist gunner position, but his parachute harness had caught on his gun mount, blocking the only way out.

"It was the first and only time I've experienced men in panic," Milliken later said. "They were screaming, clawing at me, pulling at my hair. It was an absolute jungle, an incredible experience." But the delay may have saved their lives, as the plane was still moving at high speed. When it finally halted, "You never saw 10 men run so fast. We had boots and heavy flying suits on, but that didn't slow us down. We knew it was going to explode. For some inexplicable reason, that didn't happen, but the plane was a total wreck." Taken immediately to the base infirmary, the crewmen were offered shots of whiskey by a physician.[15] Since it was 6:30 A.M., Milliken declined. Asked whether he had been frightened during the episode, Milliken replied, "I was frightened. We all were."

Milliken's crew also endured a crash landing in northern Italy within a mile of enemy lines. The mission had been to Wiener Neustadt near Vienna. The flak was intense. "We got hit, lost our number-one engine, then got hit again and lost another engine. We began losing altitude almost as we came off the target and were unable to stay with our formation. By the time we were back over northern Italy and losing altitude at an alarming rate, we knew we had to lighten the plane." The pilot ordered the crew to throw out every piece of unattached equipment: guns, ammunition, even parachutes. After jettisoning his ammunition, Milliken looked out to see what he thought was a German fighter off his right wing. The bomber was now defenseless. Fortunately, the fighter turned out to be a British Spitfire that had been sent to escort the B–24 to an emergency landing in a partially cleared and abandoned orchard.

Touching down, the plane lurched toward the orchard. "Just as we were about to hit some trees, the pilot cut the engine on one side and revved the other up and came to a halt by doing a ground loop . . . Safely on the ground, we could hear the firing on the front lines. When a British truck loaded with soldiers turned up a few minutes later, we knew then we were in friendly territory. After they drove us away from the scene, they stopped and offered us tea."[16]

On another occasion, Milliken and his crewmates were forced to bail out of their plane. Over Munich, the B–24 had run into intense flak, which knocked out the plane's hydraulic system. Although the bomber was able to return to southern Italy, the failure of the hydraulic system made it impossible to lower the landing gear. After the right gear was lowered manually, the left remained stuck. The crew tried to retract the right gear to make a belly landing possible, but it, too, was stuck. Thirty miles away from their base and low on fuel, the crew was ordered via radio to abandon the plane.

> Our pilot set the plane on automatic pilot and over the intercom gave the word to bail out. As I was preparing to jump, I suddenly saw a body fly by and then another—the pilot and copilot had left

WILLIAM G. MILLIKEN

28

the plane. For a moment, we were in a pilotless plane. I quickly bailed out and it was one of the happier moments of my life—as I counted nine other parachutes all on their way safely to earth. The plane on automatic pilot was headed out to the Adriatic Sea, but it veered back toward land. We learned the following day that it had crashed about twenty miles north of us and had run a farmer down in a field and killed him.[17]

The experience of coming under fire fostered in Milliken a deeper desire to devote his life to serious purposes. "After 10 months of flying missions and not knowing whether you'd live another day, you saw how precious life was. I thought frequently how I would live life to the fullest when the war was over. I developed a sense of wanting to give something back. I wanted to make some kind of meaning out of my life."[18]

While flying missions, Milliken remembered, "I would say to myself, if I can only survive this, I will not ever complain about anything, not fear anything, not turn away from anything . . . You wouldn't want to do it [serve in a war] again, but looking back, you wouldn't have missed it for the world." The experience of shared danger also kept the bomber's crew of five officers and five enlisted men meeting for reunions into the 1990s.

The assignment to Italy also acquainted Milliken for the first time with profound poverty. Food for the native Italians was so scarce that when a military truck ran down a dog Milliken and his tentmate had been keeping in their tent, a group of locals "ran out on the road and took him away—to eat." Reflecting on this decades later, Milliken said he realized "how fortunate I was . . . not ever having to worry about food."[19]

Military service bred skepticism of institutional routine in the young gunner. "I remember the unchanging nature of everything," he said. "The food was the same for three years. Spam and powdered eggs. Canned milk." Milliken bristled at the make-work that often attended barracks life.

His sense of justice was offended when, after he had flown more than 45 missions, a commanding officer paid a surprise inspection visit to his tent and, finding flak suits, parachutes, and equipment under the crew's beds, promptly demoted Milliken from staff sergeant to private and another crew member from tech sergeant to private.[20] Refusing to accept the unfair demotion, Milliken appealed the matter to headquarters. He was reinstated to full rank on the day he completed his fiftieth mission.

One of the few breaks during his service was a four-day stint at a rest camp close to the Adriatic Sea. "We were served breakfast, given steak and ice cream and allowed to sleep!" he marveled later.[21] The trip home from the abandoned plane in the orchard was another respite, requiring three days of travel. "I remember one night sleeping on a schoolhouse floor. It was a beautiful part of Italy—small towns, totally untouched by the war. Those were the happiest times I can remember; it was as though you were transported to another world—a peaceful world."[22]

Milliken's fiftieth mission qualified him for a rotation out of the combat theater. Driven by truck to Naples, he steamed back to Boston on a troop ship. He was in transit on the ship when he learned that President Franklin Delano Roosevelt had died. From Boston, Milliken was sent to Santa Rosa, California, to serve in a firefighting unit. He received his discharge on September 29, 1945.[23] He had been decorated with the Air Medal with two Bronze Oak Leaf Clusters, the American Campaign Medal, the European–African–Middle Eastern Campaign Medal with a Silver Service Star and three Bronze Service Stars, the World War II Victory Medal, and a Purple Heart.[24]

He emerged from military service a changed man, "young in a physical sense but with a better understanding of life . . . [M]aturing comes from adapting to other human beings who may come from different backgrounds, different parts of the world or different parts of the country." Not knowing whether he would survive the war, he said, "gives you a sense of beauty, of life and its meaning."[25]

Almost immediately after leaving the service, Bill Milliken married Helen on October 20, 1945. About 300 people attended the service at Ascension Episcopal Church in Denver. Helen had eight bridesmaids; older brother John Milliken served as Bill's best man. A little incredulous, Bill remembered almost 60 years later that he wore striped trousers, a long coat, and a top hat to the ceremony.[26]

There was no time for a honeymoon; Bill needed to return to Yale to complete his degree. His parents stayed near them on the first part of the drive east. When the first day's trip ended, both the parents and the newlyweds lodged in the same hotel. After getting out of the car, Bill's mother approached Helen and said, "Isn't he wonderful?" Both Bill and Helen remembered this as an indicator of Hildegarde Milliken's lifelong admiration of her second child.[27]

Helen remembered their year at Yale as "sociable and intellectually stimulating." Already a graduate of Smith, she attended some of Bill's classes with him and typed his papers. "I really enjoyed that year," she said.[28] Bill obtained a bachelor's degree in economics, history, and public affairs in the spring of 1946, his graduation having been delayed by two years of war service. He hoped to attend the graduate school of business at the University of Michigan the following fall—and was accepted—but his father had taken ill. His brother was pursuing a medical degree, and his sister was otherwise occupied. The responsibility of taking on the family's department store business thus fell on Bill. But he did not take it on with a glad heart.

A clue to Bill Milliken's future was his reaction to his future father-in-law, Stanley Wallbank, when Bill asked his permission to marry Helen. "He expressed the hope that I would make my career in business. I said, 'Mr. Wallbank, I have to say I have no interest in that.' He was flabbergasted."[29] Despite his application to the University of Michigan business school, Bill continued to dream of a career in public service.

For now, family and fate had something else in store. Necessity required him to return, with Helen, to his hometown. It would prove to be both a challenge and a balm to the couple, rooting them in a place they loved—though for Helen a place alien to her experience.

3

FROM BUSINESSMAN
TO SENATOR

WILLIAM MILLIKEN WAS a reluctant if dutiful businessman. Returning to his hometown after six years at Yale
and in the military, he chafed at the role of "utility man" in J. W. Milliken, Inc. "It wasn't my dream, but I felt an obligation to support my
father," he said.[1]

His father directed that Bill learn the business step-by-step. Beginning as a buyer, Bill then became a merchandiser. Eventually he rose to
general manager and vice president. By the time his father passed away
in 1952, he was prepared to assume leadership of the family business.

The Milliken store was a significant presence in the community.
Decades later both Helen and Bill remembered fondly the tearoom,
which overlooked the women's apparel department from a balcony.
Watching the shoppers while dining was a Traverse City pastime, they
said.[2]

During the early postwar years, the family renovated the store, hiring an architectural firm from New York to draw up the plans. "The
store was really very beautiful," Bill said proudly. "It was recognized as
an outstanding store not only in Traverse City but all across the
north."[3]

The Millikens were not above a little creative marketing. They
decided to exhibit a monkey in a cage in the children's department to

attract customers. Before the monkey was transferred to the store, however, Helen fed and cleaned up after it at home. In its new, colorful circus cage on wheels, the simian created a sensation in the children's department. "Its antics just fascinated everyone," Bill said. "Children would bring their mothers, and the mothers would buy things." The experiment ended, however, when the Millikens decided to provide a partner for the female monkey to cure its loneliness. The monkeys did what monkeys do, fascinating the children and bringing store employees scurrying to close the curtains on the cage. Bill and Helen laughed at the memory in 2005.[4]

Milliken received his first political appointment in 1947. Republican Governor Kim Sigler appointed Milliken to the new state Waterways Commission on August 25.[5] Using funds generated from a tax on fuel used by vessels on navigable rivers, the commission oversaw the establishment of a system of harbors of refuge, channels, and marinas along Michigan's Great Lakes shoreline. The hometown newspaper announcement highlighted Milliken's war service.

> The 25-year-old Milliken is general manager of J. W. Milliken, Inc., in Traverse City. He is a graduate of Yale University and a veteran of World War II. During service in Italy he completed 50 missions as a waist gunner in the Army Air Force. He is the son of State Senator James T. Milliken.[6]

Despite the historic election of Democrat G. Mennen Williams as governor in 1948, Milliken continued to serve on the commission until June 1955, when he resigned. Milliken had a favorable opinion of the progressive Williams. Just after Williams's upset win in the 1948 election, the Waterways Commission met with the new governor in Detroit. "I was quite excited, and the other members of the Commission were, too," Milliken recalled. "Here was a young, new governor who seemed to be a very capable guy. He had great knowledge of the issues."

Williams's great memory for names impressed Milliken, as it did many others. When the governor joined the Cherry Festival parade in Traverse City one year, Milliken sat above the marquee of the department store. "I was touched by the fact that when he came by in the parade he looked up and said, 'Hi, Bill.'"[7] Milliken also praised

Williams for running "a very clean administration" and objected to the partisanship of Republicans who sought to block the governor's program of expanded public services. "I may have had some areas of disagreement with him on issues, but I was amazed at his political skills," Milliken said.[8]

Until the end of their lives, his parents, particularly Hildegarde, doted on Bill. Both Bill and Helen remembered vividly an incident that occurred during their first winter in Traverse City. One blustery day, Hildegarde called Helen and said, "You be sure to tell Bill to wear his rubbers today."[9]

Milliken lost his parents in 1950 and 1952. Ill for some time, Hildegarde Milliken sought care at the University of Michigan Hospital in 1950. Advanced colon cancer was found, and she died three months later "after long suffering."[10] Heart troubles slowed James Milliken during his later years, contributing to son Bill's decision to assist with the family business. One Sunday afternoon in the fall of 1952, after a long walk in the woods on the Old Mission Peninsula, which divides the East and West Arms of Grand Traverse Bay, Bill stopped at his father's house to check on his condition. "When I arrived in his room," the son remembered later, "I was unable to awaken him. He apparently had died in his sleep only a few minutes earlier."[11] The man who had done so much to shape his son's conception of public service as an honorable profession was gone.

Newspaper remembrances of the former Traverse City mayor and state senator, who was 70 at the time of his death, were uniformly glowing. W. K. Kelsey said that James Milliken "never allowed partisan interest to rise above his devotion to the welfare of the people. He made the study of government one of his specialties; no problem was too involved or too dry to absorb his attention, and he usually came up with a practical answer."[12] Another commentator observed, "Senator Milliken served his district with fidelity and what is equally important, intelligence . . . his interest in politics was completely unselfish and he gave to state administration a broad measure of service beyond the capacity or even interest of the average legislator."[13]

Assuming leadership of the family business, Bill soon found that its financial position was more precarious than he had realized. "There were times when I was not at all sure we were going to survive financially," he later said. Donald Gordon, who managed the local newspaper, the *Leelanau Enterprise,* recalled that he once sold Milliken advertising space for which the department store could not pay for several months.[14]

After his father died, Milliken said, he felt the company had potential but needed an injection of capital. "I went out and borrowed a lot of money," he told Dan Angel.[15]

Under Bill's stewardship, J. W. Milliken, Inc., grew in sales volume from approximately $400,000 to almost $2 million annually. The store became a chain with satellites in Manistee and Cadillac.

Milliken often walked the mile and a half from the family home on the West Arm of Grand Traverse Bay to the downtown store. He redesigned the Traverse City storefront, adding a new marquee. He also enlarged the tearoom, oversaw the construction of a large parking lot at the rear of the store, installed an elevator, and redesigned the layout to put departments in "their location of advantage."[16] Helping Bill operate the stores was his sister Ruth, who was general merchandise manager for eight years. Their father, Bill said, called Ruth "the best merchandise manager I've ever seen in all my years of retailing."[17]

Before Bill assumed management of the company, a failed unionizing effort among store employees made "an indelible impression" on him. He sought to quell dissatisfaction and improve working conditions, reducing a 40-hour work week to 37½ in 1958 and improving benefits such as leave time and health insurance. "I think we had good employee relations in the store. There was a good feeling, a close feeling," he later said.[18]

As the business prospered, the Millikens replaced the small prefabricated house they had located on the choice Grand Traverse Bay property given to them by his parents as a wedding present with a single-level, contemporary house. Floor-to-ceiling glass on the bay side afforded the family a constant perspective on the changing colors and moods of the water.[19]

In the meantime, Bill was becoming more active in civic affairs. He headed two local Red Cross fund drives, served as president of the Boy Scouts, was president of the Chamber of Commerce, joined the Rotary Club, and served on the initial governing board of Northwestern Michigan Community College. In 1953, he participated in an intercultural exchange program operated by the U.S. State Department and

From Businessman to Senator

spent more than two months in West Germany. The experience warmed his feelings toward the West German people, he once said. He lectured to the Rotary Club in Traverse City that July on his experiences in Germany, impressing Guy VanderJagt, who would later hold the local congressional seat for more than two decades.

A 1955 front-page story in his hometown newspaper that ran when Bill stepped down from his post as president of the Chamber of Commerce featured a photograph of the boyish Milliken. The retiring chief discussed the chamber's support for a "jet air base" and its work on city traffic problems and beautification of the bay shore.[20]

One of Milliken's most important posts was his six-year chairmanship of the Grand Traverse County Republican Party, which allowed him to build a political base and forge ties with other up-and-coming young politicians.[21]

Although Helen Milliken was also active in the community, the rearing of two children occupied much of her time in the late 1940s and 1950s. Born on October 14, 1946, Bill Jr. inherited his father's features and even-handed demeanor. Elaine, the Millikens' other child, was born on June 6, 1948.

Helen remembers the early years in Traverse City as sometimes difficult emotionally: "When we moved to Traverse City after Yale, I thought it was a wilderness. There were no neighbors within a quarter mile. It felt like we were deep in the woods . . . We had very deep snow. It might have been 30 inches deep that winter. It was daunting to be in the confinement and isolation of winter. I thought I had moved to the Arctic."[22]

Compared to the Denver area, where she had grown up, the new environs "seemed like a remote wooded outpost," Helen remembers. Her mother visited the newlyweds in their cottage the first year and was told by Bill's father that as a boy he could remember Indians paddling their canoes down the bay. The next morning Helen's mother confessed to a sleepless night spent "listening for the Indians."[23]

Far from her home and lacking the stimulation of a large city or university, Helen found an outlet in community activities after Bill Jr. and Elaine reached school age. She occasionally worked in the family store, volunteered for the Red Cross, taught skiing to children, led a Brownie troop of which Elaine was a member, and joined the local garden club.

Life for the Milliken children often involved long periods of separation from their father because of the family business and his civic involvement. "I didn't see much of him at times," Bill Jr. said. "He was always working." Just as Bill's father had done, however, he tried to expose Bill Jr. to the wonder of the outdoors. The son remembers one outing with his father and a young cousin, a trip to a hunting cabin in Michigan's Upper Peninsula, not far from Sault Sainte Marie. Although the cabin lacked plumbing and electricity, to the young boy it was "a great father-son experience." He added, "The fly rod didn't make it off the wall much while we were there."[24]

Daughter Elaine inherited her father's shyness and, like Bill Jr., his features. It was not until she attended the University of Michigan Law School in the early 1970s that she came into her own as a forceful advocate for equal rights for women.

Two Traverse City experiences of prejudice during the years before he sought political office left an impression on Bill. When he proposed building a garden apartment on a parcel of land near the family residence, a local attorney who represented a neighbor "had no problem using whatever tactics he could," Milliken said. "He publicly threatened his client would sell her property to 'Negroes' if I built the apartment." The city's Planning Commission denied Milliken's rezoning request.

The Traverse City Country Club's policy of barring Jews from membership appalled both Bill and his father, who fought to reverse it. For many years, a boulder at the entrance to the club bore a sign that read "Gentiles only." Bill said he was "astounded" by the policy and the sign. After years of controversy, the club rescinded its discriminatory policy.[25]

The appealing Milliken family and Bill's persona began winning the admirers who would support his political ambitions. Bill saw an opening in the 1960 state Senate race for the Twenty-seventh District, which encompassed all or parts of seven counties in northwestern Lower Michigan. Characteristic of the moderate Milliken, the reason for his foray into elective politics was dissatisfaction with the government gridlock brought about by the conservative Republican majority in the state legislature. "I wanted to run for office because the party was really in the grip of some Neanderthals," he said. "Some of them were a disgrace to the party, and we needed a housecleaning."[26]

Because of the unusual role Milliken played in the history of the local, state, and national Republican Party, it is worth considering why he chose to be an active Republican in a state that made a claim to be the GOP's birthplace.

The claim dated from July 6, 1854, when a "fusion" meeting was held at Jackson, Michigan, between disaffected Democrats and Whigs angry about the imminent passage by the U.S. Congress of the Kansas-Nebraska Act, which permitted the expansion of slavery in areas north of the so-called Missouri Compromise line of 1820.[27]

Michigan, recently a frontier state, tended to be populated by a younger generation of transplants who seemed more willing to abandon old party allegiances than their counterparts in eastern states. In April, [*Kalamazoo Telegraph* editor George A.] Fitch editorialized, "We cannot look to any other movements of the old parties in reference to the Nebraska bill and questions touching slavery that bring any promise of success, nor to any class of old broken-winded, broken-down politicians; but we may look with a strong hope of success to see these measures consummated by the honorable and active young men of the State."[28]

The frustration and anger over the potential expansion of slavery into states and territories that Michiganians thought should be free galvanized thousands to attend the July 6 Jackson meeting. Forced to move from the city hall to an oak grove on the edge of the village, the gathering featured "patriotic tunes" and the adoption of a strong anti-slavery platform. Delegate Jacob M. Howard offered a resolution giving the fusion party the name Republican.[29] Adopted by the attendees in Jackson, the name stuck. A memorial plaque installed at the spot in 1910 reads: "Here under the oaks July 6th, 1854, was born the Republican Party, destined in the throes of civil strife to abolish slavery, vindicate democracy and perpetuate the union."[30]

In the autumn elections in Michigan, the new Republican Party slate swept to victory, with Kinsley Bingham, a former Democrat, becoming the nation's first Republican governor. Six years later the Republican Party won its first presidency with the election of Abraham Lincoln of Illinois.

Although the party was identified through the end of the nineteenth century as the enemy of slavery and the friend of African Americans, it also won a reputation for both zealotry in rhetoric and pragmatism in the handling of the rights of the emancipated slaves. A Michigan Republican, U.S. senator Zachariah Chandler, was a leader of the so-called Radical Republicans in Congress, who took a punitive attitude toward the readmitted southern states after the war. Chandler's pungent rhetoric scorched his opponents, but his commitment to the newly freed slaves was tenuous at best. Although he championed the enlistment of African Americans in the union army during the Civil War, he largely turned his back on civil rights for them when the conflict was over. A biographer wrote, "If the role of the lawgiver is to give his people what they should have but do not want, then unquestionably Chandler failed in the area of civil rights . . . [T]he Senator managed to view the problem with philosophic coolness. 'As sure as there was a god in Israel,' he once said, 'the negro would work out his own salvation.'"[31]

Beginning at about the time of the Great Depression, which followed the stock market crash of 1929, the national GOP earned a reputation as obstructionist and isolationist, opposing much of the Democratic president Franklin Delano Roosevelt's New Deal program while fiercely resisting U.S. participation in the conflict that would become World War II until the attack on Pearl Harbor. The war experience, however, inspired an independence from party doctrine on the part of Michigan Republican Arthur Vandenberg, a former isolationist in the U.S. Senate, who outspokenly renounced that cause "in favor of the internationalism of Roosevelt and Truman."[32] In Michigan and some surrounding midwestern states, a "pragmatic to progressive" strain of Republicanism dating back to the reformist impulses of President Theodore Roosevelt and Wisconsin senator Robert M. La Follette persisted, rarely controlling party doctrine but serving as an alternative to the reflexively probusiness impulses of the mainstream party. It was this brand of Republicanism that Bill Milliken's father had adopted, and it would shape the positions and values of his son as he entered elective politics.

Michigan had drawn unwelcome national attention during the 1959–60 legislative session when Governor Williams and the Republican-controlled legislature reached an impasse on a substantial state budget deficit. One of the senators participating in the impasse that led to a "payless payday" for state employees was Republican John Minnema, a three-term incumbent.

From Businessman to Senator

39

"My opponent was sort of part of the old boys network. He was part of the group of entrenched politicians practically married to lobbyists. He had a cozy relationship with special interests," Milliken said. "But he stood for the things I didn't stand for, and didn't like."[33]

Milliken acknowledged that his decision to run for the state Senate instead of the more natural choice, the state House, was "partly sentimental."[34] His father and grandfather had once held the same Senate seat, and victory would continue a family tradition.

In his March 24 announcement of candidacy in the *Traverse City Record-Eagle,* Milliken said he was "acting on a life-long interest in government and a firm personal conviction that active participation in politics is an obligation of citizenship."[35] The newspaper noted that Milliken was "already well known in Lansing" thanks to his Waterways Commission service, noted the two major expansions of the family department store, and mentioned the "national recognition" he had received during his trip to West Germany with five others in 1953. His military service also earned a paragraph.

Perhaps caught off guard by Milliken's announcement, the incumbent, Minnema, only gained comparable space on the front page of the *Record-Eagle* the next day. "I will stand by my record in the Senate as a man who has received the support of the people who stand for government by the people; government at its source," he said.[36] A former eight-year member of the Traverse City Commission and mayor of the city for one year, Minnema boasted of numerous other community credentials, including two years of service as director of the County Road Association of Michigan.

Challenging an incumbent through a primary election fight is rarely a successful mission, but 1960 was a year of change. At the end of eight years of the Eisenhower presidency, Americans were anxious about the nation's rivalry with the Soviet Union, and a growing civil rights movement was releasing new energies at home. At the age of 38, Milliken's boyish looks and charm, as well as his dogged effort to unseat Minnema, contributed to his momentum.

"I shudder to remember the work that I had to do in that campaign," Milliken recalled. "I went door-to-door. I wore out a couple of pairs of shoes. I went to all the little towns and places, and it worked."

Operating as his own campaign manager, Milliken said he "worked like a dog." Admitting that he had doubts about his chances at times, he said he remained optimistic: "I don't think anyone had ever run as hard in that district as I did."

Helen Milliken established herself as a supportive partner in Milliken's first campaign, but she admitted that her husband's decision to run was a surprise.

"I was astounded that he was going to take the plunge into this," she said.[37] "That summer, every day, I'd pack him a lunch and he'd go out to one of the counties in the district, going door-to-door. I didn't understand his passion for it. Bill was already successful. In 1960, he was gone all week most of the time. That was an adjustment. Politics makes great demands on a family."

His opponent's uncertainty on the issue of taxes played a significant role in the primary election. Minnema took several contradictory positions on whether the state should institute an income tax to ease its reliance on the property tax. At a debate sponsored by the League of Women Voters, Minnema at first hedged on the issue of an income tax but then gave the impression that he favored it, apparently catering to an audience of public-minded league members. Milliken then triumphantly produced a newspaper article in which Minnema had said he opposed the income tax. "He confirmed once again that evening that he would say or do just about anything that would please his audience," Milliken observed.[38]

Milliken, meanwhile, was unequivocal in his support for an income tax because, he said, "ability to pay was the fairest basis for supporting government services." Although most of his would-be constituents opposed an income tax, Milliken believes he won points for openly supporting an unpopular position. "I think I won in the primary essentially because I was willing to take a position—however unpopular—and he was perceived as an equivocator."[39]

In a final advertisement run just before the primary, Milliken said he would "make sound and moral business principles work in Michigan government" and touted his community involvement. He presented himself as "an experienced businessman and administrator," a volunteer in government, and "a veteran of outstanding war record."[40]

The primary election bore out Milliken's appeal, his political judgment, and his hard work. He trounced Minnema on August 2 by a margin of 9,921 to 4,250 votes, sweeping all seven counties. In the heavily Republican district, Milliken's election to office in the November general election was almost a foregone conclusion. He defeated Democrat John B. Hopkins, a motel owner, by a margin of 26,040 to 12,226.

The victory was only the prelude to a bigger challenge. When Milliken arrived in Lansing in January 1961 to take the oath of office, he found himself part of a distinct minority of moderate Republican senators. Although seven other moderates had either been elected or won reelection—among them John Stahlin of Belding, who would soon become a Milliken confidant—the conservative Republicans still dominated the party caucus. That left only one tactic to the moderates: aligning themselves with the Senate's minority Democrats in the vote on committee assignments. With the support of the Democrats, the Republican moderates succeeded in electing John Fitzgerald chair of the Senate Business Committee, "the first tangible evidence of their clout."[41] United Press International dubbed the vote for Fitzgerald a "coup" that overthrew a "GOP conservative bloc which has long dominated Michigan legislative action."[42] It was the first of many Lansing battles that Milliken would fight with the conservative wing of his own party. A "jubilant" Milliken issued a statement hailing the win.

> The Senate has projected an image of intractability in the past and the new Chairmanship of the Senate Business Committee symbolizes an action that is good for the Republican party and good for the people of Michigan. I feel that the senators who opposed the ultra-conservative bloc are speaking for the real Republican Party of the state.[43]

Milliken received a humbler assignment, the chairmanship of the Senate's Veterans Affairs Committee. It was a panel that rarely saw action, and Milliken recalled that only three bills were considered during the two-year session. Milliken's only staff support was provided by Phyllis Dell, who also served several other committees. Dell would later join Milliken's personal staff during his service as lieutenant governor and governor.

His first impressions of the legislative process were not favorable and helped fuel his ambition to move to the executive branch. Milliken found the legislative process "frustrating. You debated bills endlessly, often to little effect. The executive position, where you could move more without being a debating society, suited my temperament better."[44]

Unwilling to play the role of a quiet freshman legislator who would be seen and not heard, Milliken soon engineered a remarkable rebellion against the entrenched conservative Republican leadership. Meeting over two summer days in the Park Place Hotel in Milliken's hometown, the eight moderates fashioned what would come to be known as the Traverse City Pact.[45] It called for reform on issues ranging from civil rights to tourism. The group recommended broadening local tax bases beyond the property levy, expansion of the community college system, increased research on the causes and cures of mental health illnesses, and the enactment of laws permitting farm commodity groups to tax themselves to pay for research on and promotion of their products. The pact declared, "It is our intention to work within the Party structure to win approval of a forward-looking action program for Michigan."[46]

Perhaps archly, the *Record-Eagle* put the word *moderate* in quotation marks in its coverage of the meeting and noted that the eight men had issued a "long statement."

> The eight senators said they realized that some of their recommendations would cost more now, but that they would save tax dollars over a period of time. They also said the means of carrying out their plans for Michigan progress would be recommended after the state constitutional convention and consideration of a long-range revenue structure.[47]

The newspaper quoted approvingly the moderates' statement of support for increased tourism promotion. "No other state offers the year-round attractions which Michigan boasts, but many other states surpass us in promoting their features," said the moderates. "A substantial increase in appropriations for this purpose and a more intensive effort to develop Michigan as a tourist state will speed us toward the goal of a billion-dollar-a-year tourist industry. Tax dollars spent for this purpose will be more than repaid as the industry grows."[48]

The moderates' declaration won notice in Detroit's daily newspapers as well. Noting Milliken's role as host, the *Detroit Free Press* highlighted the willingness of the eight moderates to support increased taxes to pay for their program. The paper also pointed out the moderates' support for action on civil rights, including legislation assuring equal

From Businessman to Senator

rights for all in public accommodations and measures to assure open housing in Michigan.[49] A little over a week later the *Free Press* reported that the moderates were facing retaliation from lobbyists over their declaration and were angry. Milliken ally John Stahlin told the paper that "whisky-buying lobbyists already are trying to create an impression in my district that we are extremely liberal." But Republican national committeeman John Martin pledged that party leaders would come to the aid of any Senate moderate facing reprisals from the lobbyists.[50]

Milliken and Arnie Levin, a former *Detroit News* reporter and a Republican Party publicist, had worked together for several days to draft the document before the meeting convened on August 16. Although the moderates revised the draft before it was released, the "document that emerged was in large part Milliken's."[51] Milliken remembered the reaction four decades later. "It attracted quite a bit of press attention. It was revolutionary. Here were these upstarts trying to modernize the Republican Party."[52]

But, given the precarious nature of the moderates' voting power in the Senate and the tenacious hold with which the conservative Republicans clung to power, it would take another election to give Milliken and his allies a chance to act on their vision.

In the meantime, Milliken began to distinguish himself as a Republican concerned about equal opportunity. At the start of a decade that would be characterized nationally by tension and civil unrest over race relations and civil rights, Milliken stood squarely for full enfranchisement of all citizens.

Responding to concerns over discrimination in the screening of potential home buyers and renters, the state Corporation and Securities Commission had established a regulation barring such bias in 1960. Having provoked an uproar among some realtors and conservatives, who viewed the regulation as an intrusion on the private sector and a barrier to the "preservation" of white communities, the rule attracted opponents in the state Senate. In March 1962, Republican senator Charles Feenstra of Grand Rapids offered legislation to override the so-called Rule 9. Milliken, whose Republicanism harkened in part back to the days of Lincoln as "the party of civil rights," bucked the real estate lobby and others in his party and opposed repeal of the rule. Quoting the 1960 Republican state party platform, he said:

We believe that in the matter of the sale or rental of property no group should be allowed to interpose itself between an individual owner and the would-be buyer or renter. We vigorously condemn a screening system for the disqualification of some buyers on grounds of race, creed, color or national origin.[53]

The rule was sustained. Later Milliken explained, "The right to live where one wants to live is about as fundamental a right as there is, and I believe it supersedes so-called private property rights . . . I supported Rule 9 in 1962 because I felt it was morally, fundamentally, legally and constitutionally correct."[54] He added, "The realtors were just up in arms. [But] I felt very strongly about that. I paid a price for that. I represented a district not known for its liberal thought, and they were surprised."[55]

The stand was significant. Foretelling Milliken's later defense of African American and other minority communities as governor, it was particularly remarkable given his youth in an almost totally Caucasian community. But, as Milliken explained, "My parents taught us to view all people equally."

4

NUMBER TWO TO
NUMBER ONE

T HE 1962 ELECTION was good news for Milliken and the
   moderate Republicans. After 14 years of Democratic governors G. Mennen Williams and John Swainson, voters chose a 55-year-
old Republican, George Romney, to run the state. And they sent to
Lansing five new moderate Republican senators, giving the Milliken
faction a slender 12-to-11 majority in the GOP Senate caucus.

The election of Romney marked more than just the end of Democratic domination of the governor's office. It signified the emergence of
a new breed of successful candidate for statewide office—the moderate
Republican—and the modernization of Michigan's legislative and
executive branches. In a time of social ferment and increasing complexity, the state would soon have a new constitution—forged under
the leadership of Romney—which strengthened the powers of the
state's chief executive and spawned the mixed blessing of a full-time
legislature.

Romney was an interesting study. Born in July 1907 in a colony run
by the Church of Jesus Christ of Latter-Day Saints in Chihuahua, Mex-
ico, he accompanied his family to Salt Lake City in 1912 as a result of the
Mexican revolution. His Mormon faith shaped his life's path and outlook. Before attending college, he served as a missionary in England and
Scotland, and during his political career he was known for his absti-

nence from liquor and caffeinated beverages and his strong personal morality—and, some would say, his intolerance of the frailties of others.

Romney never completed a degree at the two colleges he attended, the University of Utah in Salt Lake City and George Washington University in Washington, DC, but he made a mark for himself in the nation's capital nonetheless as a lobbyist for the Alcoa Corporation during the 1930s. During World War II, he served as head of the government's Automotive Council for War Production, promoting the coordination of resources and materials to boost automotive production. He then served as chief executive officer of the Nash-Kelvinator Corporation and after its merger with the Hudson Corporation became chairman of the new firm, the American Motors Corporation (AMC). Based in Wisconsin, Romney won national renown for bringing the company back from the brink of failure by touting the development and sale of compact cars. His business success and influential role in drafting the state's new constitution at a 1961 convention propelled him onto the Michigan political stage.

Although Milliken regarded Romney as a "forward-looking" governor, the two men were never close personally.[1] The Romney and Milliken personalities were not always compatible. Although both men shared a taste for the initiative that a chief executive could exercise, Romney tended to operate on his own judgments and hunches, often without extensive consultation; Milliken preferred seeking consensus before acting in most situations. In addition, while Romney was a relative newcomer to politics who was starting at the top of Michigan's executive branch, Milliken had honed his skills over more than a decade prior to entering the Senate.

Romney is definitely not a typical politician. The *Wall Street Journal* quoted one friend who described him (in 1961) as "incredibly unsophisticated politically. When he meets party professionals, it's like a Salvation Army girl in a burlesque house." [Selig] Harrison summed up his political appeal as that "of a man who has made it to the top in the knifeplay of modern American business competition and yet personifies the old fashioned virtues." To the junior executive in Chicago, his rise gives reassurance that for all of our bigness there is still room at the top; and for the young man's mother, he is proof that nice boys don't necessarily get there last.[2]

Number Two to Number One

In his second two-year term as a state senator, Milliken became his party's floor leader, the second-highest position in the Republican caucus, helping to round up votes while championing causes both successful and unsuccessful. He backed legislation establishing a Construction Safety Commission to assure soundness in buildings, chaired a committee that recommended economies in government spending worth a reported $2 million over two years, and coauthored a law that provided state aid for community mental health programs designed to assist patients in living and working outside institutions. The program soon expanded to provide a 75 percent share of funding when matched with local expenditures.

Chairing the Senate Committee on Education in the 1963–64 session, Milliken helped create a scholarship program for high school graduates and sponsored a law providing bus transportation to parochial-school children, a concept he would continue to advocate during his years as governor. He sponsored, but did not win approval of, legislation providing up to two hours per week of "released time" from public schools for students taking religious instruction off school grounds.[3] Given Milliken's personal detachment from organized religion, his support of public measures for religious schools struck some as a calculation designed to attract voters of faith, particularly Catholics.

One of his most controversial—and ultimately unsuccessful—initiatives was an attempt to banish, or at least limit the number of, the billboards flanking Michigan's highways. An early signal of his concern for the state's scenic beauty, the legislation failed in the 1963–64 session and would appear again on his agenda as late as 2003, when he cochaired a state land-use commission that would recommend billboard limits.

The 1964 version of Milliken's bill would have established a "scenic area commission" to designate areas of scenic significance where typical commercial signage would be outlawed. "We are simply trying to preserve the beauty still offered in the landscape of northern Michigan especially," he said as he introduced the measure. "Billboards not only disrupt the scenery, but studies have shown that they are distracting to the motorist."[4] Although it was cosponsored by 16 other senators and approved by one committee, the bill died at the end of the 1964 session under the smothering weight of billboard lobbyists.

WILLIAM G. MILLIKEN

"This beautiful state was, and is even more so now, being uglified by billboards," he said in 2003. "It is such a beautiful state, and to allow that to happen . . . They're obscene."[5]

Milliken would always have an ambivalent attitude toward the lobbyists. After leading the moderate Republican revolution in the Senate, Milliken recalled that "the lobbyists became quite eager to be friends with us. They used the lunch hour and the dinner hour and the cocktail hour to be friends. Some of them were helpful, and some were not. I listened to them and sometimes felt they had useful, factual information in specialized areas. As long as you knew where they were coming from, you were fine."[6]

Milliken had briefly considered seeking the Republican Party nomination for lieutenant governor in 1962. Deferring instead to a Senate colleague, John Stahlin, who lost in a three-way primary election that August, Milliken held his cards for a better round and also gained an ace. "Mishandled by the old guard" before Milliken's arrival in the Senate and "more progressive than he appeared" in Milliken's view, Stahlin would become his devoted ally and fund-raiser in future statewide campaigns.

In 1963, Milliken briefly considered seeking a seat in the U.S. House of Representatives. It was the only time he seriously considered federal office. "I started campaigning in the congressional district, which went down to Muskegon. That was about the time JFK was assassinated. But the more consideration I gave it, the more inclined I was not to do it."[7] When incumbent Robert Griffin, a longtime Republican associate from Traverse City, decided to seek reelection to the congressional seat instead of making his expected run for the U.S. Senate, the route to Washington was closed for Milliken. He saw a potential opening on the state level, where he would spend the rest of his career in elective office.

Under the new state constitution, in 1964 the governor and lieutenant governor would be elected on the same ticket for the first time.[8] Despite the stiff headwinds suffered by the national Republican ticket in the wake of President Kennedy's murder and a Democratic surge in response to it, Republican governor Romney was considered popular and likely to win reelection. And he had expressed no public preference about the choice of his running mate. Milliken moved to fill the opening. After consulting with friends and receiving a noncommittal response from Romney, he announced his candidacy for lieutenant governor on March 9, 1964, the first Republican to do so.[9]

It is unclear whether Romney's flirtation with the idea of running for president as a moderate alternative to the conservative Barry Goldwater emboldened Milliken. In January, Romney had let it be known that he was willing to be drafted as a presidential candidate at the July national convention, leaving the state's Republicans "shocked and perplexed."[10] If Romney ran for president, who would fill his shoes on the state ticket? The stunning declaration by Romney "focused attention on the state GOP's need for grooming a worthy successor, a task neglected by the party to date with no apparent concern expressed by Romney himself."[11] While it soon became clear that Romney would not actively pursue national office in 1964, the rest of Milliken's time as lieutenant governor featured speculation that he might someday succeed the governor.

Pledging to help implement Romney's program if he were nominated and elected, Milliken touted his legislative experience rather than his stance on particular issues as a credential: "We have already turned a corner in the state and the future is bright. Many problems have now been turned into opportunities for constructive, positive action. We are making excellent progress . . . I believe that success in the future will depend to a considerable extent on team leadership and close liaison between the executive and legislative branches of government and citizens of the state." He said he had consulted with party officials across the state and received a "most gratifying" response.[12]

The response of political reporters was also somewhat gratifying. James S. Brooks, a reporter for United Press International, said the ticket of Romney, Milliken and Elly Peterson, who was expected to run against the incumbent Democratic senator, Phil Hart, "would appear to assure the Republicans one of their most attractive and articulate tickets in state history." Brooks added that "Milliken would lend a geographic balance to the ticket and his support of Romney's programs would certainly seem to make him an acceptable candidate with the governor."[13]

Volunteers began to multiply across Michigan. One enthusiastic supporter was a young Grand Rapids attorney, Hilary Snell. As chairperson of the Downtown Republican Club in the early 1960s, Snell had invited Milliken to make a lunchtime presentation on the issue of state taxes. He later said that Milliken's tax talk "just blew me away . . . The grasp he had on this issue, and the erudite careful understanding he had on the issue, and all its implications." As soon as he heard of Milliken's candidacy for lieutenant governor, Snell added, "I called him up and said, 'Sign me up.'"[14] Snell offered to resign from his post as assistant chairman of the Kent County Republican Party, but Milliken encouraged him to stay on, further evidence of the candidate's consideration, according to Snell. "I thought he was a sharp young senator who was everything I could aspire to be. He was smart and articulate."[15]

A young Republican activist named Keith Molin got a glimpse of another Milliken at about that time. Driving to Lansing from suburban Detroit in March 1964, Molin heard mention of Milliken's name as a possible candidate for lieutenant governor on WJR Radio. Walking into Holly's, a downtown Lansing restaurant, Molin was ordering his "standard toast and coffee" when he recognized a man sitting alone on a stool next to the wall as Senator Milliken. Surprised to see Milliken in such an unassuming posture, Molin approached him and mentioned the radio report. "What do you think?" Milliken asked. When Molin replied favorably, Milliken invited him to the announcement news conference. It was the beginning of a long political partnership.[16]

Milliken was hungry for the job and determined to show it. Shuttling from one county Republican organization to another across the state, he sought formal endorsements. "I worked hard at it. I used some of the strategies and approaches I'd used to get to the State Senate. I worked the state. I was out there. I had some wonderfully loyal people who worked for me."[17]

The fast pace of the campaign for the state's second-highest office further consumed the time of William Milliken, the father, leading to later regret. When the Milliken children, Bill Jr. and Elaine, reached high school age, each was sent to boarding school. Bill attended Suffield Academy in Connecticut and Elaine Concord Academy in Massachusetts. "They were both outstanding schools," Milliken later said, "but that meant separation for long periods of time . . . I have mixed feelings about what we did. One of the things I missed was being with my children."[18]

From the perspective of Bill Jr., the significance of his father's political career dawned slowly as the senior Milliken advanced onto the statewide stage. "I wasn't really cognizant of the [1960] senate campaign or its significance, which was that [his father] would be around less . . . As for Suffield, that was a new concept for me. I didn't wake up one morning wanting to go there, but it turned out all right." Graduating from Suffield in 1965, Bill later couldn't remember whether his parents had visited him at the prep school other than to drop him off and attend his graduation.[19]

Among other groups he courted in his bid to be lieutenant governor, Milliken consciously cultivated Catholics and other people of faith. A profile of the senator in the *Catholic Weekly* less than three weeks before the announcement of his candidacy for lieutenant governor emphasized Milliken's interest in expanding state support for non-public schools. "We are going into a whole new period in reviewing the areas in which we can constitutionally assist some of our non-public enterprises," he said. "We are going to need a lot of thoughtful and responsible consideration on both sides of the question of aiding private schools, in order to find areas of agreement." He specifically touted his bill providing public funds for transportation to parochial schools.[20]

But Milliken also had last-minute, and surprising, opposition. On July 8, while Milliken was out of the state attending the Republican National Convention, another Republican, Allison Green, the 52-year-old Speaker of the House, announced his candidacy for lieutenant governor. There were indications that George Romney preferred him to Milliken. "Personally, I think Governor Romney really preferred the Speaker," Milliken said in 2003. "He had local government experience and deep knowledge of state government."

He was also more conservative than Milliken and could act as link to and buffer against the right wing of the party, with which Romney was not universally popular. A 14-year veteran of the legislative wars, Green came from rural central Lower Michigan. Green, who faced questionable reelection prospects in November because of a Democratic-controlled reapportionment plan, argued that he could better serve the party as lieutenant governor than as the likely minority leader of a shrunken GOP House delegation.

Although Romney remained neutral in public, there was no question that he had asked Green to run before Milliken's March announcement. More than 30 years later, Green wrote to his former foe: "Early in the year, possibly in mid-February, Gov. Romney invited me to his home in East Lansing for early breakfast. When we got around to discussions I was amazed to learn that he wanted me to consider running with him in November. This idea had never crossed my mind, and the rough and tumble politics of the house seemed more exciting. He seemed to think we would make an excellent team."[21]

A party loyalist, neither flashy nor flamboyant, Green could be expected to remain in the shadow of the charismatic governor, while reporters continued to rave over Milliken's youthful good looks and unusually liberal positions. A typical example was a piece speculating on his political future in 1963.

> Milliken is Yale-educated. He is the third generation head of this city's largest department store and son and grandson of former state senators. He has the fast mind, personal charm and private wealth needed for a strong campaign.[22]

Green's entry into the race for lieutenant governor touched off a new urgency in the Milliken camp. Milliken appointed John Stahlin as his campaign manager and began running a more structured, methodical campaign. Continuing to seek county party endorsements, Milliken also began lining up delegates to the state's September party convention, trying to assure a count that would provide victory. Contributing to his eventual success were at least three factors beyond organization. A strong endorsement from U.S. representative Robert Griffin in the form of a letter to all convention delegates provided a boost. Romney's eight-to-one margin of victory in the September gubernatorial primary election over conservative former legislator George Higgins undermined the argument that Romney needed a conservative like Green to balance the ticket. Finally, Democratic Party state chairman Zolton Ferency raised ethical questions about Green's handling of a scandal involving a Tuscola County judge.[23]

Although nervous about his opposition, Milliken was the clear choice among young party workers such as 31-year-old William F. McLaughlin, who had left his insurance business to work for the Michigan GOP. "It seemed to me the old guard from outstate was the main body of support for Greene [sic] and the new young Turks in the Party were lining up behind Milliken. I don't think either one would have made a difference as far as Romney's electability went but I was thinking of life after Romney. Who would succeed him as our Party leader and as the Party's main candidate? Milliken looked like an up and coming, electable leader. I didn't think Greene did."[24]

Entering the convention on September 17, the Milliken team was confident of success. But Green had substantial support. It was not until 36 votes remained to be cast and Milliken had a lead of 864 to 636 that Green conceded and asked for a unanimous vote in favor of the Traverse City man. Asked by Romney to accept a lower spot on the ticket as a candidate for secretary of state, a position best known for handling driver's licenses and license plates, Green accepted.

Press reaction to Milliken's selection as the candidate for lieutenant governor was warm. "The Republicans wound up with a 'glamour' ticket when they picked William Milliken, a young, handsome and articulate state senator from Traverse City," read a United Press International report. The Traverse City paper was even more effusive, declaring that Milliken "possesses the kind of intelligence that is so honed and refined that it doesn't show, which in the end is what impresses most voters. They want to elect an astute and human man to office, not someone who makes them feel inferior, but someone who makes them feel more aware and alive for having met him, and this is essentially the charm and impact of the Milliken personality."[25]

Romney was correct but not warm in congratulating Milliken on his nomination by the party, merely shaking his hand and offering a brief comment before walking away.[26] Milliken recognized the coolness and proudly considered his selection a personal accomplishment. "No one delivered the office to me on a silver platter," he later said. "I had to fight for the nomination."[27] Looking back on his relationship with Romney 40 years later, Milliken characterized it as "always cordial and friendly but never a deep kind of relationship. He seemed always to be thinking I was competing against him."[28] Milliken's former aide, Joyce Braithwaite-Brickley, put it this way in 2005: "Frankly, except as required by law and circumstance, there was no personal relationship between those two governors."[29]

The fall fight to become lieutenant governor was less eventful. The voluble Romney overshadowed Milliken on the campaign trail. Although incumbent Democratic president Lyndon Johnson was rolling to a landslide, Michigan voters were developing a reputation for ticket splitting that would later serve Milliken in his campaigns for the Michigan executive office. Romney disassociated himself from the presidential candidacy of Republican Barry Goldwater, implying that the Arizona senator was too extreme for his taste. While voters in 80 of the state's 83 counties gave Johnson the edge over Goldwater, Romney more than quadrupled his 1962 edge with a 400,000-vote margin that carried his lieutenant governor along. The victory enabled Romney to "emerge as a prime prospect for the 1968 GOP Presidential nomination."[30]

But Democrats won majorities in both the state House and Senate, the latter for the first time since the reelection of Franklin Delano Roosevelt during the Depression in 1936.[31] A reporter commented that Milliken might be just the thing to help bridge the divide between a Republican governor and Democratic Senate, over which the lieutenant governor would preside. "An able speaker and bearing a hard-to-dislike personality, he will continue strong personal relationships with individual senators, the staff and the press. Most importantly he will be a backstop to Romney, and the governor's most important link with the legislature." He could be a "rising political star," Charles Harmon speculated.[32]

An article published on the eve of Milliken's swearing in as lieutenant governor noted that he and wife Helen would spend their weekdays in an East Lansing apartment and return each weekend to their Traverse City home. Helen would enroll in the landscape architecture program at Michigan State University. Paired with a photograph of the couple and their two teenaged children, who were home from boarding school for the holidays, the article suggested that the constitutional reform of the office of lieutenant governor had supplied it with new powers, making Milliken "more of an assistant governor, performing duties requested by Gov. Romney."[33] It added, in what would become a refrain of both Milliken and the reporters who covered him throughout the next 18 years in Lansing, "His main concern is putting public interest in front of narrow partisan interests—looking at the problems as problems, not from a liberal or conservative point of view." In 1966, the *Traverse City Record-Eagle* suggested that Milliken might attempt to succeed Romney if the governor didn't run again or that he might pursue a U.S. Senate seat.

Although the dynamic Romney continued to capture press attention at his second inaugural on January 1, 1965, Milliken gained a fair share. A full-page photo spread in the *Grand Rapids Press* contained, in addition to a scene of Romney giving his inaugural speech in a heavy, wet snow, photos of the Millikens entering the lieutenant governor's office in the Capitol, of Elaine and Bill Milliken Jr. watching Romney speak, and of a receiving line that featured both the Romneys and the Millikens.[34]

Emboldened by their legislative landslides in the fall of 1964, including new control of the Senate, Democrats took a shot at Milliken in his role as presiding officer of the Senate. On the opening day of session in January 1965, they voted to deny Milliken the seat on the Committee on Committees traditionally given to a lieutenant governor. The symbolic slap deprived Milliken of a seat on the panel that established other Senate committees.[35] Although Milliken could not fight the move, he successfully opposed a Democratic attempt to deny the lieutenant governor the constitutional power to cast a tiebreaking vote in the Senate. "Now it was clear to [the Democrats] that the new lieutenant governor could be tough. Bill Milliken had notched goal number one."[36]

Milliken continued to attract favorable coverage early in his service as the state's number-two executive officer. A profile in the *Detroit Free Press* noted his "easy grin" but called him a "hard battler," pointing out that he had objected strongly when the reporter suggested that he had enjoyed a "bowl-of-cherries life, department store variety."

> His forefinger flashes à la Jack Kennedy. His voice becomes harder: "No one picked me to be lieutenant governor. What I got I fought for. I decided it was a job I could provide a public service in. I made a public appearance in every county in the state . . . I feel that anything that is worth fighting for you go out and fight for it."[37]

Perhaps the strongest recommendation in the profile came from Milliken's predecessor as lieutenant governor, Democrat T. John Lesinski, who had frequently unsettled Governor Romney. "Bill's a great man," Lesinski said. "He was a fine senator—and this is no con job . . . He's a real asset to his party. He's a moderate. He's understanding. He's ready to come to an honorable compromise." Lesinski added that when Milliken had voted on party grounds against a ruling Lesinski had made while chairing the Senate he had quietly approached him and apologized privately.[38]

Less than two weeks into his term, Milliken was winning notice for his "fast-paced timetable." Milliken announced that he would hold "office hours" in county courthouses around the state and had more speaking engagements than he could fill. The *Lansing State Journal* commented that "Friends who expect him to continue his climb in politics—perhaps eventually aspiring to the governorship—won't be surprised at his determination to travel widely and become better known to voters."[39]

Another article published half a year into his term added to the speculation that the "boyish-looking" Milliken was building a constituency and name recognition for future, higher office with his meetings around the state. Instead of returning exclusively to his private business when the legislature adjourned for the summer, the *Detroit News* noted, Milliken was still working full time "at his $17,500-a-year job." In his meetings with citizens in county courthouses, Milliken told a reporter, all citizens were welcome. "It's strictly nonpolitical. Republicans, Democrats, independents, anybody can come and talk. It's a marvelous opportunity to be in touch with people who don't know where else to go," Milliken said, adding that he tried to help those in need of state services.[40]

At the same time, Milliken observed that the expanded needs of the state government were putting it on a collision course with bankruptcy. Supporting the establishment of a state income tax, as he had done since his first candidacy for the Senate in 1960, Milliken lamented the lack of urgency among citizens he met regarding the state's fiscal problems.

Such high visibility was a conscious choice. "Clearly, George Romney was by temperament and habit used to running things," Dan Angel wrote. "He could delegate powers to underlings, but he was neither prepared nor disposed to share his own executive level responsibilities. If Milliken was to have the imaginative role he envisioned, he would have to loosen George Romney's strangle-hold on state government."[41]

Moves Milliken quietly made in his early days as lieutenant governor annoyed Romney. Milliken hosted a Lansing reception for county and state Republican officials in mid-January 1965, authorized the formation of a Milliken Advisory Group that would help plan fund-raising events for the lieutenant governor, and made plans to publish a four-page newsletter, *Dateline Lansing*, which would be distributed to over 2,000 opinion leaders. Romney reportedly summoned Milliken to the governor's residence when he learned that John Stahlin was forming a statewide organization for Milliken.[42]

The lieutenant governor's busy pace tempted reporters to predict great things in his future. While not openly courting it, Milliken did nothing to dampen the speculation. He later recalled: "I used to joke . . . that every time I shook [Romney's] hand I felt his pulse."[43]

But the lieutenant governorship is an office that, like the U.S. vice presidency, almost inevitably humbles its occupants. When President Johnson flew over Michigan and Ohio to inspect tornado damage in the spring of 1965, at Romney's request, Milliken joined him in Toledo and accompanied him to Minneapolis. But while making phone calls in the Minnesota airport he missed the presidential flight back to Toledo. Although news coverage described Milliken as "embarrassed," he made a quick recovery, boarding the press plane, which typically landed before Air Force One, and reaching the Toledo airport before Johnson. "He was the first to greet the tired Johnson as he stepped down from his sleek blue and white jet."[44]

Another embarrassment was Romney's occasional jealousy of Milliken's visibility. When the *Detroit News* reported one Sunday morning that the lieutenant governor had asked for and received an appointment with Detroit's Democratic mayor, Jerry Cavanagh, to "patch up old state-city feuds and negotiate a new era of peace," Romney exploded.[45] Milliken had read the article before the call and realized the governor was not likely to approve of his lieutenant's initiative. "I thought it was ill-advised now to attend the meeting, and I could truthfully tell him I had already canceled it . . . He was very sensitive about things like that," Milliken said.[46]

Milliken remembered another incident that illustrated the famous Romney temper. One year Romney, Robert Griffin, now a U.S. senator, and Milliken all converged on Traverse City's annual Cherry Festival parade. When the parade marshal asked the men who went first according to protocol, a governor or a U.S. senator, Romney, according to Milliken, made it clear that as chief executive of the state the governor always leads. "It was not becoming," Milliken said of the way Romney expressed himself.[47]

The governor and lieutenant governor had their most significant clash in the winter of 1966. Seeking to unseat Democratic incumbent Patrick McNamara for a U.S. Senate seat, the governor invited Milliken early in the morning to his Bloomfield Hills residence for a private meeting and proposed that Milliken seek support for the GOP Senate nomination at that weekend's state party convention as a consensus primary candidate, avoiding what Romney feared would be a bloody battle. When Milliken told the governor he preferred remaining in the state executive branch and had no interest in seeking the Senate seat, Romney, according to Milliken, grew angry. Jabbing his finger at Milliken, he said, "Look, no one gets a free ride" in the Republican Party. Romney then stormed off, leaving a nonplused Milliken wondering whether he should fetch his coat. Romney cooled off enough to get it for him.[48] "Forgive me, forgive me," the governor repeated in apology.[49]

When McNamara unexpectedly died in March 1966, Romney appointed Robert Griffin, then a Republican U.S. representative, to replace him. Griffin won election that November and reelection in 1972. He would be a consistent Milliken ally in Washington.

Despite the Romney-Milliken tension, the governor gradually began deploying Milliken in a number of new roles. One reason was necessity: traveling the nation in hopes of cultivating support for a future campaign for the presidency, Romney was out of the state for approximately 100 days in 1965, leaving Milliken in charge. But the two men also gradually developed a cordial if not close relationship, giving the governor enough comfort to assign him to help on specific projects. Romney appointed Milliken cochair of his Human Resources Council, which tried to marshal volunteer resources to solve social problems; gave him the lead role in a panel charged with recommending ways of cutting state government expenses and improving efficiency; and asked him to monitor the threat of widespread teachers' strikes in Michigan school districts during the fall of 1965.[50]

The strike assignment put Milliken in the headlines, even though it amounted to little more than acting as a state cheerleader for the resolution of local school district contract disputes without strikes. An example of the high profile the assignment generated was a front-page article in the *Detroit Free Press* headlined, "Milliken Tells Schools to Seek Court Action."[51] In it, the lieutenant governor said he was urging school boards unable to settle contract issues with their teachers to seek injunctions to force the instructors to return to the classroom. "This forced idleness must cease," he said. Milliken later regarded the role of monitoring teachers' strikes as an insignificant assignment. "The governor wanted to know, what were the strikes that were imminent?" he said. "My job was to see how serious the problem was going to be. He was always worried that if there was a major flare-up across the state it would be disastrous."[52]

Number Two to Number One

More substantive—and also highly visible—was Milliken's role as chair of the cost-cutting Total Research for Improved Management (TRIM) team. Under Milliken's leadership, the panel revoked permanent assignments of state cars to officials, improved inventory control at the Liquor Control Commission, and claimed the credit for saving taxpayers more than $150,000 annually.[53]

At his side during his service as lieutenant governor was Don Gordon, his chief of staff and a longtime associate from the Traverse City area. A past owner of the weekly *Leelanau Enterprise*, Gordon had served a term as a state representative and was Milliken's alter ego for years. Gordon helped Milliken chart a course somewhat independent of Romney but always respectful in public of the governor's prerogatives and ultimate decision-making authority. Still, Gordon was well aware that Romney and Milliken were not close, observing that the governor held his number two at arm's length. He said that the substantive assignments Milliken received as lieutenant governor were taken, rather than received, from Romney. Although Milliken often served as acting governor, Gordon said, "He didn't get much help from Romney's staff."[54]

Another aide, Fred Grasman, who had worked on Romney's 1962 campaign before returning to college and then joined Milliken's lieutenant governor staff, remarked that there is "an inherent conflict" between the two offices and staffs. "There never was a good model for a governor and lieutenant governor to work together," Grasman said. "Milliken kind of picked some of the issues he liked to work on, and Romney went along."[55]

Nothing stopped reporters from wondering about Milliken's future, particularly when Romney's presidential ambitions became clear. After the landslide reelection of Romney and Milliken as a ticket in November 1966, the chief of the Lansing bureau of the *Detroit Free Press* wrote that "this 44-year-old with the looks of a matinee idol, an astute businessman's mind and more than a touch of political magic, may step out [into the limelight] for good" if Romney either became president or resigned to seek a fresh challenge.[56]

Before Romney could make his bid for the presidency in the Republican primary process, however, events conspired to undermine his candidacy. One of the most significant was the Detroit riot of 1967. Triggered by a police raid on an after-hours drinking establishment in the inner city of Detroit on July 23, 1967, the riot lasted five days, left 43 people dead, injured 1,189, and resulted in the arrests of over 7,000 people.[57] Outrage among African American residents over charges of police brutality and the lack of quality housing and jobs has long been cited as a primary cause of the riot.

In addition to the near-catastrophic toll in human life and property, the riot took a political toll on Romney. He and President Johnson initially differed over whether to send in army troops as well as the National Guard to police the troubled area; Romney balked at the suggestion before relenting. Some observers said he was thinking first of the political implications of the riot, since the use of the army's 82nd Airborne unit from nearby Selfridge Air Force Base would suggest that the state had lost control of a civil problem.

Detroit's health plummeted still further after the riot, with so-called white flight accelerating and the overall population sinking from 1.8 million in 1950 to less than a million in the 2000 census. It also "led to an increased fear of the city among suburbanites which continues to this day."[58]

The riot had a lingering, searing effect not only on Detroit but on the entire state, its race relations, and suburban-Detroit relations. In 2004, the director of the Wayne State University Center for Urban Studies, Kurt Metzger, told the *Detroit Free Press,* "People are still using the excuses that came from the riot for staying out of Detroit and rejecting any responsibility for the problems left behind in Detroit. A lot of people in the suburbs don't even want to know about the other side of the story of the riot—the history of housing discrimination, the abuse by a segregated police force, the pressures that built up."[59]

In the same *Free Press* article, the Rev. Edgar Vann Jr., the pastor of Detroit's Second Ebenezer Baptist Church and a prominent religious leader, remembered, "It was absolutely surreal in the black community, as well. It was terrifying. This army was camped in our streets, shooting people."[60]

"What came out of the riots was an opportunity to consider what caused them in the first place," Milliken said. "The plight of the black population was finally seen as something to get damned serious about."[61]

Before the riot, Romney had tapped Milliken to demonstrate the state's concern for struggling Detroit. Attending the opening of the

GOP's Community Service Center on Woodward Avenue in April, Milliken had pledged to lend his energies to the party's effort to provide housing, counseling, and referral services to urban residents. The brainchild of state party chairperson Elly Peterson, the center bypassed the traditional state party structure. "Our primary task was to solve people's problems. We worked on everything from getting street lights fixed to finding baby formula," said GOP activist William McLaughlin, who later became the state party chairman. "We solved many problems and did indeed attract new young blacks to our cause."[62]

Although widely praised as a sign of the Republican Party's renewed commitment to urban and minority residents, the experiment did not win many lasting allies. McLaughlin blamed the harsh conservative rhetoric of President Richard Nixon and Vice President Spiro T. Agnew after their election in 1968 for disaffecting African Americans in Michigan and other places. But the party's outreach in Detroit and the riot itself had a lasting impact on Milliken that would help shape his gubernatorial record and legacy.

With Romney on the campaign trail, it fell to Milliken to try to acknowledge the anger and despair of the state's African Americans after the riots by promoting "fair housing" legislation that would bar discrimination in the sale or rental of housing. The governor tapped his lieutenant to drive the bill through the legislature while Romney took an international tour to promote his foreign policy credentials. Milliken declared the legislation "absolutely essential to the health and integrity of this state and this society."[63] When Senate Republicans balked at the measure during a special session in December 1967, Milliken used unusually tough language, telling the legislators that they would "look damned good in their seats Christmas Eve if the job is not done."[64] The House of Representatives rejected the legislation on December 21 by a vote of 55 to 47. Milliken said, "I think what happened here is a disgrace, but I don't despair . . . This is an idea whose time has come." He added that, while "enlightened legislators" had supported the measure, "lesser men have sought refuge from responsibility behind walls of rhetoric and mountains of delaying amendments."[65]

Milliken was willing to challenge Republican audiences to demonstrate their commitment to equal rights. At the annual Lincoln Day dinner of the Muskegon County Republican Party in early 1968, Milliken "left many area old line [R]epublicans shocked at the apparent liberalism displayed by their fair-haired and popular Lt. Gov."[66] The audience offered only "scattered and then more reluctant applause" when Milliken said, "One of our greatest challenges is to provide for adequate, decent housing for low-income families. Above all, this means the right for any man to buy or rent any house or apartment he can afford."[67]

Romney's continued pursuit of the presidential nomination provided numerous opportunities for Milliken to try on the governor's political clothing. By late November 1967, Romney was in effect declaring Milliken acting governor and heir to the office. "The lieutenant governor will act with full power and authority," he said at a meeting with reporters before leaving on a brief vacation and an extended tour of Europe and other locations that would keep him out of Michigan for 30 additional days. "The members of the executive staff will report to him . . . We are fortunate to have as able and experienced a man as Lt. Gov. Milliken . . . I have no question about his providing the necessary policy and direction to keep the state functioning as effectively as if I were here . . . My contact while I am away will be with him."[68] To Capitol reporter Bud Vestal, the words were as "close as Romney has come to saying Milliken will be his inheritor."

The speculation over Milliken's future as Romney's successor continued through much of the winter of 1968. But a comment Romney made on a political program hosted by Lou Gordon on Detroit television in September of the previous year would turn out to be the undoing of his presidential hopes. He said he had been "brainwashed" by American generals into supporting the Vietnam War effort while touring Southeast Asia in 1965. Carrying heavy freight in the cold war era, the term suggested that Romney did not have an independent mind, in fact, that he had been programmed by the generals, just as the Chinese did a U.S. serviceman in the movie *The Manchurian Candidate*. The comment touched off a furor in the news media. Romney was unable to sustain his candidacy and dropped out of the race two weeks before the February New Hampshire primary.

But Romney was not so seriously injured politically that he had lost his national value. As a thrice-elected governor of a northern industrial state and a moderate Republican, Romney would still have political currency with a Republican president. After Richard Nixon won the 1968 Republican presidential nomination, talk of Romney as a member of a Nixon cabinet flourished. Milliken has vivid memories of that time.

In October 1968, with Nixon ahead of the Democratic challenger, Hubert Humphrey, in the polls, the Republican candidate traveled to a rally at the Saginaw airport, where Romney and Milliken would greet him. "I remember riding with Romney, and as usual he liked to go fast," Milliken said. "He pressed the State Police driver to speed up. He was so eager not to be late that he leaped from the car and ran across a field."[69]

After Nixon concluded his speech, he approached Milliken and said with a smile, "It's good to see you again, Governor." Milliken reflected, "In retrospect, this was the first time I understood that if he won he might appoint George Romney to his cabinet."[70]

Nixon's narrow victory in November intensified the speculation. Not long after the election, Milliken received a call from Romney. As Milliken remembers it, the governor said, "I wanted to call and tell you that I have accepted [Nixon's] offer to join the cabinet, which of course means you will be governor."[71]

By now prepared for the news, Milliken said one of his first impulses was to call reporter George Weeks, at the time the foreign editor of United Press International (UPI) in Washington, and ask him to serve as his press secretary. Weeks accepted. The two men were acquainted from their Traverse City days. Don Weeks, George's father, had served as city editor of the *Traverse City Record-Eagle* and secretary of the Traverse City Chamber of Commerce, organizing the city's National Cherry Festival beginning in 1931 and the statewide observance of an annual Michigan Week in May beginning in 1955. Don Weeks had also served as a pallbearer at the funeral of William Milliken's father. The younger Weeks had followed Milliken's political career while reporting for UPI. He remembers visiting the lieutenant governor at his Traverse City store and remarking to himself with some surprise, "Here's somebody gung-ho about addressing the problems of the cities."[72]

Weeks helped Milliken get off to a good start with the hard-bitten Capitol press corps and would also help him establish and sustain a style of openness with reporters that would serve his political fortunes well. Weeks proved to be a good manager. He would later succeed Don Gordon and William Hettiger as Milliken's gubernatorial chief of staff.

Despite the occasional differences and lack of personal chemistry between the two men, Romney bequeathed Milliken critical resources. First, his three successful campaigns for governor in 1962, 1964, and 1966 had put many Michigan voters in the habit of electing a moderate Republican to the state's highest office. Second, many of the young men and women inspired by his political persona had devoted themselves to the hard work of rebuilding the party after 14 years of Democratic rule, creating a firm foundation for Milliken's future. Third, he had taught Milliken much about the governorship both by example and by providing the opportunity for the lieutenant governor to fill in for him during his absences. Fourth, and perhaps least measurable, was the impression Romney created of "Michigan on the move."[73] His activist program of tax reform, education funding, civil rights, business promotion, and conservation was difficult for Democrats to characterize in the terms they had successfully used against the GOP "Neanderthals" in the legislature that had acted as obstructionists throughout the 1950s. To both the nation he had sought to lead and millions of Michiganians, Romney projected the image of a state that was energetic, progressive, and determined. Milliken would benefit from that legacy.

Looking back on the slightly more than four years he spent as lieutenant governor, Milliken said the most valuable part of the experience was not any particular accomplishment but the process of getting to know Michigan, its people, and its government better.

Those years opened up a period of statewide political opportunity for me. Although I believe I made some valuable contributions to state government and to education in this period, it was the time spent in the area of personal growth that provided the greatest opportunities. I had time for study, reading, listening and achieving a statewide understanding, an enlargement of my own view.[74]

If there was any doubt that his "own view" was sharply different in some ways from that of his predecessor, it was dispelled even before Milliken ascended to the governorship. January 1969 brought a season of change to Michigan's Capitol and set a tone in Lansing that would persist for nearly 14 years.

5

FIRST IMPRESSION

Although George Romney was still governor of Michigan when the annual State of the State message was due in January 1969, he relinquished the constitutional task of setting forth the year's agenda to his lieutenant governor. In Romney's January farewell address to the state, he described Milliken as "experienced and able" and urged citizens to extend to him "the same understanding and consideration that you've given me."[1]

In the same farewell address, he suggested that the state should handle secular education while churches concentrated on "religious and moral instructions." Three days later, as Milliken enjoyed his "moment of glory" in delivering the State of the State message to the legislature, he broke with Romney on the issue by endorsing state aid to parochial schools. Reporters noticed.

> Governor-to-be William G. Milliken set out forcefully and dramatically Thursday to establish himself as his own man in state government, unfettered by the policies of Gov. Romney . . . Utilizing the forum of the State-of-the-State message in a jammed House chamber, Milliken picked the politically sensitive issue of Parochiaid and a position diametrically opposed to Romney to underscore the break.[2]

Milliken had indeed expressed sympathy for the budget problems of religious schools, adding, "It would be tragic if circumstances should cause the private schools and colleges, religious-affiliated or otherwise, to deteriorate and disappear."[3] A closer look at the speech by the same newspaper's editorialists revealed the governor-to-be attempting to strike a balance on the issue. The *Detroit Free Press* noted on its opinion pages that Milliken had added that public aid to the private schools would have to conform "with our constitutional restrictions" and that the legislature would have to find a source of revenue to pay for it. Fretting that Milliken might "find it difficult to hold the Legislature to his own interpretation of what is constitutional and what is fiscally sound," the newspaper said that Romney's comments had been "an unintentional unkindness to his successor" because they had forced him to address the issue before he had the authority to contribute to a solution.

Milliken's decision to address Parochiaid, in the eyes of some observers, was based not just on a desire to distinguish himself from Romney but also on the belief that he could court traditionally Democratic Catholic voters. Expecting strong opposition from Democrats in his upcoming 1970 election campaign, and running in a year that was traditionally hostile to the party of an incumbent (and at the time Republican) president, Milliken knew his chances could come down to a few thousand votes. It was one of the relatively few times he would be suspected of such a blatant political calculation.

Milliken uttered in his first speech as de facto governor a significant phrase that would serve for some as his political epitaph. He said he hoped his administration would be "known for its compassion, its idealism, its candor and its toughness in pursuit of public ends."[4]

The priorities outlined in the thematic speech were not typical for a Republican governor, although in some ways they expanded on those of his predecessor. In a significant change of emphasis, Milliken elevated "concern for our natural environment" to "a high place on our state agenda."[5] Noting overwhelming voter passage the previous November of a $335 million clean water bond and a $100 million recreation bond, Milliken said they represented a mandate for "immediate action by governments on every level." Referring to the motto on the state seal, he said "We tell our visitors, 'If you seek a pleasant peninsula, look about you.' Let us never be forced to add, 'But don't go near the water.'" He decried "the ravaging and wasting" of the state's natural resources.[6]

The other top priorities mentioned by Milliken in the speech included "human rights and crime" and "urban oriented government." Balancing support for the equal opportunity laws important to minority populations with the concerns about crime that were widespread in suburban, primarily white communities, Milliken stressed the former. "It is often suggested that laws cannot and will not change the minds of men. This half truth has served far too often as a rallying cry for those who opposed expressing, in law, the simple precepts of social justice. Law unenforced is, of course, a mere passive good wish. But law enforced does change human behavior and a change in behavior has a most definite effect on the minds of men."[7]

Milliken's forceful call for action to address urban problems was a striking utterance for a Republican governor. "Those citizens of Michigan who live in remote parts of the state—remote from the urban centers in a geographical sense—where urban problems seem so very, very far away, cannot sit smugly by, in tranquility, while our cities sink in despair," he said. "For the most practical and moral lesson which experience offers is simply this: that the well-being of each of us, and the quality of our own existence and that of our children, is bound up with the lives and well-being of countless others whose lives may never directly touch our own."[8]

Deliberately avoiding specifics, Milliken followed up the speech after he officially became governor with special messages to the legislature on water pollution (February 6), urban affairs (February 18), and education (April 4). In the messages, he laid out an activist program. The urban affairs message bristled with proposals, including the identification of nonprofit organizations to sponsor urban housing projects; a $50 million low-income-housing bond; increases in welfare funding, including $3.5 million in incentives for welfare recipients to acquire jobs; increased funding for community mental health programs; funding for urban mass transit; a pilot program to foster small businesses owned and operated by African Americans; and the establishment of a new Governor's Office on Urban Affairs in Detroit.[9]

Milliken's concern about urban Michigan, particularly the industrial cities of the southern Lower Peninsula, had been refined during his time as lieutenant governor according to Fred Grasman, a key staff member during Milliken's transition. "An outstate Republican being responsive to the needs of urban constituencies—it was extraordinary," Grasman said. "He had developed a worldview about the conflict between urban and rural Michigan and the need to bring them together."[10]

Milliken's appointment of a University of Michigan political science professor, John T. Dempsey, to head the Detroit office won both praise and criticism.[11] The latter came from two quarters: African Americans, who pointed out that Dempsey was white and not necessarily in tune with the concerns of urban residents; and Detroit Mayor Jerry Cavanagh, a Democrat. The mayor accused Dempsey of having supported Cavanagh's opponent for reelection. Milliken brushed off the criticism, saying that Dempsey would run the urban affairs office "objectively, responsibly and in no way politically." He also defended Dempsey's commitment to equal rights, noting that the professor had served as cochairman of the state's Civil Rights Commission since 1967.[12]

The response to Milliken's other early moves was warm. Legislators of both parties praised the January 9 speech, hailing Milliken's call for improved relations between the executive and legislative branches—sometimes strained under Romney. Republican Senate leader Emil Lockwood lauded Milliken's "sincere feelings that he wants cooperation between the executive office and the Legislature."[13] In one notorious incident during his years as governor, Romney had accosted Lockwood outside his office. When Lockwood failed to express support for the governor's position on an issue, Romney grabbed the senator by the lapels and ripped one loose.[14]

The *Detroit Free Press* said that Milliken's goals on urban affairs "ought to be the cause for mild rejoicing in Detroit and for general dancing in the streets if he can follow through. We will have a sympathetic administration in Lansing, and we can expect a genuine state effort to deal with our problems."[15]

Even before the speech, the unnamed "Capitol observers" that populate political columns were expressing hope for the Milliken era, telling one reporter that they expected Milliken "to be more of a team player than Romney and less emphatic about imposing his views on others."[16] On the other hand, noting his "nice-guy" image, some observers questioned his ability to govern. "The Legislature would eat him for breakfast every morning," said an unidentified Democrat.[17]

But in the same article it was noted that "a new Milliken, tougher than the pleasant fellow who seemed reluctant to twist arms as a floor leader," had emerged when he sought the lieutenant governor's office in 1964 without seeking or getting Romney's blessing.

Milliken's hometown newspaper was particularly proud of its first native son to serve as governor. In an article published the day after Milliken took the formal oath of office on January 22, 1969, the *Traverse City Record-Eagle* described the state's new chief executive as "youthfully handsome at 46" and complimented "his lovely wife."[18] Covering everything from Milliken's family tree to Helen and Bill's two pedigreed Siamese cats, the feature called the new governor "young in appearance but . . . mature in his thinking and outlook."[19]

The ceremonies accompanying Milliken's swearing in were simple. After a telephone call from Romney breaking the news that the U.S. Senate had confirmed his cabinet appointment and that he had been sworn in and was officially resigning, Milliken took the oath of office from state Supreme Court chief justice John R. Dethmers in a "very informal ceremony," said secretary Phyllis Dell.[20] Dethmers apologized for not wearing his robe. Milliken made an impromptu speech of 203 words and afterward celebrated with close friends over lunch at the Kellogg Center at Michigan State University.

Milliken sounded a note of eagerness in his brief message. "I don't know if Michigan is ready for Milliken, but I can assure you that I am ready for the job—and eager to get started on it."[21]

Members of the team with which Milliken surrounded himself shared one trait: utter loyalty to a man who they believed was the most ethical, kindest, and ablest politician in Michigan. Charlie Greenleaf, who served for a time as Milliken's education adviser, remembered his first impression of the governor in a job interview:

> He was obviously a polite, urbane, thoughtful kind of person. I immediately liked him personally. You could tell he was interested in the issues. He wasn't worried so much about my credentials as he was about the fact that I was a guy who would work hard, and had a personal interest in educational policy.[22]

The two linchpins of the Milliken staff would turn out to be George Weeks, then the press secretary and later the chief of staff, and Joyce

Braithwaite (later Braithwaite-Brickley), who became appointments director in late 1969. In the contrasting personalities of the affable, mild-mannered Weeks and the intense, politically gifted Braithwaite, Milliken seemed to find a perfect balance.

The appointment of Braithwaite as appointments director, a position in which she would handle both hundreds of personnel recommendations and the governor's relations with the state and county Republican Party, illustrated Milliken's fundamental open-mindedness. A single mother with two young sons who had risen from an insurance company secretary to a top state party worker and Milliken's aide, Braithwaite was unfaltering in her dedication to the new governor. "He didn't look at you as a man or a woman, a white person or a black person," she said, reminiscing about the Milliken years. "He looked at your ability to contribute, your concern for solving problems. He judged you only by your performance."[23]

Mentored by Elly Peterson, the first woman to head the Michigan Republican Party and a candidate for the U.S. Senate in 1964, Braithwaite lacked a college degree but had something far more valuable: she innately understood the rough-and-tumble world of politics. Those who thought Milliken was too nice to be governor soon realized that in Braithwaite he had an aide fully capable of returning devastating fire to his critics and foes. She also offset what some reporters regarded as the staid Milliken image. The *Detroit Free Press* declared that she was

> without question the most important and influential woman in Milliken's front office. She is also hyperactive and uninhibited and one of the few members of Milliken's inner circle who ever laughs out loud or cries in public . . . Warm blood—not ice water—flows through her veins, a condition that will surely go down as some sort of medical miracle in the annals of the efficient but passionless Milliken years.[24]

Braithwaite handled Milliken's appointments process deftly. In over a dozen years of recommendations to the governor, her candidates rarely hit the rocks of a difficult Senate confirmation despite the fact that the opposition Democrats controlled the chamber for eight of those years. While delegating considerable authority to Braithwaite, Milliken reviewed each name and made the final decision. Milliken later said that she "thought the way I did. I thought we shared values. When it came to the appointments that really mattered, she made sure I knew everything."[25]

At first, the duo of Weeks and Braithwaite mixed like oil and water. Braithwaite believed Weeks was too open with reporters about the inner workings of the governor's office; Weeks, a former reporter, believed in cultivating his former colleagues with the fertilizer of news tidbits and leads. Ultimately Milliken took note and in a characteristically restrained way urged the two to make peace. "I wish the two of you would get along," Braithwaite-Brickley remembers the governor telling her quietly. The two soon patched up their disagreements.[26]

In fact, Weeks's openness and candor with reporters turned out not only to serve his boss well but also to reflect Milliken's self-confidence and ease with the press. Remarkably by modern standards of media management, Milliken allowed reporters to station themselves in the reception area of his office, where they would often stop staffers and ask questions. The governor's news conference room was adjacent to his personal office, permitting reporters to observe the comings and goings of Milliken and his aides and visitors.

"He was remarkably open," said former *Detroit Free Press* Capitol correspondent and columnist Hugh McDiarmid. "I was very impressed when I came here [from Ohio in 1975] to walk into his secretary's office. You could walk right into the chief of staff's office. You could pound on Joyce Braithwaite's door and talk to her. You could stake out the governor and follow him down to his car . . . If you wanted something from Milliken, you could get it, firsthand or secondhand."[27]

The beginning of Tim Skubick's career as a Capitol correspondent and host of the public television program *Off the Record,* which focuses on Michigan politics and personalities, nearly coincided with Milliken's governorship. He echoed McDiarmid's observation about the governor's accessibility. "You could literally go in and sit in his office and monitor him all day, who was going in and out," Skubick said. "His relationship with the press was very good. We had disagreements, but we respected each other."[28]

Milliken said he was determined "never to tell a lie" to reporters. "I will confess to, on occasion, turning the fog machine on or telling the press I would not answer a question or saying I didn't know the answer.

But I never said something I knew was untrue . . . I wanted there to be a policy and feeling of openness with reporters."[29]

So good were Milliken's relations with reporters that scandals and exposés were few, as were occasions when they took advantage of him. A notable exception that Milliken remembered ruefully was an interview with *Detroit News* reporter Charlie Cain. Asked whether he sometimes considered his job a "pain in the neck," Milliken laughed and said, "Sometimes, it's a real pain in the ass," then told the reporter his remark was off the record. The remark appeared in an article by the reporter the next day. "I called [the reporter] and said, 'For God's sake, why did you report that when I told you it was off the record?' He said, 'You told me it was off the record *after* you said it.' So on that technicality he felt free to use the statement."[30] Press Secretary Weeks told Milliken that Cain was right. "You don't go off the record retroactively," he said.[31]

More typical of Milliken's treatment by reporters was a "day in the life" article published a month after he became governor.

'If you were the kind of kid who got in trouble all the time, your mother would have said, Why can't you be like Billy Milliken?' That's the way Michigan's new governor was described by a Capitol worker close to the executive office . . . His career is that of a man who works steadily and with quiet determination toward his long-range goals and on a day-by-day basis.[32]

The feature reported on Milliken's daily routine, beginning with a "dip" in the State Police indoor swimming pool in East Lansing. By 8:30 A.M., he had started work at his office on the second floor of the Capitol, reviewing a speech he would give at lunchtime. After a staff meeting, Milliken hosted members of the Michigan Banking Association at a meeting about legislation and legislators and accommodated a photographer who wanted a photo of the governor signing a proclamation. The president of the Michigan Good Roads Federation told the governor in a meeting that the $1.6 million Milliken proposed for a State Police task force should be spent on roads. State representative Rusty Hellman, a Democrat from the Upper Peninsula, told Milliken he would offer an amendment boosting the appropriation for Michigan Technological University, which was located in his district.

The day continued with the luncheon speech to the Michigan Association of Broadcasters at a hotel across the street from the Capitol and meetings with legislators, a member of the state Board of Education, and five school principals from Holland. Leaving the office at 5:30— early for him, the article insisted—he headed to Southfield, just north of Detroit, for a Lincoln Day dinner speech to Oakland County Republicans. "He makes few gestures as he talks and keeps his hands clasped to the sides of the lectern. His voice is even," the reporter noted. "He's a static speaker and lacks the evangelical fervor of his predecessor, George Romney." An unnamed aide told the reporter that the staff was trying to improve the governor's delivery. Milliken's day ended at about 1 A.M., when he returned to the apartment he and Helen shared in East Lansing.[33] They would soon move to a Lansing home donated to the state by a millionaire to serve as the first official governor's residence.

In some ways, the transition was more difficult for the new governor's wife. Helen had lived an unassuming life largely out of the public eye even as the wife of a lieutenant governor. She'd driven herself to classes at Michigan State University, where she was pursuing a degree in landscape architecture. "It was not a big deal to me or other people in my program that I was the lieutenant governor's wife. I remember picking up kids that were hitchhiking," she said.[34]

Saying she had not given much thought in advance to the rumors that Romney might join the Nixon cabinet, Helen said the sudden change in their lives took her by surprise. "It happened so fast, to me. It was just sort of 'wham.' We moved from our cozy little apartment to the governor's residence, a very large ranch-style house with only two bedrooms," she said, adding that she spent considerable time gardening at the new home. "It was therapy."[35]

More than her husband's job and their residence was changing. As first lady of the state, an unofficial but daunting job, Helen Milliken was expected to make frequent public appearances and deliver the formal speeches that she had largely shunned in the past. Even more significantly to the future of the Millikens, she would begin a journey from quiet politician's wife to outspoken activist on issues ranging from the arts and environmental protection to equal rights for women. She termed it her "radicalization." By the time the Millikens retired from Lansing, Helen would be a symbol of hope to some and a lightning rod for criticism to others.

A glimpse of the Millikens during the early years of his tenure as governor and their stay in the new governor's residence is revealing. Aide Fred Grasman said Milliken "had a defined sense of who he was. You'd never see him without a coat and tie. I'd deliver mail to him at his residence on Saturday, and he'd be wearing that coat and tie."[36] Milliken preferred small gatherings to large, Grasman said, recalling that Milliken didn't host the entire executive office staff at the residence.

Grasman often accompanied Milliken on trips during his 1970 election campaign. "You never knew what he was thinking. He had a very distinct set of boundaries that helped protect him. You can't go through the public like that without retaining a zone of privacy. He didn't talk about his family or religious beliefs . . . [and] he wouldn't tell you what he thought about a person. He was pleasant, and he rarely used profanity."

Grasman said that he rarely saw Milliken angry. On one occasion, as he was shaking hands in public, a hostile Democrat offered a palm that turned out to contain a glob of spit. Milliken, Grasman said, gave no sign of his anger in public, but privately he fumed.[37]

The incident was indicative of the tension that characterized the 1970 Michigan race for the governorship. Thinking Milliken was far less well known, more soft-spoken, and more vulnerable than Romney would have been, Democrats launched an all-out effort to take the governor's office for the first time in eight years. But both parties would be fractured by dissension. Thirty-nine-year-old Democrat and state Senate minority leader Sander Levin, who represented Detroit's Oakland County suburbs, clashed with former state party chairman Zolton Ferency in a bitter August 4 primary. When Levin defeated Ferency, the latter refused to endorse him, and some of Ferency's supporters defected to Milliken.[38]

The Michigan Republican Party had its own internal conflicts in the fall campaign. Although Milliken's candidacy was unopposed within the party, his inability to bring about peace in that year's U.S. Senate race would dog him through Election Day.

At the party's state committee meeting on February 21, 1970, Milliken and state party chief William McLaughlin hoped to forge a consensus behind a single candidate for the U.S. Senate nomination. Conservative Robert Huber (coincidentally, a Yale classmate of Milliken's but not a friend) had been waiting in the wings; liberal Donald Riegle, a U.S. House member from Flint who would later switch parties and become a Democratic member of the U.S. Senate, was mulling over his candidacy. Then former governor Romney's wife, Lenore, expressed interest in the nomination, generating considerable excitement. "The more you heard 'Lenore' the more exciting it became to many," McLaughlin later wrote. "We all believed the name 'Romney' was a magical political name. Lenore Romney had been an outstanding First Lady. She was articulate, spirited and very intelligent."[39]

But the February 21 meeting did not result in the anticipated party consensus designation for Lenore Romney. Instead, in a confusing meeting chaired by the governor, the former governor's wife made a poor impression in her speech while the young, dynamic Riegle generated a standing ovation. McLaughlin said, "Lenore was dull and showed no fire. She was probably, as the front runner, too conservative. The result was to contrast the young, hungry Riegle with the aging grandmother."[40] After three ballots, with Riegle still not openly declaring his candidacy but awakening enough excitement to tempt state committee members, Romney fell short by 15 percent of the 75 percent required to be designated the consensus candidate, suffering a "public humiliation."[41] Lenore Romney's husband was outraged.

Reporters had a field day speculating what the former governor was up to. Both Detroit dailies charged that the angry George Romney had "retaken command of the Michigan Republican Party from his successor, Gov. Milliken."[42] The *Detroit News* observed that "Romney's reassertion of power was quick and brutal, and the full force of it fell squarely on Milliken. It may well have irrevocably damaged the governor's ability to lead his party."[43]

That was an overstatement, but the impression that George Romney was ordering Milliken to fix things damaged the new governor. Even worse, the apparent weakness of Lenore Romney's candidacy only encouraged the conservative Huber to run as a "maverick" in the primary, defying the state party hierarchy. The result was a bitter, divisive primary that undermined Romney's candidacy. Her narrow victory over Huber in August left her weakened and considered unlikely to defeat the popular incumbent Democrat, Phil Hart.

Meanwhile, Milliken was staking out positions both principled and risky. In March, he told a news conference that he supported granting women the right to choose an abortion. Although not yet the pivotal issue it would later become in the Republican Party, abortion generated fierce emotions in 1970. Milliken would never abandon his pro-choice stance.

> I believe women, under appropriate conditions, should be permitted to make an individual judgment and that the result of this judgment should be respected and protected by law . . . I believe very deeply in the strength of the family as a basic unit of our society. There are those who argue that this strength would be eroded by proposed changes in our abortion laws. I would argue that our family units would be strengthened if we give women the decision as to whether or not they will bear children.[44]

A month later Milliken chose James H. Brickley, the former U.S. attorney for eastern Michigan and a former Detroit City Council member, as his running mate for the office of lieutenant governor. Intended to give geographic balance to a ticket headed by a governor from northwestern Lower Michigan, Brickley was in many respects a mirror of Milliken: thoughtful, principled, not flamboyant, and unable to win the hearts of the increasingly conservative base of the party.[45]

As university campus protests against the Vietnam War multiplied following President Nixon's bombing of Cambodia in May 1970, Milliken distanced himself from his party's national leader. Saying that he had "serious reservations" about the Cambodian incursion, Milliken held back harsher fire, pointing out that Nixon had "facts and a perspective that no other American can have."[46]

The war and the strident rhetoric of both supporters and foes contributed to a divisive, feverish political tone that year. Republican Party chair William McLaughlin remembered years later a campaign visit to Midland, Michigan, by Vice President Spiro Agnew on behalf of Lenore Romney. Agnew was the darling of the so-called conservative silent majority and the bête noire of the antiwar cause. He said:

> [I]t was to see and hear Agnew, not Lenore, that drove thousands to the rural airport. And among the crowd was a vocal group of stu-

dents and anti-war protestors complete with signs and strong vocal chords. Chanting "Sieg Heil" and "Lenore, we don't want your (bleep) war," they were already in their places, in the best seats when I got there, a good hour and a half before the rally was to start.

The *Detroit Free Press* best described his morning. "His [Agnew's] words were frequently lost amid obscenities and anti-war slogans shouted by a group of several hundred youths who filled the back of the airport hangar where he spoke." Agnew railed at them, as I remember, with great glee. "That's exactly what we're running against in this country and with enemies like that, how can we lose? . . . You're pathetic," he said.[47]

By and large, however, Milliken continued to strike a high-minded tone in his campaign, distancing himself from the harsh rhetoric of Nixon and Agnew. In his formal announcement of candidacy on June 9, he declared, "During the seventies in Michigan, indeed in the nation, our best hope—our only hope—is to conduct our affairs in an atmosphere of reason, respect and civility . . . In that same spirit, I will go directly to the people with a vigorous campaign—a campaign based not on personalities, but on issues; not on narrow partisanship, but on sound public policy."[48] When McLaughlin let slip the comment to a reporter that "Republicans who vote for Hart and Levin are criminals just like the criminals walking in the streets," Milliken had Chief of Staff Don Gordon call him to request an apology to Hart.[49] It was given.

Milliken's candidacy for a full term as governor was running against the grain in a state with growing presidential unpopularity and a top of the ticket Senate race in which the Republican, Lenore Romney, was at one point down 67 to 24 percent in a *Detroit News* poll. But the state's struggling economy was perhaps the biggest obstacle to Milliken's election. The state's unemployment rate continuously topped the nation's, and when United Auto Workers members struck against General Motors in the fall unemployment reached more than 13.5 percent in Muskegon, the highest rate in the country.[50] The state's treasury suffered under the weight of reduced payroll taxes and increased unemployment and welfare benefits. An $11.6 million budget deficit was forecast to rise to as much as $50 million because of the strike.[51]

But Milliken had several strong cards in his hand. First, he had laid out and begun seeing the fruition of an aggressive program of education reform, pollution control, anticrime measures, and urban affairs. Second, he managed to appeal to independent voters by avoiding the most severe of the Republican rhetoric of the year and showing he could work with some Democrats in the legislature. Third, he was a strong opponent of a measure on the ballot that November that would amend the state's Constitution to ban state aid to parochial schools, winning him the affection of the powerful Michigan Catholic Conference. Levin supported the Parochiaid ban. Finally, Milliken enjoyed strong media relations, including endorsements from many of the state's major daily newspapers, including both of the Detroit dailies.

The *Detroit News* said Milliken had "worked hard, spoken softly, performed well in a job of crushing responsibility. In fractious times he has restored an attractive element—civility—to state government . . . Particularly we note the minimum of political bickering between Milliken and a politically divided Legislature. It reflects his adherence to a pledge to recognize that both Republicans and Democrats want to serve their state well."[52] The *Detroit Free Press* highlighted the governor's attempt to link the fortunes of cities with that of the entire state. "Gov. Milliken has done as much in less than two years to bridge the gap between outstate and urban voters as most governors do in several terms. This is important for the state . . . We must rebuild the city and protect the countryside, we must achieve equality of treatment and opportunity and build an atmosphere of realistic optimism."[53]

Milliken performed well in head-to-head competitions with Levin. The *Detroit News* flatly declared him the winner of an October 5 debate before the Economic Club of Detroit, typically an audience friendly to Republicans. Getting the last word in the debate, as political writer Robert L. Pisor noted, Milliken charged that Levin had introduced 44 bills "with press releases and publicity" since announcing his candidacy for governor, but none had been enacted into law. Turning Levin's campaign attacks on the incumbent around, Milliken asked, "Is that leadership?" Pisor said Milliken spoke "almost sorrowfully" as he attacked Levin.[54]

Lest anyone think him too genteel to knock heads in the reelection effort, Milliken summoned Republican district and county chairpersons to Lansing in mid-October to demand a greater effort on behalf of the GOP ticket. At the closed-door meeting, Milliken reportedly said:

"I have a memory like an elephant, and I will remember those who helped and those who did not." An article quoting Milliken said that state Republicans were "increasingly concerned that their party has remained dangerously lethargic and complacent in the face of opinion polls indicating Milliken is in a tough race and other statewide GOP candidates are in even more serious trouble."[55]

As the campaign neared its climax, Milliken was forced to alter his working style, increasing the number of "handshaking" and other events that he found unpleasant, even distasteful, according to his campaign manager, Keith Molin. The privacy-loving chief executive had to show his hunger and determination for the job. "The governor learned it was going to be more frantic and fast-moving than his usual deliberate style," Molin said. "There was lots of personal invasion. That was very difficult, probably more for Helen than the governor."[56]

Given the closeness of the race, anxiety over the first-time use by the City of Detroit of computerized balloting in a general election was understandable. Detroit historically offered a solid base of Democratic votes. The new vote-tallying system raised the specter of election fraud in the minds of some Milliken supporters. As early as June, campaign manager Molin and others had begun studying problems that might arise with the computerized punch card system. Still, few were prepared for the election night debacle that occurred. Thousands of ballots were damaged by moisture on a rainy election night, and there were reports that a ballot box containing punch cards had fallen off the back of a truck.

It took more than 42 hours after the polls closed on Tuesday, November 3, to declare a winner in the race for governor. It was Milliken. His edge over Levin was a bare 44,000 votes out of 2.6 million cast. Meanwhile, and predictably, Lenore Romney was swamped by Phil Hart in the Senate race. And the anti-Parochiaid constitutional amendment, while swelling the turnout of Catholic voters in opposition, was approved by the electorate overall. Democrats swept the other statewide offices of attorney general and secretary of state and made gains in the legislature. Milliken's win clearly reflected his personal popularity in a sharply divided state.

Milliken had won by carrying "outstate" Michigan, including 68 of the state's 83 counties, and by narrowing the margin by which Democratic, urban Wayne County backed Levin. The *Detroit Free Press*

James W. Milliken (*second from left in foreground*), the grandfather of William Milliken, began a three-generation tradition of service by the Milliken family in the state Senate. Here he is pictured with his colleagues on the Senate floor. James W. Milliken served there in 1898, 1899, and 1900. (Photograph courtesy of George Weeks.)

Born on March 26, 1922, in Traverse City, William G. Milliken showed a characteristic sunny disposition at an early age. Throughout his political career, his ability to charm critics and opponents served him well. (Photograph from the Milliken family collection.)

The young Bill Milliken enjoys a summer day with his maternal grandfather, Charles T. Grawn, who served as president of Central Michigan State Normal School, later Central Michigan University, from 1900 to 1918. An authority on Swedish literature and the Swedish educational system, he also was president of the Michigan State Teachers Association. (Photograph from the Milliken family collection.)

The Milliken pets were part of the family. When the family dog, Gyp, got loose one day and wandered through the neighborhood around the Millikens' Washington Street home, the sheriff shot the dog. "My father never forgave him for that," William Milliken said. (Photograph from the Milliken family collection.)

Bill Milliken entered Yale a year before the United States entered World War II. He enlisted in the Army Reserve Corps in September 1942 and volunteered for service in the Army Air Corps in February 1943. His war service delayed his graduation from Yale until 1946. (Photograph courtesy of George Weeks.)

Milliken's high school basketball team won the Michigan state championship. He later played on the Yale squad (*back row, second from left*) but admitted his talent for the sport was modest. (Photograph courtesy of George Weeks.)

Milliken was decorated with the Air Medal with two Bronze Oak Leaf Clusters, the American Campaign Medal, the European-African-Middle Eastern Campaign Medal with a Silver Service Star and three Bronze Service Stars, the World War II Victory Medal and a Purple Heart. (Photograph courtesy of George Weeks.)

Milliken flew 50 missions in 10 months with his comrades, surviving several brushes with death, including a flak wound. (Photograph courtesy of George Weeks.)

After marrying Helen Wallbank of Littleton, Colorado, on October 20, 1945, Milliken was photographed for one of the few times in his life wearing a hat. There was no honeymoon. The young war veteran had to return to Yale to finish his studies. Accompanying her new husband, Helen found the year at Yale "sociable and intellectually stimulating." (Photograph from the Milliken family collection.)

The Milliken family at the father's office in the 1960s. Daughter Elaine and son Bill Jr. are at the right. (Photograph from the Milliken family collection.)

Declaring his candidacy for lieutenant governor in 1964 without the support of the incumbent Republican governor, George Romney, Milliken defeated Allison Green, Romney's choice, at the party convention that summer. Milliken served slightly more than four years as Romney's lieutenant. The two men were never close personally, although they shared a progressive brand of politics. (Photograph from the Milliken family collection.)

Milliken's affable demeanor at the many public events he attended during his 22 years in elective office barely concealed the discomfort of the essentially private man with the glad-handing and costuming that those events required. (Photograph courtesy of George Weeks.)

Of all the rituals of public life, Milliken most enjoyed his frequent greeting of young people. (Photograph courtesy of George Weeks.)

Milliken meets with President Gerald Ford of Michigan at the White House. The partnership of the two helped win a $600 million commitment from the U.S. Department of Transportation for mass transportation in southeastern Michigan. It was a gift on which the politically and racially polarized suburbs and City of Detroit could never capitalize. (Photograph from the Milliken family collection.)

Milliken championed his fellow Republican's 1976 party nomination when President Ford was challenged by Governor Ronald Reagan of California and delivered the nominating speech on Ford's behalf at the Republican National Convention in Kansas City. (Photograph from the Milliken family collection.)

marked his victory by noting, "The people . . . showed they like and appreciate Bill Milliken's gentility, his intelligence and his decency. They selected him to govern again over a worthy opponent who ran a strong campaign and who had many other factors in his favor."[57]

Despite his breathtakingly close defeat, opponent Sander Levin remembers feeling no bitterness toward Milliken. "There was a feeling then that our campaign should not be basically about character assassination. I retained a respect for him after the campaign—the years since have vindicated that," Levin said in 2005.[58] Some analysts suggested that the moderate temperament and demeanor of both men had made it difficult for voters to choose between them.

The campaign not only marked the emergence of William Milliken as a statewide political winner but also the emergence of Helen Milliken as an active statewide campaigner. On one Wednesday afternoon in September, she had worked a nine and one-half hour day, ranging from a speech to the Warren Beautification Council to press interviews with "society" editors to a "Ladies on Parade" fashion show.[59] "At first I looked upon [campaigning] as something that had to be done, but I learned a great deal, and I think I learned to be much more effective. I could go out and tell the people my husband meant what he said," she offered in a postelection interview.[60] The same article addressed the mock "battle" between the governor and his wife over the hem height of her skirt. It would not be long before Helen Milliken would become a political figure in her own right, speaking on matters more substantive than women's fashions or even her husband's sincerity.

With the electoral battle behind him, Milliken could govern with new authority, but he sounded a note of conciliation: "The outcome of the election only emphasizes how much we need to work together to achieve the goals we hold in common. With the Legislature so closely divided, with Democrats holding top administrative posts, we must be willing to compromise honorably and to share credit for our accomplishments."[61]

It was time to put the Milliken creed of bipartisanship and civility to the test for a full four-year term—or more.

6

THE GREEN GOVERNOR

To understand William Milliken's reputation as an environmental governor, it is critical to study two things: his times and the beauty of the area surrounding Traverse City, where he grew up and to which he returned almost weekly during his time as Michigan's chief executive. Milliken "survived 14 years in office" by jumping in the car many weekends, going home to Traverse City, and coming back on Monday, said Capitol correspondent Tim Skubick.[1]

The drive from Lansing to Traverse City, mostly on limited-access highways, took about three hours. During that time, the governor's state automobile moved from the intensively cultivated farmland of south-central Michigan through a perceptible ecological boundary just north of Clare, where the agricultural land yields to forest. To many Michigan citizens, that boundary is where "up north" begins on weekend trips to escape the stresses of everyday life. To Milliken, it represented the first clear sign of home. From there to Traverse City, he could breathe easier, knowing he was in a portion of the state that was recovering some of its ancient grandeur after the ravages of the late-nineteenth-century lumbering era.

While at home in Traverse City, he was able to enjoy from the floor-to-ceiling window in his living room a panoramic view of the West Arm of Grand Traverse Bay, the color and texture of the water changing with sunlight and storm. His longtime environmental and natural resources policy adviser, Bill Rustem, credited the bay and the surroundings in general with shaping Milliken's views on conservation.

"He grew up in a very pretty area of the state," Rustem said. "If you start from that perspective, you end up believing in protecting the outdoors. I think he always believed that people from the urban areas of Michigan should have the kind of opportunities he'd had as a child to enjoy swimming and just being outdoors."[2]

Although he rarely fished after childhood and never hunted, Milliken spent considerable time outdoors. He walked, skied, and during his later years as governor jogged frequently in the woods near the tip of the Old Mission Peninsula, which juts into Grand Traverse Bay for some 20 miles. There he frequently found the seclusion and peace necessary to anchor him during his years in public life. "There's almost always no one else there," he said. Acknowledging he had "a need to be by myself at times," Milliken described "the renewing experiences that one has in nature."[3]

Milliken's attitude toward hunting and fishing was tolerant, but he was not personally engaged. He recalled with disgust attending a shoot with several other state senators organized by an influential manufacturer during the early 1960s.

I foolishly accepted the invitation . . . All these cages were in front of us. They would open up a cage and prod a pheasant to come out. These birds had never been free before. They were disoriented, they were easy targets.

I was so damned disgusted with that. It was a terrible experience. To see these domesticated birds—I took one shot and stopped. I never went to that lodge again.[4]

Rustem, on the other hand, was an enthusiastic hunter and angler. He took the Millikens to a remote state park near Craig Lake in the western Upper Peninsula in 1980, where they slept in a rustic cabin, fished, canoed, and watched eagles rise above the conifers. Capitol reporters had sport with the idea of the polite, formal governor in the backwoods. "The governor just doesn't look like a lumberjack," wrote Robert Longstaff, the chief of the Booth News Service in Lansing.[5] "He looks undressed if he's not wearing a tie . . . He's quiet, refined, dignified—the sort who would wear a robe on a midnight dash to the outhouse . . . the kind who would say 'excuse me' if he bumped into a bear . . . or mourn if he stepped on a wildflower."

"As Governor, I always encouraged outdoor recreation and sports," Milliken said. "I consider these to be an outlet for a lot of people. Somehow, the idea of going out to kill for killing's sake is repugnant to me. But I respect that there are people who just live for it."[6]

Another personal connection to the outdoors was Helen Milliken. Like Bill, she was an avid downhill and cross-country skier. As a child, she had also developed a love of the outdoors while camping as a Girl Scout. Her love of gardening also linked her to nature. As the years passed, more and more observers credited her with being an influential behind-the-scenes voice for conservation in the governor's realm. As her husband began to speak out on the issue, so did she. Lamenting the mounting toll of pollution in early 1970, she said, "But our young people are this country's greatest hope. And nature, over the centuries, has displayed astounding resilience in the face of man's destructive ways."[7] She touted her husband's program, declaring that he "has made the quality of our environment one of the principal concerns of his administration."[8]

Milliken came to office in 1969 at a time when the national and state environmental crisis was reaching a new level of severity, triggering a public clamor for action. On June 22, 1969, the oil-fouled Cuyahoga River caught fire at Cleveland, resulting in national publicity that helped create momentum for the federal Clean Water Act of 1972. Michigan was far from immune to pollution problems. Black plumes of smoke were a typical sight in the state's industrial cities, especially in Downriver Detroit. The Rouge River often ran orange or black with the wastes dumped by Ford Motor Company, and hundreds of miles of Lake Michigan swimming beaches were considered unfit for public use at times because of high bacteria counts.

Most significantly, in Milliken's first spring as governor a long-running battle over the use of the toxic pesticide DDT in Michigan was coming to a boil. In the late 1950s, an ornithologist at Michigan State University (MSU), Dr. George Wallace, had documented significant bird kills on campus resulting from the use of high concentrations of DDT to treat Dutch elm disease.[9] Cited in Rachel Carson's landmark 1962 book *Silent Spring,* Wallace's research contributed to fears of a world characterized by "a strange stillness . . . a spring without voices."[10] Citizens and civic groups, including the League of Women Voters, rallied across the state against DDT use and formed the Michigan Pesticides Council, a volunteer group committed to the eradication of the so-called hard pesticides. This class of chemicals was new to the world. Unlike most natural substances, the hard pesticides take hundreds of years to break down and accumulate in the fat of animals, including humans, posing health risks scientists were struggling to define.

But the chemical industry that manufactured the pesticides and the agricultural sector that used them defended DDT and other chemicals, claiming that they represented the best hope of promoting farm productivity and the health of trees and other organisms afflicted by pests. An MSU horticulturalist, John Carew, urged Americans "to accept some injury to restricted segments of our wildlife population in return for the irrefutably better standard of living we now enjoy because of agricultural chemicals."[11] During most of the 1960s in Michigan, citizens fought the farm interests and natural resource agencies warred with agricultural agencies.

Then came a startling discovery that doomed DDT in Michigan and put it on the road to elimination in the United States. The U.S. Food and Drug Administration, while examining interstate shipments of coho salmon, a large fish with significant stores of fat initially stocked in Lake Michigan in 1966 by the Michigan Department of Conservation, found high levels of DDT and seized 14 tons of fish. Coupled with findings by the Michigan Department of Agriculture (MDA) of another pesticide, dieldrin, that resulted in the impoundment of 500,000 pounds of salmon, the DDT discovery generated front-page headlines across Michigan. It threatened Michigan's thriving new Great Lakes sport fishery. With the health of the tourism industry, as well as the people who ate the fish, at risk, the state's agricultural commission canceled most uses of DDT in April 1969, making Michigan the first state to do so.[12]

Rather than dampening public concern, the DDT ban only renewed public doubts that government was doing enough to protect air, water, and human health. By the end of 1969, plans were under way for a national Earth Day, to be held on April 22, 1970, to express citizen concern about environmental degradation. The University of Michigan in Ann Arbor, on a trimester system that would put April 22 in the midst of final exams, would anticipate the national Earth Day with its own observance in late March.

Attempting to get out in front of the issue, and with the help of Michigan Department of Natural Resources (DNR) director Ralph MacMullan, Milliken sent a special message on the environment to the legislature on January 22, 1970.[13] As the first Milliken administration document to set forth a comprehensive environmental strategy, it deserves close examination. It began with the following statement.

> The preservation of our environment is the critical issue of the Seventies. Unless we move without delay to halt the destruction of our land, our water, and our air, our own children may see the last traces of earth's beauty crushed beneath the weight of man's waste and ruin . . . We are already the most affluent nation on earth, but we have paid too high a price. We have paid for this affluence with the beauty of our landscape, the purity of our air and the cleanliness of our water.[14]

Milliken's message included a 20-point program. Three of them resulted in significant new laws passed that year. One made agreements between the state and water polluters to clean up their messes enforceable in court; a second spawned the Great Lakes Shorelands Act to help conserve the state's more than 3,000 miles of Great Lakes coast; and the third fostered the Natural Rivers Act, which was designed to protect the scenic beauty and environmental health of designated rivers and streams of high quality.

What Milliken proposed that did not result in significant reform is also noteworthy. He appointed a special commission on land use to address urban sprawl. More than 30 years later, he would serve on another governor's land use leadership council, as the state had still failed to produce a coherent policy and program on the management of growth. As governor, Milliken also resumed the fight against billboards that he had begun as a state senator, calling for a new law and a "comprehensive plan for enforcing existing billboard regulations . . . People escaping to the countryside for recreation and leisure should not be subjected to visual pollution which destroys the landscape they have traveled to enjoy."[15] Although that effort would not succeed, *Detroit Free Press* outdoor writer Tom Opre called Milliken's 1970 special message "one of the finest documents of 'awareness' yet seen in political circles . . . [It] capsulizes a vibrant, effective leadership to heading off Michigan's environmental deterioration."[16]

Policy adviser Rustem, referring to Milliken's frequent use of such special messages to galvanize public opinion and legislative action on environmental and other topics, observed that he "used the bully pulpit for policy better than any of his immediate predecessors or successors. He was at the helm of the state government policy process."[17]

But in 1970 it did not always seem that Milliken was at the helm of the environmental ship. One after another, seismic shocks struck the state and the Great Lakes region, forcing the governor to respond in a sensitive election year. The first jolt was an announcement in March 1970 of the discovery of the toxic metal mercury at dangerously high levels in fish taken from the Saint Clair River, Lake Saint Clair, and the Detroit River, waterways shared with Ontario. Notorious for causing the death or deformity of 111 persons who had consumed fish and shellfish from Minamata Bay in Japan between 1953 and 1960, mercury as an aquatic pollutant was a serious concern. Although it was a Dow Chemical Company facility in Sarnia, Ontario, that caused most of the Saint Clair river and lake pollution, Milliken supported aggressive efforts by the Department of Natural Resources to crack down on the Wyandotte Chemical Company, which was dumping 10 to 20 pounds of the highly toxic metal into the Detroit River every day.

A greater challenge to Milliken was the question of what to do about fishing in Lake Saint Clair, which is adjacent to the northeastern suburbs of Detroit and a highly popular recreational resource. The science was uncertain. Would consuming Lake Saint Clair sport fish pose significant health risks? Both commercial and sport anglers who enjoyed the lake bristled at the idea of limits on fishing. Milliken's handling of the issue illustrated his concern for hearing the views of experts. He summoned not just agency directors but technical and legal experts from the lower levels of state government to advise him.

A young fisheries biologist at the time, Jack Bails, remembered the summons. "When you are in an agency and you're called over to the governor's office, you're a little worried what you should do, how you should act. But it was easy. He was good with people. The surprising thing to me was, Milliken wanted to talk to the lowest-level person with the most information," Bails said.[18] "He'd ask the right questions, he'd pay attention to what was going on . . . You could almost see the wheels turning in his head."

Bails added that Milliken in the private meetings never raised, or hinted at, the political implications of the fishing decision, unlike the practices of later governors with whom Bails met. "I got spoiled," he said. "After Milliken, it seemed like the first thing you ended up talking about in those meetings was the political considerations."[19]

After hearing from the experts, Milliken commendably decided he couldn't put the health of Lake Saint Clair anglers at risk. On April 11, he announced that he was issuing an executive order closing the Saint Clair River and Lake Saint Clair to fishing as "a precautionary measure."[20] A few days later he announced support for legislation requiring users of toxic materials who discharged wastewater to register with the state, calling it a "truth in pollution" law. He reiterated his support for the bill in a 30-minute airplane tour of Detroit River pollution sites on April 15, accompanied by reporters. He said the state had need to "know precisely what industries are dumping and the time these are occurring."[21] Later in the year the legislature agreed to Milliken's proposal.

The tempo then quickened for the governor. On Earth Day, April 22, he spoke on four college campuses. Before about 1,900 students at Michigan State University, he touted his truth in pollution proposal but added that the government could not solve the problem of pollution alone. "The government, despite what some people may think," he said, "is neither omniscient nor omnipotent. It can't be everywhere, catching empty bottles in midair before they land in a trout stream, dissuading every businessman from erecting another billboard." He urged citizen responsibility.[22] As a measure of the growing campus volatility over the Vietnam War, "a small group of radical students and non-students" drove Milliken off the stage during a question-and-answer period, some waving Viet Cong flags.[23]

Milliken recalled the temper of spring 1970 on the state's college campuses. Visiting Central Michigan University on Earth Day, he recalled, "I was surrounded by students. There was one young woman who wanted to scream and shout; she jumped up and down on the hood of my [state] car and dented it . . . It was a volatile time."[24]

While students stormed on campus, older environmental activists from across Michigan organized to pass a new law called the Michigan Environmental Protection Act (MEPA). Drafted by University of

Michigan professor Joseph Sax at the behest of the West Michigan Environmental Action Council, the proposed law essentially deputized any citizen who could afford an attorney to protect the environment by granting him or her standing to sue in a court of law. The business community fought the legislation tooth and nail. The state Chamber of Commerce predicted that the proposal "would create a serious threat to the operation and growth of business and industry." But hundreds of citizens, mostly supporters of the bill, turned out for a series of public hearings.

At first, Milliken did not commit himself on the measure. His legal adviser, Joseph Thibodeau, raised questions about it at the legislative hearings and proposed amendments. But by May Milliken had come on board and endorsed passage of House Bill 3055. After it was signed into law on July 27, 1970, it would become identified as one of the signal accomplishments of Milliken's tenure and a model law for other states.

In 2004, 22 years after his retirement from office, Milliken "took the unusual step of filing a third-party brief" in the Michigan Supreme Court's consideration of whether to gut the law by striking down its grant of standing to any citizen. "This is a crucial decision of the Michigan Supreme Court. Much is at stake," Milliken said.[25] In the 2004 case, the court did not strike down the citizen-standing provision.

Milliken took the offensive at the annual meeting of the Michigan United Conservation Clubs (MUCC), the state's largest outdoor organization, in June 1970. He outlined what he called a "major principle" behind his environmental program: "Those who utilize natural resources of water and air in manufacturing should assist the state in financing the costs of monitoring waste discharges into these resources."[26] Known as "surveillance fees," the polluter-pay program passed but was repealed in the early 1980s.

As the decade deepened and environmental values came to occupy mainstream voters, if not lawmakers, Milliken elaborated on his initial commitment in gestures both small and large. During a tough battle, his insistent offer of a state plane to fly a reluctant state senator, Oscar Bouwsma of Muskegon, back to a Capitol committee meeting to provide the necessary quorum for a vote on a proposed Inland Lakes and Streams Act was critical to the law's passage.

Milliken's appointment of an environmental activist, Joan Wolfe, to the state's Natural Resources Commission (NRC) was important both symbolically and substantively. Wolfe was a hero to environmentalists as the founder of the West Michigan Environmental Action Council, which had pushed for MEPA and other landmarks in environmental law. As the first "environmentalist," and the first woman, to serve on the commission, Wolfe won praise from the *Detroit Free Press* as a "refreshing" choice, her appointment coming in the wake of "a heavy-handed attempt to force Gov. Milliken to keep the DNR board 100 percent masculine."[27] Wolfe herself praised the governor for the appointment, saying it was "a very courageous move" in light of the enemies she had made fighting for clean air and water.[28]

An even larger gesture was his decision to supply the first signature for a citizen petition drive to enact a beer and soda beverage container deposit law in 1976. Under industry pressure, the bill had died several times in the legislature. In signing the petition first, Milliken was taking a position opposite that of beer and soda wholesalers and the retailers who would be required by the law to take back the deposit containers.

Wayne Schmidt, a staff ecologist for the MUCC, observed that Milliken "nearly always knew that line between right and wrong for Michigan's natural resources. Never was there a more unambiguous case—real and symbolic—than the bottle bill." Milliken lent natural resources adviser Rustem to the MUCC during the campaign for the measure. Helen Milliken helped galvanize garden clubs across the state to contribute to the drive, which collected 400,000 signatures and resulted in passage of the deposit law by a margin of two to one on the November 1976 ballot.[29]

Milliken also challenged a powerful Michigan employer, and a major contributor to the Republican Party, when he backed a proposal by the Department of Natural Resources to limit the phosphorus content of laundry detergent. Scientists had determined that detergent phosphate was a leading culprit in the gross outbreaks of algae that had contributed to the "death" of Lake Erie, which had lost most of its value as a recreational lake. Soap and detergent manufacturers at first questioned the science, then said it would be cheaper to treat phosphorus at sewage treatment plants than remove it from products, and finally alleged that without phosphorus clothes could not be satisfactorily cleaned. Adamantly opposed by the Amway Corporation of Ada, near Grand Rapids, the Michigan DNR's proposed phosphate limit resulted in a phone call to the governor from Jay Van Andel, cofounder of the corporation.

"I can still remember how incensed he was. He was adamant, but so was I," Milliken later said.[30] "There was always a constant suggestion from industry that anything you wanted to do to solve a chemical pollutant problem would hurt the bottom line. But it was so evident [that phosphorus] was harmful that I knew we had to do something." Milliken disregarded Van Andel's urging and in an aggressive use of his executive powers transferred decision-making authority on the matter from the state's Water Resources Commission, which had balked at enacting the rule, to the Natural Resources Commission, where longtime ally and commission member Hilary Snell was tasked with ensuring that the rule was adopted. In February 1977, the panel approved the rule. The beneficial water quality effects were almost immediately realized. In 1978 and 1979, the amount of phosphorus dumped into the Detroit River by the city's mammoth sewage treatment plant declined by 40 percent, reflecting the new controls. Because the river supplies over 90 percent of the lake's inflow, the Michigan action was a significant contributor to the recovery of Lake Erie.

With the exception of the phosphorus issue, where the two men saw eye to eye, NRC member Snell said Milliken never discussed with him how to vote or pressured him to vote a certain way on a matter before the panel.[31] Snell briefed Milliken regularly on DNR issues, usually on Friday afternoons at the end of the three-day monthly commission meeting.

> One time I was really concerned that an issue was really going to hurt him politically. I was concerned that the issue be handled a certain way—I was convinced that was the position I ought to take on the merits. But I thought if I did that it could hurt the governor. I called up Phyllis [Dell, Milliken's secretary] and made an appointment to see him. I told him all that. He leaned across the table. He said, "If you think that's the way to handle it, Hilary, then go ahead and don't worry about the political side. Good government is good politics." I sure as hell never forgot that.[32]

Snell also recalled a telling incident reflecting the governor's concern about treating citizens with respect. During the 1960s and 1970s, emotions ran high in the Upper Peninsula over whether to permit the hunting of does in order to keep deer numbers down. Many sportsmen's groups strongly opposed a doe season, fearing it would undermine the deer population, while DNR biologists said there was no scientific argument against it. Commission meetings frequently featured hours of testimony on the issue from impassioned hunters. "One DNR official got angry about a letter from a deer hunter and fired off a rude letter telling this guy where to get off," Snell said. "The Michigan Deer Hunters Association got this 'very intemperate' letter and put it in the hands of the press in five minutes." When Milliken learned of the DNR's letter, he summoned the commission members to his office and lectured them on the agency's responsibility to work with the public. "We all sat there, and everyone listened," Snell said, smiling.[33] Milliken's office then issued a news release saying he had responded to the uncivil treatment of a citizen.

If there was one environmental issue that displayed the influence of Helen Milliken on her husband, it was the debate over whether the DNR should authorize oil and gas drilling in the Pigeon River State Forest. Assembled from cutover lands in the northern Lower Peninsula in the 1920s and 1930s by P. S. Lovejoy of the Department of Conservation, the state forest, popularly known as the Pigeon River Country, grew to become one of the peninsula's few large-scale wild areas by the end of the 1960s. Outdoor writer Gordon Charles wrote that a "motorist can travel twenty miles in any direction without seeing a house, cottage, fence or anything else manmade. There is no other place in Michigan's lower peninsula like it."[34] A haven for hunting and fishing as well as increasing numbers of backpackers, the forest was an expanse of 90,000 acres when Shell Oil Company announced in July 1970 that it had made a major oil and gas find in the heart of the forest. The industry and its backers in the legislature soon squared off against conservationists and environmentalists.

A forester with the DNR and Pigeon River defender, Ford Kellum, noting Helen's well-known interest in gardening, wrote her a letter urging her to take a personal interest in the issue. "Mrs. Milliken, I think you could do the most good by, somehow, getting to the DNR commissioners and persuading them to keep the Pigeon River Country off-limits to oil developments no matter how refined their plans are," he wrote.[35]

"He said he knew I was a gardener and that I appreciated the out-doors. I had known nothing of the [Pigeon River drilling] issue before that," she remembered. "I said to Bill, I think you and I should go over there. And we did. It's a marvelous place, not only wilderness but stunningly beautiful."[36]

Conservationist David Smethurst, a Gaylord public school teacher who enjoyed hunting in the forest, accompanied the Millikens, along with the DNR's Ned Caveney and a State Police trooper assigned to the Millikens' security, on a hike of the Pigeon River Country. The trip would be filmed for the *Michigan Outdoors* television show, which was syndicated statewide, as a means of rallying support for what was then regarded as a local battle. Originally intended to be a ski tour, the trip became a hike when rain melted the snowpack. As the hikers moved down the trail, they stopped occasionally while the approximately 60-year-old Gene Little, carrying "a huge TV camera two or three times larger than the ones I see on the shoulders of TV guys now," according to Smethurst, filmed them walking and talking for the program.

> Pretty soon, Mrs. Milliken asks to borrow my backpack and is picking litter up off the trail. Those skiers left their cookie wrappers and the melted snow revealed their waste. We walk on, and on. Pretty soon Gene is huffing and puffing. We stop more often for him. I walk ahead with Ned and Mrs. Milliken and look behind. Gene is still slogging along, but the Governor is now carrying his TV camera . . . I made up my mind about the Millikens that day. Good people make good leaders.[37]

Helen Milliken spoke out both publicly and privately against drilling in the Pigeon River Country. In January 1975, she responded to Kellum's request by writing the Natural Resources Commission members to say, "Our wilderness areas are so few and the pressures on them so relentless. The Pigeon River Country is unique in its qualities of beauty and wilderness. It seems to me this public land should remain unspoiled, a part of the heritage of all the people of Michigan."[38]

With his wife's enthusiastic support, William Milliken repeatedly called for protection of the forest from oil drilling, but after the domestic oil price shocks of 1973 and 1979 industry influence over the legislature grew. Even a historic 1979 Michigan Supreme Court decision

The Green Governor

blocking drilling under the state Environmental Protection Act did not mean victory for the conservationists. Oil industry friends in the legislature introduced bills to exempt the Pigeon River project from the act and other environmental laws. Under pressure, the two sides agreed to a legal settlement that allowed some drilling in the forest while placing other areas off-limits and defining the conditions under which the drilling could be done. Smethurst credited Milliken with playing a pivotal role in what he ultimately regarded as a successful compromise. "Gov. Milliken held firm and told people he would veto any bad legislation and kept telling [both sides] to work out a deal and compromise. He was not directly involved in the details. But his backbone supported us and enabled the compromise to happen," Smethurst said, hailing the fact that the drilling is scheduled to end by about 2020.[39]

Milliken's voice was guarded, but ultimately critical in stopping two environmentally destructive federal forays into Michigan. In March 1976, the state Department of Natural Resources announced that it had been contacted by the U.S. Energy Research Development Administration (ERDA) about testing salt deposits in northeastern Lower Michigan as possible storage sites for high-level nuclear waste.[40] Such waste can remain radioactive for hundreds of thousands of years. The deposits were considered favorable for radioactive waste storage because of their stability and isolation from water. Late that summer newspapers reported that three sites in Alpena and Presque Isle Counties, not far from Lake Huron, were on the federal list. Adams Point, a small peninsula jutting into Lake Huron southeast of Rogers City, was considered "much the best . . . site in the northeastern U.S."[41] The idea of burying radioactive waste in Michigan, especially that close to one of the Great Lakes, sparked a furor across the state. A Republican ally of Milliken's, U.S. representative Phil Ruppe of Houghton, whose district included the proposed northeastern Michigan sites, expressed rage over what he called "a typical bureaucratic sneak play." The agency had not consulted Ruppe before beginning its local studies.

Milliken had another Republican ally in Washington, President Gerald Ford, who until 1974 had represented the Grand Rapids area district in the U.S. House. On July 8, the governor wrote Robert C. Seamans, director of ERDA, to insist that Michigan be given a veto over the siting process. "I believe that scientifically gathered information and the views of local citizens and governments on this project are crucial factors in the decision-making process." While not taking a formal position on the siting of radioactive waste in Michigan, Milliken ordered state DNR officials not to cooperate with test borings that ERDA officials had planned to make. In late September—only a few weeks before Ford would stand for election to a full term—Milliken received a promise that Michigan would have a final say on the site.[42] By the middle of the following year, he had exercised the veto, pulling Michigan out of the process, citing the inability of the federal agencies to assure the state of the radiation exposure limits it would apply.

"This created a dilemma for the state," Milliken wrote to a U.S. House subcommittee. "We could either trust the federal agencies to guarantee the protection of public health and safety and continue in the program in spite of the lack of details, or we could respond to concerns that were raised and withdraw from the program." Siting of a facility, he said, "cannot come at the expense of the safety of our citizens or the integrity of our environment."[43]

Another federal scheme with significant environmental and political implications emerged in early 1973. It became known that the U.S. Navy was considering burying cables six feet underground over a 1,200-square-mile area of the western Upper Peninsula. The cables would emit low-wavelength signals that would strike the ionosphere and then return to earth, penetrating the oceans and signaling nuclear submarines in the event of nuclear war. This "doomsday trigger," known initially as Project Sanguine, "presumably would be used only to order the retaliatory firing of intercontinental ballistic missiles in the event of a nuclear attack on the U.S."[44] By 1974, both Wisconsin and Texas had rejected the scheme, leaving only Michigan under serious consideration for the estimated $1 billion project.

In fact, thinking the project would produce jobs, some Upper Peninsula legislators had invited the navy to brief them on the project. Senator Joe Mack of Ironwood said the project "would be the biggest thing that ever hit the U.P." He attacked "people from Ann Arbor and Detroit coming here to save our peninsula. We don't have Ford and Chrysler up here and our people need work."[45]

Environmental organizations "choke with fury when they think of 1,400 miles of 25-foot wide lanes that must be cut through forests in order to lay the cable," the *Detroit Free Press* reported. The navy called that scenario unrealistic, saying it would follow existing roads and utility rights-of-way wherever possible, minimizing forest intrusions. There were other objections. Initial testing of the extremely low frequency (ELF) waves suggested that they could increase blood pressure, cause genetic mutations, and affect plant growth.[46] Milliken's press secretary, George Weeks, a principal adviser, urged Milliken to say that he was "opposed to the Sanguine project, or at least have great reservations about it but that before a final decision is made, it is important that the views of the people of the Upper Peninsula be heard."[47] But Milliken refused to take a position other than to say that he wanted the navy to meet a number of conditions before he would support the project. In the spring of 1976, he began to take heat for what the *Free Press* called his "conditional invitation" to the navy the year before to continue considering Michigan for what was now called "Project Seafarer."[48] The newspaper urged him to make "a bold and firm decision now . . . to [ask the navy to] leave the UP as quickly as he invited it in last year." And, while some Upper Peninsula newspapers touted the project as a job producer, four communities in the vicinity of the proposed project rejected Seafarer that month in advisory referenda by overwhelming margins as high as eight to one. Environmental groups were joined by peace activists, who argued that the system would promote rather than deter nuclear war. One group of protestors smeared the carpet in Milliken's office with ashes.[49]

In August 1976, U.S. representative Ruppe, who had taken several differing positions on the project, surprised Milliken with a letter released to the news media that urged him to exercise his veto immediately. The project had grown to "a minimum of 2.6 million acres, 25 percent of the Upper Peninsula," Ruppe said, and he attacked what he considered a lack of candor by the navy in explaining its full environmental and health implications.[50] Milliken again demurred, but he assured Ruppe that he would veto the project if the congressman's constituents continued to oppose it after all the studies were completed.

With incumbent Gerald Ford facing reelection in a few days, the president wrote Ruppe and Milliken on October 31, 1976, pledging that the project would not be built in Michigan without the governor's approval. Democratic challenger Jimmy Carter had already made the same commitment.[51] Milliken announced that he would veto the project. But after Carter's victory the governor received a letter dated March 17, 1977, from Secretary of Defense Harold Brown, saying only that his agency would "give very great weight" to the views of the people of Michigan. The less than total reassurance gave the governor an instant out from the project.

"Mr. Secretary, I object," Milliken wrote. After citing substantive arguments against the project, he declared, "I object to the periodic backsliding on the assurances the people of Michigan have been given about how their voice would be heard on Seafarer."[52] Ultimately, the navy installed a much smaller, far less disruptive system in the forests of the western Upper Peninsula and northern Wisconsin. Known as Project ELF, the system operated only from 1985 to 2004.[53]

The management of the issue was not Milliken's finest hour politically. Determined not to prejudge the merits of the project until an environmental review by his own appointed task force as well as navy studies were done, Milliken was ultimately almost deserted by former project supporters in the Upper Peninsula before exercising his "veto." While he won a few plaudits for sticking to facts until 1977, his withholding of judgment raised doubts in the minds of some environmental critics about the depth of his commitment. Meanwhile, the few remaining backers of the project characterized Milliken's ultimate veto as "political cowardice."[54]

Of all the environmental health issues that Milliken addressed during his 14 years as the chief executive of Michigan, the controversy over contamination of the state's food chain by a fire retardant known as PBB (polybrominated biphenyl) threatened his reelection and lasting reputation most significantly. Examining why this is so underscores both the weaknesses and the strengths of the Milliken executive style, as well as the response of the political system to the problem of chemical exposures.

In the late spring of 1973, the Michigan Chemical Company in St. Louis accidentally shipped a fire retardant with the brand name Firemaster to Farm Bureau Services, a supplier for thousands of Michigan farmers, in place of Nutrimaster, a cattle feed containing magnesium oxide. Firemaster was a brand name for PBB, used to reduce the flammability of plastics and electrical circuits. The mistake apparently happened at a time when Michigan Chemical ran out of preprinted bags and hand lettered the trade names of the two products in black, contributing to a worker's error in misidentifying the bags.

Farm Bureau Services sold the mislabeled feed to, among others, dairy farmer Fred Halbert of Battle Creek. Halbert purchased 65 tons, and after one week of feeding it to his cows in the fall of 1973 he noticed that the animals were sick. They lost their appetites, lost weight, and produced 25 percent less milk. When Halbert stopped feeding the Firemaster pellets to the cows, they showed signs of recovery. He resumed feeding them with the Farm Bureau product and noticed the symptoms of illness again.

In October 1973, the state Department of Agriculture's head diagnostician inspected the herd and at first suspected lead poisoning. But not until May 1974 did the department determine, with help from Halbert's son Rick, a chemical engineer, that PBB was the poison.[55] The department then tested feed and farm products across the state. Ultimately, the state slaughtered 23,000 head of cattle, 1.5 million chickens, and thousands of pigs, sheep, and other farm animals. About 500 farms in 58 of the state's 83 counties were quarantined. The Velsicol Chemical Company, which acquired Michigan Chemical Company, and Farm Bureau Services were stung by approximately 800 lawsuits. The state spent more than $21 million to deal with the problem.[56]

"Never before in the history of the United States had there been such an incident of extensive contamination of food products by a toxic substance, so there were no precedents to follow in resolving the problem," the Department of Agriculture reported in its final summary of the crisis in 1982. "Because of the complexity of the problem there was widespread public misunderstanding, which greatly increased the difficulty of reaching the goals."[57]

This commentary after the controversy subsided mirrored Milliken's view more than 20 years after he left office. "I wish I had more effectively carried the story to the public as an educational issue. I didn't adequately explain what had happened. No one had deliberately set out to put the poison in cattle feed. People always assumed it was due to some fault or failing of government . . . It got out of hand."[58]

More than a public relations debacle, the PBB disaster was an example of sluggishness and indifference on the part of bureaucracy in responding to a contamination issue in the chemical age. It was an example of the damage that can be done by diffused executive responsibilities in a state government. Finally, it was a genuine health threat, though apparently not on the scale feared in the mid-1970s. The fact that approximately 95 percent of the population of Michigan had residues of PBB in their bodies in 1981 was a signal that something had gone terribly wrong.[59]

The state Department of Agriculture had long been considered the friend of farmers, but in the second half of the twentieth century it was an equally close partner of the leading farm lobby group, Michigan Farm Bureau, to which the agency frequently turned to get support for its budget in the legislature. And there was another conflict. "The agency that's regulating is the agency that depends on the vitality of the industry," said Dick Allen, a farmer and veterinarian and a state senator from 1975 to 1982. The MDA "didn't move nearly fast enough . . . There were some people saying early on, we should condemn these herds. But MDA didn't want to put farmers out of business."[60] He added that Milliken and other state officials were sensitive to the fact that "to condemn a herd, that ends a way of life. You inherit a herd."

Allen said the state made all of its substantive errors in the first three months after realizing PBB had contaminated the food chain, hesitating before taking decisive action to quarantine the most affected farms, slaughter the most affected livestock, and destroy contaminated dairy products. He estimated that only 200 pounds of PBB ultimately "got into humans," with most of the heaviest impact felt by the families on the farms that used the tainted feed.

That impact was real. The state for more than two decades maintained a study group of over 3,500 persons from the most highly exposed farm families in the state. Researchers reported in 1995 that women in the group with the highest levels of PBB in their blood had an increased risk of developing breast cancer.[61] A second study, published in 1998, revealed increased risks of digestive cancer and lymphoma among members of the group with the highest PBB blood levels.[62] A third study suggested that girls born to women who had the highest levels of the chemical in their blood reached menarche six months earlier than those whose mothers had been less exposed. Other research had suggested that for every year earlier a woman has her first menstrual period, the risk of breast cancer increases by 5 percent.[63] The final verdict on PBB's human health consequences will not be rendered until sometime in the middle of the twenty-first century. The verdict on the state government's performance came a lot more quickly.

Most state officials admit they should have acted more quickly to remove contaminated animals and food from the market. But they were hampered by the relatively new problem of toxic contamination. The result was that it took months after PBB was discovered for the extent of the contamination to be understood . . . The delays took a toll on the public and the image of government.[64]

Since Milliken was the head of that government, and, in Allen's view, initially did not pressure the agency to do more, he was among those who paid a price, even though he did not have direct authority over the MDA. A five-member citizens' commission appointed by the governor, not the governor himself, hires and fires the director of the agency. Designed to insulate agencies such as the DNR and the MDA from constant political whipsawing, the system in this case led to open disagreement between the governor and the agency, further undermining public confidence. When a scientific advisory panel appointed by Milliken recommended a "tolerance" or health-based standard for PBB in food 60 times lower for meat and 300 times lower for milk than the extant state standard, Milliken urged the MDA to lower the number. Director B. Dale Ball and the Agriculture Commission refused, infuriating Milliken.

"His direction was one of thwarting and frustrating my efforts," Milliken said. "He really defied me."[65]

The agriculture agency chronically mismanaged the release of data about PBB contamination, confirming the fears of many that it was trying to cover up the problem. For example, in February 1977 the department did not divulge meat tests that showed PBB in more than 10 percent of samples of grocery items, triggering headlines that the MDA had "suppressed PBB findings."[66] An aide to the governor told him, "I have a very real concern about the fact that information appears to have been suppressed from you as well as from the public on this matter."[67]

Making things worse for Milliken and the state government, something had to be done with all the slaughtered animals, and no community wanted to be anywhere near a PBB dump. A landfill near Kalkaska was constructed only after the local county commission sued and won a temporary injunction to stop it. Another, built at Mio, resulted in the governor's only hanging in effigy during his 14 years in office. He never forgot the day he traveled to the community to "discuss and reason with them" and spoke with his effigy behind him and a near riot in front of him. "But I was in good company. [Attorney General] Frank Kelley was also being hung in effigy," he said.[68]

For a time, it appeared that the mishandling of the PBB contamination might terminate Milliken's career. Democrats in the legislature seized on it as a symbol of Milliken's lack of aggressiveness. A year before he would face reelection for a third term in 1978, House Speaker Bobby D. Crim, ordinarily a cordial competitor, blasted Milliken for taking credit for signing a bill reducing the state PBB tolerance level. "Democrats see Milliken particularly vulnerable on his handling of PBB, should he decide to seek reelection next year . . . PBB, pure and simply, is a political issue and the Democrats will try to make it a campaign issue."[69]

The tactic didn't work. Milliken deftly turned the issue around late in the 1978 campaign, adding to his staff as an agricultural adviser Rick Halbert, the man who had identified the initial PBB contamination in his father's herd. Milliken said, "The state has created a number of effective mechanisms to deal with PBB and other toxic materials. [Halbert] will, in a sense, perform a watchdog role over these functions."[70] Milliken swept to an easy reelection.

Both the governor and the agencies he headed had learned at least one lesson: the political sensitivity of chemical contamination. In the late 1970s, Milliken and the Department of Natural Resources responded swiftly to the growing discoveries of contaminated sites— old dumps, abandoned factories, and tainted groundwater—across industrial and agricultural Michigan. At Milliken's request, the state began making emergency appropriations to clean up some of the worst sites. After he left office, the cleanup program would become a major task of the state.

Late in his tenure, Milliken championed the most important environmental cause of all for Michigan—protection of the Great Lakes. Although the size and beauty (and usefulness to humankind) of the lakes has been apparent to all generations of Michiganians, including the aboriginal peoples, it wasn't until the late 1970s, with the signing of the amended U.S.-Canada Great Lakes Water Quality Agreement, that government agencies committed to treating them systemically.[71] The new pact explicitly called for "an ecosystem approach" that encompassed not just the water but also the land, air, fish, wildlife, and humans of the Great Lakes Basin.

Milliken's role in advancing the issue was the use of his bully pulpit. In 1982, after publicity about the danger of exporting Great Lakes water to Montana through a coal slurry pipeline and a U.S. Army Corps of Engineers study of the declining High Plains Ogallala Aquifer raised concern about threats to the lakes, Milliken convened a summit on Mackinac Island to address the issue. There he urged "strong collective action" by the Great Lakes states and Canadian provinces to resist water export.

> The simple truth is that there are growing threats to our Great Lakes system. There is a growing threat of diversion of Great Lakes water to other regions of North America. I, for one, strongly believe that jobs should be located where adequate supplies of fresh water exist, rather than attempting to move water to other regions . . . I am convinced that we must reaffirm our commitment to a clean and healthful water supply in the Great Lakes . . . I believe that the states and provinces should have a greater voice—and a greater opportunity to cooperate among ourselves.[72]

After leaving office on the first day of 1983, Milliken became president of the Chicago-based Center for the Great Lakes, a nonprofit organization that served as a source of policy and public education in support of a regional Great Lakes Charter and Great Lakes Toxic Substances Control Agreement signed by the governors and premiers of the Great Lakes jurisdictions in 1985 and 1986. Milliken's call for a Great Lakes consciousness in Michigan helped shape the issue for the following several decades. No governor could be seen as neglecting or harming the Lakes and expect to be popular.

Admiration of Milliken's leadership on environmental issues was not total. Jeff Dauphin, who worked at the West Michigan Environmental Action Council from 1974 to 1980, said that on the major solid and hazardous waste issues of the era Milliken and the Republicans "were mostly tag-a-longs rather than leaders."[73] But this was a minority view. Joe Stroud, a longtime editorial page editor of the *Detroit Free Press,* hailed Milliken as embodying "the very best qualities in our state . . . The laundry list of legislative and administrative achievements during his administration is an important measure of his legacy . . . He has understood that conservation meant places to fish in the city, and places to find solitude on trout streams."[74]

As the years after his governorship passed and no successor seemed to make quite the same personal and moral claim on the environmental issue, conservationists and environmentalists began to look back with yearning and to realize that whatever differences they had with Milliken he was still the greenest governor of the twentieth century. His reputation grew steadily. In 1997, when the Michigan United Conservation Clubs invited him to speak at a banquet, a defensive Republican governor John Engler, who was constantly under fire from the MUCC and other groups on habitat, clean air, and clean water issues, released a letter to the former governor applauding Milliken's record—and promoting his own.[75] Engler appeared worried that Milliken's record would overshadow his, and in 1998, an election year, he proposed a $500 million environmental bond in his State of the State message.

At the MUCC banquet, describing urban sprawl as a "plague on the land" and calling for reform in state policies that promote it, Milliken struck a note that he had repeatedly hit as governor.

> The truth is that the quality of human life in Michigan depends on nature. The natural beauty of our state is much more than a source of pleasure and recreation. It shapes our values, molds our attitudes, and feeds our spirit . . . In Michigan, our soul is not to be found in steel and concrete, or sprawling new housing developments or strip malls. Rather it is found in the soft petals of a trillium, the gentle whisper of a headwater stream, the vista of a Great Lakes shoreline, and the wonder in children's eyes upon seeing their first bald eagle. It is that soul that we must preserve.[76]

Although Engler did not act on land use issues, in 2003 newly elected Democratic governor Jennifer Granholm appointed Milliken and former attorney general Frank Kelley to cochair a panel to deal with urban sprawl and the revitalization of cities. In August 2003, the panel released a report with hundreds of policy recommendations.[77]

In the end, the image of Milliken the guardian was as important as any of the more than three dozen major environmental and conservation laws he signed during his 14 years as governor.[78] His periodic emergence from retirement to act as the state's conscience on the environment prevented even worse political attacks on the framework of laws he helped put in place during the 1990s and the early twenty-first century.

Although his successors openly intervened in and reorganized the structure of the Department of Natural Resources, Milliken "respected the concept that the role of natural resources management in government should be as nonpolitical as possible," said Howard Tanner, DNR director from 1975 to 1983. "Both the [Natural Resources] commission and the Governor worked to find common ground whenever possible and do what was best."

Milliken's single greatest legacy may have been an ethic of conservation. "If he said he was going to do something, he did it," said Tanner. "If you have integrity, nothing else matters. If you don't have integrity, nothing else matters. He had integrity."[79]

Mark Van Putten, who directed the Great Lakes Natural Resources Center of the National Wildlife Federation in Ann Arbor and ultimately became president of the federation, looked back on Milliken's years as follows: "Governor Milliken's environmental leadership exemplified the bipartisan tradition of natural resources conservation and environmental protection that distinguished the 20th century. It's a lesson elected leaders of the early 21st century would do well to learn as it's the key to meeting the environmental challenges of the future, as it was in the past."[80]

7

AN ACTIVIST GOVERNMENT

WILLIAM MILLIKEN viewed government not as a passive referee among competing interests but as an active force for the protection of the vulnerable and the equalizing of opportunity. Milliken never abandoned his belief that government could marshal the better impulses of citizens to improve society.

Early in his first year as governor, he jumped into a simmering educational debate with both feet, investing enormous political capital and taking significant risks.

For decades, Michigan had relied on a system of school finance bankrolled chiefly by the local property tax. Because the value of residential and industrial property largely determined the revenues that could be raised, faltering urban core cities with significant enrollments of minority students often had deteriorating schools, while fast-growing suburban areas, with a disproportionate percentage of white students, had the best-funded schools. But in some cases the roles were reversed. In the 1970–71 school year, the mostly white Wayne-Westland school district west of Detroit levied 36 mills of property tax. Coupled with state aid, its total per-pupil spending was $830. River Rouge, then the richest school district in the state because of the heavy industry located there, levied 21 mills of property tax and spent $1,260 per pupil on its mostly African American students.[1]

In his 1969 State of the State message to the legislature while he was still technically the lieutenant governor, Milliken outlined the reforms whose attainment would concern and vex him through many of his nearly 14 years as chief executive. "We must develop a vastly improved state aid formula to help equalize educational opportunity, and we must do it as quickly and effectively as possible . . .We must improve our system of financial support to take undue pressure off property taxes."[2]

Pressure for school finance reform began to strike Milliken almost immediately after he took office. "The governor who lets this crisis build unchecked, in its present advanced state, is risking a cruel day of reckoning for himself and the state," the *Detroit Free Press* editorialized in March 1969.[3] Hoping to galvanize the legislature to act, Milliken himself termed the state's education problems "a crisis" in April 1969. "The school finance structure is inequitable, and inadequate . . . inequalities of educational opportunity continue and increase, particularly in the inner cities . . . nonpublic schools are becoming less adequate and are threatened with the prospect of at least partial closing," Milliken said to the legislature. "What is clearly needed is solid and total reform of our educational system, and a clear blueprint for the future."[4]

James Phelps, a former teacher, joined Milliken's education team in June 1969. He recalled two key facts about his job interview with the governor. "Number one, he asked no questions about my political affiliation. He didn't know and didn't ask if I was a Republican or Democrat," Phelps said. "Number two, he wanted somebody whose advice would be independent of the educational interest groups."[5] Milliken's hope was that a truly independent group of education advisers would enable him to navigate among interest groups that had competing interests and demands.

Phelps's initial assignment was to help staff, along with Robert Jewell, an education reform commission to be appointed by the new governor. Milliken hoped the panel would break a stalemate within the array of education lobby groups in the capital, ranging from the Michigan Education Association and the Michigan Federation of Teachers to the Michigan Association of School Administrators and the Michigan Association of School Boards. The twin issues of inequitable financing of schools and an overreliance on the local property tax had generated considerable political controversy but no reform during the 1960s.

Teachers' groups and school districts sought more money with few or no state strings attached; a majority in the state legislature was unwilling to provide new funding without reform.

In an unusual move, Milliken himself chaired the commission, even though doing so would make him politically accountable for its work. "It was recommended to him that he choose someone from outside to chair it," said Phelps. "That way he could be at arm's length from the commission if it came up with something that wasn't politically attainable. But he said no, the only way it's going to work is if it's identified with me, if I make it a personal priority."[6]

In addition to putting himself on the line as chair of the commission, Milliken chose not to pack the panel with representatives of the various education lobbies. Instead he appointed six citizens, ranging from the president of Western Michigan University to businessmen. When the lobbies complained of their lack of representation, the governor's office created an advisory panel that included them. "They couldn't agree on anything other than they wanted more money for schools," Phelps said.[7]

The governor spoke to members of his commission in his Capitol office as they began their work. But his educational message was less important in Phelps's recollection than a gesture he made.

> The room was packed. There were more people than chairs. He got up from behind his desk and started setting up and arranging chairs. He didn't say, "Hey, Jim, get us more chairs." It wasn't a calculated move, that's just the way he was.[8]

Milliken's panel took its reform model from recommendations made by Dr. James B. Conant, former president of Harvard University and a leading national critic of U.S. public education. Long a proponent of local financing of schools as a way of assuring local control of them, Conant changed his position in light of the funding inequities that resulted. "When I began visiting school after school to do my study of the American high school," Conant told the *Detroit Free Press* while promoting Milliken's reforms, "I suddenly became aware of tremendous differences in the quality of local schools and school systems. Then I saw the inequalities in the amount of money school systems have. It was at that point that I began to change my views."[9]

When the panel issued its report, Milliken's belief that the state should be more than a weak, partial financier of education was apparent. "The organization of public education at the state level in Michigan is a classic case of arrested development," the group said. Pointing to a provision in the state's 1908 Constitution that required the state "to continue a system of primary schools whereby every school district in the State shall provide for the education of pupils," the panel concluded that the state government had not advanced beyond that mandate despite changing times. It "still plays a passive role, generally exercising only its custodial charge to 'continue' local school districts and see that each provides for its pupils."[10] Instead, the commission said, "there must be accountability to the Governor and to the Legislature, and through them, to the people for the great stakes that this democracy has always risked on the success of the educational enterprise."[11]

Milliken's panel recommended that the use of the local property tax to fund education be replaced with a uniform statewide property tax to equalize funding. Districts would be allowed to raise an additional 3 mills for enrichment programs. The money would be distributed based on "the basic unit in the educational process—the classroom," the task force report said. "The budget process should be established to guarantee a maximum ration of certified personnel to students."[12] Because teachers' and administrators' salaries varied within regions of the state, the dollar amount to fund such personnel would still vary somewhat.

The other significant reform recommended by the Milliken panel was the adoption of a "systematic, statewide evaluation of its educational program . . . to identify underachieving pupils, specify their areas of deficiency, and develop programs to help them improve."[13] This recommendation was ahead of its time. The idea of a regular statewide assessment of student proficiency would not be codified nationally until the No Child Left Behind Act of 2001. Advanced by the state Department of Education with the support of Milliken, the Michigan Educational Assessment Program (MEAP) was established in 1970, providing a snapshot of how both students and schools were performing.[14]

Milliken sweetened the pot by promising an extra $183 million in state aid for 1970 and 1971 if the change was enacted. But the recommendations stalled in the legislature. In November 1969, Milliken chided the unions representing public school teachers for not giving the plan their full support. "I am not about to propose the pouring of millions of dollars into our existing education system unless we start down the road to fundamental education reform," he warned.[15] But he was unable to win the votes he needed to enact the package before his campaign to win election in 1970.

The governor came back with a new proposal in 1971. This time he made a 15-point education reform proposal to the legislature that went beyond his 1969 plan. To replace the $1.1 billion lost due to the cut in local school property taxes, he called for a 2.3 percent hike in the state's personal income tax on top of a 1 percent increase he had earlier requested for general operating revenues. In addition, Milliken wanted a 2 percent value-added tax on business and industry.[16] This change aroused opposition among the legislative members of his own party. Meanwhile, Democrats refused to back the income tax increase unless Milliken supported making the tax progressive instead of a flat-rate levy. Milliken joined his fellow Republicans in opposing this. Some local school officials raised the specter of state control of schools as a result of state financing, increasing resistance among lawmakers and the public. The issue again stalled in the legislature.

As Capitol correspondent Tim Skubick put it: "The new governor boldly proclaimed in April 1971 that, 'if the governor's plans were adopted, 1971 would be the last year in which property taxes will be used to finance regular school operating costs.' 1971 came and went. No deal."[17]

In 1972, another educational log was thrown on the fire. A U.S. district judge in Detroit, Stephen J. Roth, ordered busing for the purpose of integrating public schools in Detroit and its suburbs. This raised a volatile and ethically ticklish issue for Milliken. Suburban communities angrily opposed the idea of their largely white student bodies being bused great distances into inner city schools and receiving inner city pupils in their own schools.

Milliken walked a delicate middle course. He told African American lawmakers in private, before making an address that was televised statewide, that he opposed busing to achieve school integration in most cases. However, in his televised speech he also said he opposed a constitutional amendment to ban busing of students, arguing that in a few cases it might be a useful remedy. And he called on all parties to work together civilly. "I hope each of us, as we approach the problems in the months ahead, will speak to each other with calm voices, listen to each other with respect, and work together with enthusiasm."[18]

The response was generally warm. "We do not accept the shallow accusations being made by a few who are calling the governor a bigot, a racist and worse," said the *Lansing State Journal*.[19] "Gov. Milliken is no racist and those making the charges are only pouring gasoline on the flames by such a tactic." Although his opposition to busing did no lasting damage to his relations with African American voters, it temporarily frayed his working partnership with their representatives. But correspondent Skubick called the governor's address "a masterful job," saying that his confidence, optimism, and spirit of conciliation helped dampen racial tensions.[20]

The courts did not resolve the issue of busing before it faded away in the 1980s and early 1990s. Meanwhile, the struggle over school finance lingered. In 1972, frustrated by the legislature's impasse on school finance reform, Milliken organized a petition drive to replace the property tax with a sales tax increase. Midway in the process of collecting signatures, he dropped his petitions and joined forces with the Michigan Education Association, which did the legwork to place Proposals C and D on the November ballot.

The proposals were complicated but included three critical features. First, they reduced property tax bills statewide. Second, they replaced the lost revenue with a 2 percent increase in the state income tax and a tax on business profits and payrolls to pay for education. Third, they would commit the state to distributing the money to maintain a base level of education service statewide. Milliken recommended that this be a ratio of 49 professional staff members for every 1,000 pupils. The *Detroit Free Press* endorsed the twin proposals, calling them "necessary because the present millage system of financing schools has almost broken down. It is under attack by both the court and by taxpayers, who know that it is unjust."[21]

But there were harsh critics. George Platsis, a Lansing attorney, tried to get Proposal C removed from the ballot on the grounds that false and misleading statements had been made in order to place it there. "I believe Proposal C is nothing but a disguised tax increase," Platsis said at a news conference, "a loss of control over annual local millage requests and [the onset of] state control of education . . . The proposal is both meaningless and ineffective for any purpose except to create the appearance of a voter mandate to increase the personal income tax."[22] Milliken fired back, saying, "In the days that remain until the people vote on this issue, I expect to see and hear a barrage of misinformation and innuendo from the critics of Proposal C."[23]

But the opposition was formidable. Fearing loss of their control over schools, the Michigan Association of School Boards opposed Proposal C in a 159 to 73 roll call vote just before the public balloting. State senator Harry DeMaso, a Battle Creek Republican who headed the Senate's Finance Committee, said that the campaign for Proposal C was relying on "half truths and blatant lies." He added, "No one is telling them what they're going to end up paying, not to mention the loss of local control over schools. And once they find out, they're against it. The truth is there in black and white in this proposal but the backers are obscuring it. They are leading people to believe they will pay no more property taxes and that's that."[24]

The governor put his personal prestige behind the passage of the two proposals, giving frequent speeches and media interviews supporting them. "Milliken aides say the governor is working as hard as if he were running for re-election," a reporter noted. Milliken expressed unusual open dissatisfaction with lawmakers, calling the stalemate over his reform proposals since 1969 "the system at its frustrating worst. The need was so plain and the solution so clear."[25]

But the need was not so clear to voters. Handing Milliken a "smashing defeat," they turned down both Proposals C and D by margins of approximately 60 and 70 percent, respectively.[26]

The *Detroit Free Press,* which would prove to be a reliable backer of much of the Milliken program, lamented: "We have a growing suspicion that there are more people in Michigan who like to talk about tax reform than want to do anything about it. Gov. Milliken tried to do something, and he has been politically embarrassed for his efforts. We hope that he will not let this defeat divert him from his goal."[27]

Although polls conducted the weekend before the balloting showed Proposal C narrowly ahead, when Milliken called Phelps to get his prediction of the likely outcome his education adviser was pessimistic since "no" votes on ballot proposals tend to peak on Election Day. "Do you have a backup plan if it loses?" Milliken asked. Phelps said he did, and it became one of the successful education reforms Milliken was able to bring about, the so-called equal yield formula that narrowed the gap in tax capacity among districts.

Milliken indeed came back to the education issue almost immediately. In a special message to the legislature on education delivered on February 7, 1973, he noted that the Supreme Court had, a month after the failure of Proposals C and D, ruled the system of school aid based largely on the property tax unconstitutional because it deprived some pupils of equal opportunity.[28] Coupling these developments with the November defeat of the third millage renewal proposal in a row in Detroit, the state's largest school district with 13 percent of the state's enrollment, Milliken again portrayed the educational finance system as being in crisis.

> In rejecting Proposal C, the people said they were not ready to accept a major change in the method of collecting and distributing monies for education. I accept and respect their decision. However, I do not believe, nor will I accept, that the public was condoning the inequities which the present system imposes on both students and taxpayers.[29]

Milliken once again proposed a big increase in the state's financing of education with an 11.3 percent boost, the largest from year to year in the state's history. But he also insisted on the equal yield formula to "assure that one mill of property tax effort will bring the same dollars per pupil in virtually every school district." Under the proposal, the state would compensate for a depleted local tax base by making up the difference between what a poor district could raise with a mill of taxation and a statewide standard.

The problem this sought to cure was a hardship for both schools and property owners in poor districts. As the reformers explained later, under the existing formula a homeowner living in a poor district would have to pay 50 percent more in property taxes than the owner of a home of equal value in a wealthy district to generate the same amount of funding for his or her child's education.[30]

Working with a sponsor, Senator Gilbert Bursley, a Republican from Ann Arbor, Milliken fought for passage of the new measure with a vigor equal to the unsuccessful battle he had waged for the previous year's ballot proposals. The equal yield bill reshaped the politics of education in Lansing, silencing much of the opposition to previous reforms and attracting the support of school boards across the state. The proposal did not come attached to the specter of a state takeover of local schools. It merely added state funding to local efforts in an attempt to provide a more equitable education for all schoolchildren. Despite 15 extended sessions of the Senate Appropriations Committee in March 1973, during which opponents tried to water down the proposal, the bill passed the full Senate on April 5 by two more votes than the bare minimum needed.[31]

The House of Representatives' Appropriations Committee, controlled by Democrats, had its own idea. Brushing the Milliken-Bursley reform aside, the panel adopted a plan that would lower the operating taxes of most school districts to a common 20-mill level and create a common expenditure per pupil within several years. More expensive than the plan Milliken supported, the alternative also punished districts that taxed themselves more, the opposite of the Senate plan. But the full House balked at the strategy and adopted a plan similar to that of the Senate. In late July, both houses agreed on a compromise plan that essentially kept faith with the Milliken position. The "equal yield" legislation became law on August 14, 1973.

"The irony of the situation," Phelps recalled, "was that the Democratic plan by and large helped the Republican parts of the state and the Milliken plan helped the Democratic parts. The Democrats did not want their plan to pass. They wanted to keep Milliken from having a success. [Democratic] Representative Bill Keith, with the help of Jerry Dunn, a lobbyist, led a revolt of 14 representatives to pass the bill."[32]

At the signing ceremony for the bill, Milliken said, "It is wrong that the wealth of a school district should affect either the quality of education a child receives or the tax rates paid by his parents and neighbors. This act will virtually eliminate property tax base wealth as a factor in school finance among districts."[33]

One of the reasons for the measure's success in the legislature may have been Milliken's willingness to give credit to others. The reform legislation was known as the Bursley bill rather than the political property of Milliken by the governor's choice. Phelps said Milliken was also unruffled by the fact that the reform would help relatively poorer urban schools with Democratic voting majorities.

> I said, "Governor, the impact of this is going to be heavily felt in Democratic districts. It helps mostly the poorer urban and rural districts, the ones with the highest property tax and the lowest amount of revenue raised per mill." He said, "Is this the right thing to do?" I said, "Yes." So he asked me how we could get it implemented.[34]

The 1973 reform was perhaps the pinnacle of Milliken's educational achievements. His related effort, an attempt to reduce reliance on property taxes for schools, continued to falter. Meanwhile, the rage of homeowners facing skyrocketing property tax bills continued to mount. A 1978 ballot proposal to eliminate the property tax for schools and pour state tax money into vouchers that could be used at private schools was soundly defeated. Milliken backed a 1981 proposal that would have lowered property taxes, increased the state income tax, and earmarked all lottery profits for education. In a special May election, the proposal was decisively defeated despite the governor's support. He left office without having delivered on one of his top initial educational priorities. It would be another 12 years after he departed before voters would in essence choose to cap school property taxes and hike the state sales tax to provide more equal funding for local schools.[35]

A scandal in Michigan's mental health system tested Milliken's leadership and his commitment to the most vulnerable. Promoting a state role in assuring compassionate treatment for the mentally ill was a family tradition. As a state senator, Milliken's father had taken a personal interest in boosting funding for mental health, including a hometown facility. In a 1948 campaign advertisement, James T. Milliken had called himself "one of the strongest legislative champions of financial aid to improve working conditions and salaries at the State Hospital in Traverse City. Further he has always held a sympathetic attitude toward the unfortunates committed into this institution and has been a valiant supporter of bills designed to improve the general hospital conditions."[36]

But in February 1978 Detroit newspapers broke the story that workers at the Plymouth Regional Center for Developmental Disabilities routinely abused patients, touching off a firestorm. Milliken ordered a State Police investigation as well as a report from the chief of the Department of Mental Health, Donald C. Smith. He also made personal, unannounced visits to several of the state's mental health facilities.

Craig Ruff, then a Milliken aide, accompanied Milliken on some of the visits. Staff members at some of the facilities did not initially recognize Milliken. Ruff said both men were deeply affected by the sight of "people plainly medicated, numb to the world."[37] The Plymouth facility was a "particular hellhole," where abuse had resulted in visible bruises on some of the patients. Relatives were often denied access to patients. Milliken, he said, "was concerned that there had to be zero tolerance for abuse and neglect. These [patients] were wards of the state." In a report to the legislature, Milliken deplored the abuses.

To investigate the allegations of abuse at the Plymouth Center, Milliken appointed a task force headed by Wilbur Cohen, a former secretary of the U.S. Department of Health, Education and Welfare. He also directed agency chief Smith to appoint a panel to deal with the problem of abuse in the state system of mental health facilities.[38] Smith's report documented 31 allegations of abuse at the Plymouth Center, 223 at the nine other centers for the developmentally disabled, and a total of 130 substantiated abuse cases in the state system. Some 52 of these were acts of abuse committed by employees against residents. In the summer of 1978, the twin investigations and a lawsuit filed on behalf of the residents by their parents resulted in the firing of 29 state employees. Milliken escaped the scandal largely untarnished because of his quick response to the disclosures.

During the Milliken years, especially during economic downturns, the budget and role of the state Department of Social Services (DSS) expanded dramatically. Milliken consistently defended increased transfer payments to disadvantaged adults and families against attacks launched by conservative Republicans and Democrats and sought to limit reductions in welfare spending during the chronic budget crisis of his last two years in office. "Some of the hardest decision making occurred during the budget crisis of 1981 and 1982," Milliken said. "There were recommendations to cut very sharply in the area of welfare and social services. I would say, 'We're not going to do that. It hurts too many people.' Some of my critics said I lacked toughness. But I just felt too many people were in need of protection and we couldn't neglect them."[39]

By 1981, the DSS bureaucracy included 15,129 workers, making it the largest agency of state government.[40] The agency's total budget neared $3.5 billion. In 1980 alone, the general assistance welfare case-load of the state skyrocketed, increasing by 71 percent.[41] But even the runaway growth of the agency's budget failed to keep pace with the cost of necessities for the poor. Between 1971 and 1981, the purchasing power of welfare benefits for the average family of three, when adjusted for inflation, fell by about 30 percent, even as nominal spending increased by 64 percent.

From 1975 to early 1982, Milliken's DSS director, John Dempsey, served as the point man for the administration in articulating the role of government in serving the disadvantaged. When he died in April 1982, the *Saginaw News* said that he had served the poor as "their compassionate advocate against efforts to trim social spending beneath levels he thought were decent."[42] Milliken called his death "a profound loss for all of the people of Michigan."

Milliken's faithfulness to the ideal of government was sustained even when he disagreed with the programs he was charged with administering. After voters approved a ballot proposition in 1972 to create a state lottery—which Milliken opposed on moral grounds—the governor decided to make the best of it. He summoned Gus Harrison, a longtime corrections official who had risen to head of the department and had a reputation for running a clean agency. Harrison recalled: "He said, 'I wasn't for it, I was opposed to it. But now that I've got it, I want it to be the best in the country.'" He instructed Harrison to set the lottery up and provided his support when called upon.[43]

According to Harrison, Milliken was determined to protect the integrity of legalized gambling. "He told everyone to leave me alone. He built a wall around me, and that made things a lot easier. He just asked me to report periodically on my progress." When, a year after the voters had approved the proposal, Harrison said he was ready to sell the first tickets, Milliken asked him to hold off until after the Thanksgiving holiday.

To promote the lottery's kickoff, Harrison asked the governor to sell the first ticket with news media watching. "He rolled that around in his head a while," the lottery chief said. Milliken not only personally opposed the lottery, Harrison said, but also "never warmed to the idea of asking people to part with their money." Ultimately Milliken agreed to sell the ticket, standing next to a blind vendor in the basement of the Capitol.[44]

"I not only respected him but I liked him," Harrison said. "He had a quiet air about him. He was always patient, attentive. There was something that impressed you about him."

C. Patrick Babcock, who served Milliken as director of the state offices on alcoholism and drug abuse and services to the aging, as well as legislative liaison and director of the departments of labor and mental health, described Milliken's view of his job as running "a values-based state government . . . It was a caring government. We haven't had a governor like that since."[45]

Added Charlie Greenleaf, an adviser to Milliken on education issues early in his tenure: "He was far more issue oriented than he was partisan or ideological. He was committed to solving problems. That was what government was about to him."[46]

8

GOVERNOR OF ALL
THE PEOPLE

A s GOVERNOR, William Milliken found himself attempting
to bridge a state with one of the biggest racial divides in the
nation. The 1967 Detroit riot, long regarded as a turning point in the
decline of the city, had dramatized a process of "white flight" and
inner-city despair dating back to just after World War II. By 2002, 20
years after Milliken left the governor's office, Michigan's divide was the
worst ever.

According to the U.S. Census, Michigan is the most segregated
state in the nation. Five of the 25 most racially segregated metropolitan regions in America—Detroit, Saginaw, Flint, Benton Harbor,
and Muskegon—are in Michigan. The next closest state is New
York, with four. Two more Michigan metropolitan regions—
Grand Rapids and Jackson—almost made the top 25.

Census figures also show that Michigan has the most segregated
public school systems in the nation. For example, 613,000 students
attend public schools in 83 school districts in Wayne, Macomb, and
Oakland counties, according to an analysis by the National School
Boards Association. Roughly 180,000 of those students are black
and 82 percent of black students are enrolled in just three districts—
Detroit, Highland Park, and Inkster. Some 90 percent of white stu-

dents—540,000 kids—are enrolled in Detroit-region schools where 10 percent or less of the students are black.[1]

That he was unable to stop these worsening trends does not mean that Milliken failed to try hard enough. Instead, the lesson of his legacy is that from the 1970s on more politicians gained than lost votes in the suburbs and rural areas of the state by playing the race card against Detroit. Milliken's attempt to depict the state as "one Michigan"—a state of racial diversity and tolerance—was also largely unsuccessful because of economic and social factors reaching far beyond the boundaries of the state. And the national Republican Party that he continually urged to embrace the aspirations of African Americans ultimately found greater rewards in exploiting the racial fears of whites.

The Michigan Republican Party stood for fairness in the 1960s. Under the leadership of Elly Peterson, its first female state chair, the party deliberately cultivated support from young African Americans. For the first time in decades, the GOP chose an African American, George Washington, to run on its state ticket in 1966 (for the post of secretary of state). Peterson also touted an "involvement program" designed to promote voluntarism by party members in distressed inner cities, including Detroit. "Elly recognized that the Republican Party could never be the majority Party without the involvement of minorities," said her successor as state chair, William McLaughlin. "In addition, the Party didn't deserve to be successful if it was an all-white Party." The party opened a full-time action center in Detroit to help city residents get services from government and the private sector. Milliken was supportive.[2]

Milliken's values of racial tolerance, forged in childhood, were compatible with this kind of Republicanism. Although there were few African Americans or members of other racial minorities in his hometown of Traverse City, Milliken was given a belief in fairness toward all by his parents. He said his father's "sense of fairness has been, all of my life, a great influence. It provided an example for me. It made doing the right thing easy for me."[3]

As a state senator, Milliken had resisted efforts by members of his own Republican caucus to overturn the so-called Rule 9, which outlawed discrimination in the sale of housing. As governor, he would have a chance not only to stop discrimination but to promote equal opportunity.

Milliken had publicly aligned himself with the efforts of the Rev. Martin Luther King Jr. to promote racial tolerance and equality. As lieutenant governor, he participated in a 1965 freedom march down Woodward Avenue in Detroit, along with former governor G. Mennen Williams, prior to a speech by King attended by 15,000 at Cobo Hall.[4] The *Detroit News* characterized King's remarks as a "plea against ultra-militancy and hate by some Negroes," but in fact the speech emphasized the objective of equal rights for all citizens. Milliken promoted that value throughout his tenure.

Not long after becoming governor in 1969, Milliken's efforts at racial harmony won special notice from the *Detroit News*. Hoping to defuse continuing tensions between Detroit police and the African American community two years after the catastrophic riot, Milliken invited young militant African Americans to an 80-minute meeting. Although participants were skeptical, leaders of the African American community believed that "the governor is sincere in his efforts to hear what black voices are saying."[5]

Milliken by that time had already made a number of moves unusual for a Republican governor in an attempt to end what he described as the "tragic estrangement" between African American voters and his party. His appointments of African Americans, including David Duncan as his chief adviser on job training and mental health and Lowell Perry as a member of the Ferris State University Board of Control, won praise during a time of racial tensions on campuses. Carole Williams was appointed to the Civil Rights Commission, and Myron Wahls, head of the state's leading association of African American attorneys, was appointed to the Michigan Employment Security Commission (and later the Michigan Court of Appeals). Milliken also called on the Michigan State Police to step up recruitment of African American troopers and asked other department heads to increase the hiring of racial minorities.

"Milliken has even sought out—by unannounced visits to 12th Street where the fuse was lit for the 1967 Detroit riots—the opinions and complaints of black store owners, shoppers and hangers-on," the *Detroit News* reported. "He has talked to leaders of the Urban League in Detroit, visited its 12th Street Academy for school dropouts, talked economic and inner city redevelopment with leaders of Urban Design, Inc., an association of black architects and constructions firms, and learned about black contributions to American art and culture from Brothers Unlimited spokesmen."[6]

The second man Milliken appointed to head his Detroit office, Roy Williams, was an African American who "did a lot to sensitize the entire staff to race," said George Weeks, a key Milliken aide.[7] Williams had credibility as a liaison to leaders of the Detroit African American community such as Martha Jean, "The Queen," a radio personality who also spearheaded nonprofit organizations serving the disadvantaged. In memoranda to Milliken, Williams wrote conversationally about the governor's best approach to community leaders.[8]

Although Milliken's outreach to African Americans did not win him significant support in Detroit for his 1970 election bid, he had laid the foundation for one of the most remarkable partnerships in Michigan political history. That partnership joined Milliken, the mild-mannered, white, northern Michigan Republican, and the decidedly not mild-mannered African American Detroit mayor, Coleman Young, who had lived in the city's "Black Bottom" neighborhood as a child. Elected in 1973, Young was the first African American mayor of the city and served until 1993. During that time, he became a hero to African Americans nationwide and in Detroit and an easy target for white suburban politicians hoping to inflame subterranean racial prejudices. Young's sometimes profane style and attacks on the white power establishment infuriated many suburbanites—and were a world apart from Milliken's style.

"For two decades, Young was a dominant personality in deeply segregated southeast Michigan," the *Detroit Free Press* said when Young died in 1997. "His opinions and actions constantly stirred controversy. Merely mentioning his name could touch off arguments. Most blacks revered the mayor; many whites loathed him."

"In that time, no other figure embodied any other city in America in the manner that the mayor came to embody Detroit," wrote Lonnie Wheeler, coauthor of Young's 1994 autobiography.[9]

The two men—the patient, civil Milliken and the brusque, results-oriented Young—increasingly found common ground and formed a friendship that transcended the political business they conducted.

Born in Tuscaloosa, Alabama, in 1918, Young moved with his family to Detroit five years later. Young served in the military during World War II as a member of the famed African American Tuskegee Airmen, sold real estate, and became active in the labor movement in the late 1940s. United Auto Workers president Walter Reuther banished Young from the Congress of Industrial Organizations (CIO) in 1948 for supporting third-party candidate Henry Wallace instead of Democrat Harry Truman for president. In 1952, Young won national notoriety for defying the U.S. House of Representatives' Un-American Activities Committee, refusing to answer its questions about his membership in left-wing organizations at a Detroit hearing. In an exchange with committee counsel Frank Tavenner, a white Virginian, Young upbraided his questioner for pronouncing the word *Negro* as *Niggra* in his recollection. "The hearings were as big as the damn World Series in Detroit," Young later wrote, "and they were broadcast live on radio, which meant that the whole city heard me reprimand the government counselor."[10]

The friendship between the white politician from Traverse City and the African American politician from Detroit did not get off to a promising start. Young and Milliken served together in the state Senate after Young's election to it in 1964 and Milliken's election as lieutenant governor the same year.[11] Milliken thought of Young as "overly partisan" at the time.[12] And he was aware that upon becoming mayor Young "was suspicious of me at first. I think in time he came to recognize my concern was genuine. We began to put our distrust of each other aside. Then our relations developed into something that meant a great deal to me and I think to him. As I look back on Coleman Young and that relationship, I consider that to be one of the most meaningful and important friendships and alliances I had in my entire 14 years as governor. We were able to work together constructively to solve critical problems, and I think that's what the state needed."[13]

In his autobiography, *Hard Stuff,* Young described Milliken as "a wealthy moderate from a rural background that did not share a social hemisphere with Black Bottom . . . When he ascended from lieutenant governor to governor in 1969 upon George Romney's appointment as HUD [Housing and Urban Development] Secretary in the Nixon cabinet, I had little reason to believe that Milliken would depart from the course of his right-wing predecessor. But I've never had a more productive relationship with a public servant."[14]

Early proof of Young's impression of Milliken was a coarse but fond joke he cracked about the governor at a mid-1970s Press Steak-Out

Dinner in Detroit. Both the mayor and the governor spoke. Young, who never before was known to have said a kind word about a Republican, said, "The governor is governor because he is a fine gentleman . . . In fact he is such a gentleman that he steps out of the shower to take a piss."[15]

Bob Berg, who served as Milliken's executive assistant for public affairs and his chief speechwriter from early 1977 to the end of his last term in December 1982, and then worked as press secretary for Young from January 1983 to the end of 1993, saw the relationship from a singular perspective. Also a state Capitol reporter before joining Milliken's staff, Berg conceded that the politicians were "two guys who had come from about as different a background as you could imagine. But they had some similarities that made them a good team politically."[16]

Among the similarities, Berg included the fact that both men could have made far more money in private life than in politics but were devoted to public service, both were personally engaging, both had a "social conscience," and both were honorable in the terms that matter to politicians. "If either one of them shook your hand on something on a deal, you didn't need to bring lawyers in to make it legal. You could count on it."[17]

One of the most important and difficult projects that brought the two men together was the so-called Detroit equity package. Detroit ran continuing budget deficits in the 1970s, and Milliken wanted to help. But he had to have a rationale. As Young saw it, Detroit had been paying 100 percent of the cost for city institutions that benefited the entire state, including the Detroit Zoo, the Public Library, and the Institute of Arts. To compensate the city for these expenses, Young suggested that the state provide aid to the city. Milliken agreed despite Young's self-acknowledged unpopularity outside Detroit. "Detroit had become a code word for black, and in turn my name had become a code word for Detroit," Young said. "It was not politically expedient for Milliken to work closely with me, but he had enough integrity to screw the politics and get on with what was right and necessary."[18]

By the time Milliken succeeded in bringing the National Governors' Association annual conference to Detroit in 1977 to symbolize the city's comeback from the catastrophic riots a decade earlier, reporters described the relationship as a political marriage of convenience.

The Young-Milliken "romance" has led to millions of state dollars to bail out Detroit city government. The governor describes it as "equity" for Detroit—and he promptly declares war whenever balky Democratic or Republican legislators try to stop it. Result: Milliken looks like a progressive Republican, a savior of the cities . . . Young is facing a primary battle next week at the polls. All the rosy remarks about the rebirth of a city won't hurt at all. And Milliken—who may run for something next year—could gain black support and Democratic votes because of his chumminess with the mayor.[19]

Detroit Free Press political columnist Hugh McDiarmid termed the 1977 governors' meeting in Detroit "somewhat of an experiment." Milliken said it was unlike any previous such meeting. "We're going to take the governors out of their hotel and into the city. They're going to see the good parts and the bad parts . . . We're going to use Detroit, with all of its warts, as a workshop . . . an urban laboratory."[20]

The Detroit area news media were more than up to the task of identifying the warts. McDiarmid pointed out that the governors would enjoy a "stylish, very exclusive" inaugural event in Grosse Pointe Shores at the "gold-plated" Edsel Ford estate.[21] Another *Free Press* reporter, Susan Watson, mocked the governors for using "carpeted" Port-a-Johns at the Grosse Pointe reception and sending their spouses on a shopping trip in the fashionable suburb of Birmingham.[22] The Associated Press called the failure of four of six governors to show up for a tour on Detroit's crime-fighting efforts "disappointing."[23] And a suburban newspaper, the *Macomb Daily,* noted that Milliken's emphasis on revitalizing Detroit had "prompted some criticism from outstate and suburban interests, who feel they aren't getting their share of financial attention."[24]

But the event delivered much of its intended benefit in the end, said the *Detroit News.* "It will probably take years to wipe out Detroit's reputation as the 'murder capital of the world.' But the nation's governors are now in a position to help remove the stain," it said after the event ended. "Many governors spoke highly of Detroit. But all the governors were able to carry the word back to their states that 'Detroit isn't so bad after all.'" Commending Milliken for bringing his peers to Detroit, the article ended with a suggestion: "What the Republican Party needs more than anything else is three dozen William Millikens."[25]

Michigan's governor made national headlines during the conference. Appearing on the television show *Meet the Press* on September 11, he responded to a question from syndicated columnist Marianne Means about the low self-identification of voters as Republicans in opinion surveys. "It ought to be a clear lesson to the Republican Party across the country," Milliken said, "that unless it becomes a more moderate, broad-based party, it's not going anywhere . . . I think any policy of the Republican Party, or for that matter the Democratic Party, which attempts to write off blacks is not only morally wrong but is politically stupid."[26] Milliken also told the *Meet the Press* panel that he supported Democratic president Jimmy Carter's Panama Canal treaty, which would relinquish control of the waterway to Panama, differing with his fellow Republican governor Pierre S. du Pont of Delaware.

Milliken also conveyed his urgency about the problems of the cities to the nation through his welcoming address to the governors. "Cities have always been the center of civilization as we have known it. We are now at the point where we will determine whether our cities become monuments—or death mounds—of our civilization," Milliken said. "If we can't solve our urban problems, we can't solve the problems of America."[27]

When the national economy plunged into recession in late 1979, Detroit's economy sank like a stone. Always heavily reliant on auto manufacturing and supply for its job base, the city and surrounding areas were damaged by another sudden rise in gasoline prices and the switch by consumers to more fuel-efficient, foreign automobiles. Detroit's unemployment rate hovered around 18 percent in 1980 and close to 30 percent among African Americans.[28] With Milliken's support, in 1980 Young lobbied the legislature successfully for a new state law that soon permitted a "quick take" of private property to facilitate the clearing of a 462-acre site of developed Detroit to provide the site for a new General Motors plant. On the grounds that the creation of the jobs was a public purpose, the legislature agreed to give the city authority to condemn hundreds of homes and other private properties. The human tragedies associated with the dismantling of a low-income, ethnic neighborhood that the news media dubbed "Poletown" caused a national furor but led to the creation of 3,000 jobs Detroit badly needed. "We had an opportunity not only to maintain an automotive foothold in the city, but to do so with a state-of-the-art facility that would place Detroit back in the industrial vanguard, where it belonged," Young said.[29] The mayor credited Milliken with persuading the new Reagan administration to stand by assurances of federal aid that President Jimmy Carter and federal cabinet officials had made before Carter was unseated in 1980.

Despite the angry annual battles over the Detroit equity package, Milliken continued to try to channel state assistance to the state's largest city, especially as its problems worsened in the 1980–82 recession. In his 1982 budget, Milliken proposed a $40 million "distressed cities" program that would have earmarked 77 percent of its funds for Detroit while also boosting the equity package from $28.4 to $33.3 million, with a $4 million boost for the Detroit Institute of Arts. The recommendations "virtually guarantee another long, lively, and probably acrimonious series of Detroit vs. non-Detroit debates in this year's session of the Legislature," the *Detroit Free Press* said.[30] The equity package survived, but the distressed cities initiative did not.

Still Milliken refused to turn his back on the city. He told a reporter in early 1981 that he wanted to "buck" outstate resentment of the city and said he was troubled by legislators' attitudes toward Young. "I personally believe that Mayor Young has done an excellent job in Detroit," Milliken said. "He has cut costs, taken some hard measures and made no bones about his willingness to confront the special-interest groups to try to bring the city back into manageable proportions. That city is in very deep distress today . . . If Detroit should fail, Michigan will be in such trouble that we will find it difficult to recover. We are tied together."[31]

As the years passed, Milliken's attention to Detroit paid political as well as personal dividends. He heavily lost the African American vote in Detroit in both 1970 and 1974, but in 1978 he pulled off the shocking feat, for a Republican, of carrying Wayne County, which contains Detroit. No Republican candidate for governor had done that since 1946. Milliken's 114,567-vote Wayne County deficit in 1974 became a 5,311-vote edge in his race against Democrat William Fitzgerald. Young publicly endorsed Fitzgerald but "privately let it be known that he preferred Milliken," the *Detroit Free Press* said.[32]

A 1980 *Detroit Free Press* survey of Detroiters gave Milliken the top ranking among all white politicians in the poll. African Americans gave him a positive score of 56 percent versus a negative score of only 20 percent. Young, meanwhile, had an approval rating of 93 percent among African Americans in Detroit, but only 43 percent among whites.[33]

On the other hand, helping Detroit increasingly cost Milliken with legislators and some voters outside the city's boundaries. When Milliken successfully urged suburban legislators to approve preliminary funding for a light-rail system for Detroit, several progressive members of the state House who supported the plan lost their seats in the 1980 election. The specter of African American Detroit and the increasingly unpopular Young was used by Republicans to tarnish the light-rail supporters. Milliken's Democratic successor, James Blanchard, sought to distance himself from Young in order to hold on to voters outside of the city. Elected in 1990, Republican John Engler abolished general assistance welfare for able-bodied males, a large population in Detroit, and fought fiercely with Young over state budget priorities.

A Republican who many thought of as a potential governor in the Milliken mode, former state House Speaker Paul Hillegonds, moved from rural Allegan County to Detroit after leaving public office to head a nonprofit organization called Detroit Renaissance, which was devoted to renewing the city's economic base. Skeptical of Milliken's program of aid to Detroit when he was in the state house, Hillegonds saw things differently in 2004. "My journey has taken me to Detroit," he said. "This experience has brought me closer to where [Milliken] was philosophically. Detroit is key to the state. When he promoted the equity package, there were those who said it was just a bunch of grants to please his wealthy patrons and buy votes in Detroit. But actually it was his idea for tax-base sharing, and it came out of his commitment to social equity," Hillegonds said.[34]

He added, "Milliken had a passion for social justice. That's why he's still loved in Detroit. The black community could spot a phony. They knew he really cared."

Ultimately, the combined efforts of both Young and Milliken were far from enough to promote a true economic renaissance in Detroit. Detroit's economy continued to struggle into the early part of the twenty-first century, with the city's mayor, Kwame Kilpatrick, announcing a $214 million deficit in early 2005 and the possibility of laying off 2,000 city employees as Detroit's unemployment rate topped 15 percent. "The city has lost almost a million residents since its peak growth period during the 1950s," the *Detroit Free Press* reported. "Estimates show that the city may lose another 50,000 in the next five years. Many of those leaving are higher-income residents."[35]

The city's problems, which were structural and related to national trends, included the shrinking domestic auto industry, the decline of manufacturing, the explosion in growth in the Sunbelt states, and population demographics. They were not something Milliken or his predecessors or successors could do much to change. But by signaling that state government was trying to help Milliken may have helped dampen the worst of the city's despair.

Milliken remembered his work with Young and city residents fondly. "I think I was always greeted in Detroit within the black community with warmth and with respect," he said. "I don't recall any occasion in the black community where I did not get that treatment. I think my personal interest in civil rights was recognized. The community recognized also that I had a good relationship with Coleman Young and that we were able when I was governor to direct many dollars there to deal with the problems Detroit had."[36]

Beginning at about the time Milliken took office, however, the national party, and later the Michigan GOP, benefited from reversing the policies of active state help for Detroit and other urban centers. With the exception of a 1995 law reducing pollution cleanup standards to facilitate new development in contaminated urban areas, the Michigan Republicans that ran the state in the 1990s promoted few large-scale reforms of benefit to the cities. Simultaneously, candidates in conservative, largely white Macomb County and some other Detroit suburbs ran campaigns heavy with innuendo against African American Detroit, a practice Milliken publicly deplored.

The relationship between the two men from dramatically different backgrounds survived their careers in public office. Milliken and his wife Helen remained in touch with Young after his 1993 retirement and visited him once at his condominium in Detroit for a far-ranging conversation about politics. Young inscribed a copy of his autobiography to "Bill Milliken, Michigan's greatest governor, and my good friend," in March 1994. When the former mayor died in 1997, Milliken delivered one of the eulogies and was warmly received by the crowd.

Any balance sheet that measures the genuineness of Milliken's concern for racial minorities and women as political constituencies must take note of the fact that the governor had few African American advisers on his personal staff. On the other hand, through his appointments director, Joyce Braithwaite, he named hundreds of African Americans and women to state boards and commissions. In one agency, the Department of Licensing and Regulation, the Milliken team broke up the "lily-white old boys' club" on many professional licensing and certification boards, said the man who ran the department, William Ballenger.[37] At the close of Milliken's final term, 3 of the state's 19 departments were headed by African Americans, including the first black woman to run a state agency.

To characterize Milliken's relationship with Young and his view of Detroit as the sole measure of his concern for opportunity for citizens of all races and creeds is an exaggeration, of course. But in his ability to forge a friendship with a man of strikingly different background, temperament, and political style Milliken demonstrated the same open-mindedness and sincerity toward nearly all that won him the growing respect of Michigan voters. In administering the state, Milliken was as close to color-blind—and gender-blind—as any governor in the state's history. His goal of one Michigan remains elusive but tantalizing.

9

MORE THAN A FIRST LADY

Few michigan governors' spouses have come from more conventional surroundings, and had a more eventful journey to a surprising destination, than did Helen Milliken. The daughter of staunchly traditional Colorado parents, Helen at first hewed to the family line. By the time she left public life, she was identified as a passionate advocate for the equality of women, reviled or deeply admired by thousands.

Helen's father, Stanley Wallbank, graduated from the University of Colorado with a law degree in 1918 and married Nellie Sillik a year later. The marriage, which lasted 52 years, produced Helen, sisters Elaine and Elizabeth (also known as "B.J."), and a brother, Lincoln. Stanley Wallbank practiced probate, corporation, aviation, and insurance law and remained active as a Phi Gamma Delta.[1] He was also a fierce Republican and political conservative. Helen said later that she didn't understand how conservative he was until she attended Smith College and studied political history. "It was an eye-opener," she said.[2]

Helen Milliken acknowledged that she didn't think about the place of women in society while growing up. "I never had a glimmer of a thought about that as a child," she said in 2003. "It never occurred to me that women could and should be setting goals. I was raised in an era where women were supposed to be educated, literate, find a good husband, and provide a good home . . . It was serendipity and history. I was born at a time when the role of women in society was changing."[3]

Her courtship with Bill Milliken during World War II continued the education that had begun with her enrollment at Smith. When her father suggested to Bill before the marriage that his future son-in-law might want to become a business executive, the younger man demurred. "I think Bill was more than a little put off by that conversation," she said. "But my father had started from scratch. He was a postman's son. One of six children."

Bill largely shielded her from his war experiences as they continued their relationship by mail while he was serving in the military during World War II. "I didn't really have a sense of what he went through until long after," Helen recalled. "Bill has started talking about his war experiences 55 years after the fact. I've heard stories I never heard before . . . I think that experience has a profound impact on a person in many ways. Being exposed to the violence and impact of war and the terrible things that happen—that changes you."[4]

After the war and their wedding, Helen enjoyed accompanying Bill to Yale, where he finished his degree in 1946. Although the couple lived in a one-room apartment and shared a bathroom and refrigerator with others in the building, she remembers the time fondly. It was one of the few periods in their first four decades together in which they were free of family, career, and political demands. Their lives underwent a significant change when Bill opted to run for elective office.

Although at first she was "astounded" by Bill's state Senate candidacy in 1960, she loyally supported her husband then and during his tenure as lieutenant governor, slowly advancing into the limelight herself as a speaker and public figure. The few duties of a lieutenant governor's wife left her time to enroll in Michigan State University's landscape architecture program, where she was one of the few female students. In some ways, this was the happiest time of their married lives.

In a rare public glimpse of her life at that time, the *Detroit Free Press* pointed out that being Michigan's "No. 2 Lady" and pursuing a college degree were challenging. On Wednesday, January 13, 1965, her thirteenth day as the wife of the lieutenant governor, Helen was up before seven, the newspaper said, to make breakfast for her husband. "He likes a big breakfast, bacon and eggs and everything," she said.[5]

More Than a First Lady

At nine o'clock that morning, the newspaper reported, she was in class at Michigan State, but she skipped out halfway through her next class to drive to the Capitol. "There she headed for her favorite seat near her husband's old desk in a corner of the senate chamber to watch him bang down the gavel precisely at noon to open the legislature."[6]

Adding to the picture of an unusual woman with dual interests in her family and her own career, the profile said:

> Mrs. Milliken is an attractive straightforward woman with curly brown hair and brown eyes that crinkle when she smiles, which is often . . . When she talks, she looks straight at you and doesn't flap or gush like some women do. She says what she has to say and then is quiet . . . She has thought—though not too seriously—about someday becoming a professional landscape architect. "I think it would be fascinating, and I would love it, but there are a lot of things that have to be resolved along the way" . . . Like political futures.[7]

The sudden change to first lady in 1969 was jarring. "I didn't really think [of Governor Romney's possible departure] in terms of us," she said. "Maybe I was just compartmentalizing in my mind." The Millikens moved from a "little apartment" in East Lansing to the new official governor's residence in Lansing, which had been donated to the state by Howard and Letha Sober. That gave Helen added responsibilities. She was hostess for countless receptions at the residence for political and personal friends of the first couple.

On the other hand, the first lady didn't rely on a large personal staff, as others had done. One person assisted her in upkeep of the residence, and Helen herself shopped for groceries and transported them for weekends spent at the governor's summer residence on Mackinac Island. "Bill just felt we needed to cut corners wherever we could," she said, but Helen's unpretentious style likely had as much to do with the decision to forgo a small army of assistants.

A national publication, the *Christian Science Monitor*, suggested that Helen was learning from her husband. In a 1969 feature on three governor's wives, the newspaper described Helen as a "small-town Michigan girl" (apparently overlooking her Colorado and Smith College background) who had become "urban-minded." Reporter Gail Osherenko said that the governor had "made Detroit and its ghetto and city problems his special interest. And Mrs. Milliken is being swept away in it, too." In nearly stereotypical terms, Helen was quoted as saying : "My husband is very compassionate. I never had his degree of social awareness before. But I'm learning."[8]

But a genuine glimpse of her converging interests appeared later in the piece, which noted that "the tug cityward" had resulted in her membership on the board of Detroit's Brewster Douglas housing project, where she merged her husband's "social concern with her concern for quality environment—and where she sees the demands of the 20th century challenging all the state's citizens."[9]

From the start of her tenure as first lady of Michigan, Helen gave public signs that while she could match her predecessors in the standard dimensions of graciousness and enthusiastic support of her husband she was not merely a reflection of him. During her husband's first gubernatorial election campaign in the autumn of 1970, she confided to a reporter that she disagreed with her husband's support of state aid to private and religious schools. Because of its complicated wording, however, she was uncertain how she would vote on a proposed constitutional amendment to ban such aid that was on the November ballot.

"We've talked about it and we both understand," she told the *Lansing State Journal*.[10] "We just have different feelings on this question."

Political disagreements weren't frequent during their marriage. The two saw eye to eye on most issues. "I can't think of an occasion where I said, 'You blew it.' We thought a lot alike on issues," she said in their retirement.[11]

A 1970 article described the sacrifices she was making to support her husband's political career. She had given up her studies toward the degree in landscape architecture—temporarily, she said then, though she would never find time to resume them in the face of her new duties as first lady. The intense pressure of the governor's job also brought changes in the couple's pattern of living. She mentioned that she and her husband had taken a two-hour bicycle ride in Traverse City the previous day "to get away from the pressures."[12]

Moving from the relatively obscure role of a lieutenant governor's wife to that of first lady of Michigan was not an easy transition. Faulting herself for not being "a classic stump speaker," Helen later confessed that she had felt great apprehension when Bill became governor

More Than a First Lady

in January 1969. "It was learning by doing. You found as you go out and become immersed, and you found something you believe in, [that] you forgot all your reservations and tried to connect."[13]

Joyce Braithwaite, the longtime Milliken adviser, put the transition in different terms. When Helen married Bill, Braithwaite said, "She didn't have a clue that there would be a public role for her."[14] After half a decade as first lady, she agreed to do an interview with Capitol correspondent Tim Skubick on his weekly television show *Off the Record,* which is known for its tough grilling of political guests.

> The first lady's answers were living testimony to her honesty coupled with a sharp respect for what her words could do to her husband. At one point she was asked about her voting record and possible support for non-Republican candidates. She confessed that she did not vote the straight Republican ticket but declined to name names. Asked if that was to avoid political embarrassment for her husband she said, "You're absolutely correct on that point."[15]

When the 1970 campaign called, she answered, despite being, as a reporter put it, "essentially a rather private person with a penchant for gardening and landscape architecture. Although poised and confident, she is not the flamboyant, outgoing type, and radiates the air of an essential introvert who is doing her best under difficult circumstances."[16] But by 1970 she had gained confidence and was outspoken in her criticism of highway billboards, a position that alienated potential contributors to her husband's campaign from the outdoor advertising business.

Reporters instantly took to her. Initially, many of them were society reporters and female, likely to comment on the first lady's character and style. After a speech to the Southeastern Michigan Beautification Council in the fall of 1970, a *Detroit Free Press* reporter observed, "She makes you feel as though it would be fun to dig with her or maybe go camping with her because you could share a quiet experience or get the work done and then later you could talk about it or laugh about something funny that had happened . . . She declined to represent herself as an environmental 'expert.' Instead she characterized herself as a dirt gardener and concerned citizen."[17]

Another reporter, identifying her as "Mrs. William Milliken," made note toward the end of an article that the governor's wife had launched an "attack" on air, water, and solid waste pollution and had requested the support of the Shiawassee County Republican Women's Club for a ban on throwaway bottles and cans. But the bulk of the article spoke of "the details that women like to hear: of the domestic changes [being wife of the governor] had brought into her life; of the social activities in which she participated, and of the opportunities it gave her to push her own special cultural interests."[18] Among the details in this sphere covered in the piece were the fact she had three homes to manage, the family's dwelling in Traverse City and the Lansing and Mackinac Island official residences.

Another example of the traditional coverage of a first lady was a short caption accompanying two photographs of Helen in the small-town *Davison Index* in May 1971.

> Incidentally, for the fashion minded, Mrs. Milliken wore a bright red dress with the newest, just below the knee length. A white patent cinch belt circled the waist of the modified circular skirt and white buttons accented the Cossack neckline. Also very "in" were her crinkle white patent boots. A smashing white capelet coat completed her ensemble. Mrs. Milliken wears very little makeup and wears her brown hair in a tousled cap cut. She is taller than you might expect and uses her expressive, no-nonsense hands to good effect when she speaks.[19]

Suggesting how the first lady might be a potent political asset for her husband, another photo on the same page depicted a standing ovation for the apparently abashed Helen Milliken. Noting that she was "obviously overwhelmed," the *Index* added, "Her impressive poise vanished for several seconds and was replaced with a shy, almost embarrassed smile."

Helen's first major public cause was promotion of the arts. Well within the traditional bounds of a first lady's influence, the arts were also a genuine interest of the governor's wife. Building on an idea conceived by E. Ray Scott of the Michigan Council for the Arts, Helen enthusiastically promoted a mobile art museum and laboratory on rails called the Artrain. "It was a wonderful adventure," she remembered. "Among its visitors, there were children who had never seen a work of art, never seen an artist creating a work of art. This helped address that."[20]

The debut of the Artrain placed Helen on the front pages of newspapers around Michigan, including the *Detroit News* on September 22, 1971. Wearing a conductor's hat, she was depicted riding the train into Detroit's Fort Street Union Depot to provide a preview of "five railroad cars filled with paintings, sculpture and other artifacts."[21] She told the *News* that the exhibit had inspired several cities to form community arts councils and inspired talk of a performing arts center in Escanaba, one of 14 northern Michigan cities the train visited.[22] National Endowment for the Arts chairperson Nancy Hanks praised the train, which received over $15,000 in Endowment funding, on a 1971 visit to Michigan.[23] It was still operating in 2005.[24]

By 1974, as her husband set his sights on a second term, Helen had come into her own politically. Frequently interviewed on political topics, she made it clear that on the campaign trail she would emphasize the issues that mattered most to her—environmental cleanup, transportation, the arts, and women's rights.[25] A United Press International reporter described Helen in both the old and the new terminology used for women in politics. Describing her as "attractive" and "soft-spoken," Joanna Firestone also recorded Helen's assertion that the decision to seek another term was a joint one considered for many months. In case there was any doubt that Helen was aware of the tedium and sacrifice of privacy involved, she told Firestone, "Politics is a little like climbing a mountain—you start out with high hopes and the challenge and excitement of it, then the obstacles set in. And sometimes it gets very tough to breathe."[26]

Regarding Helen Milliken as political gold in 1974, the governor's campaign published a brochure, "Meet Mrs. Milliken: Michigan's First Lady."[27] The document highlighted Helen's interest in urban issues, environmental decay, and the arts. On pollution problems, she said, "Our attitude toward the environmental crisis should be one of alarm, but not of despair. Man had the capacity to make the mess; he certainly has the ability to clean it up. Smoke and discarded bottles and billboards and oil wastes cannot defeat us; only our apathy can."

One reason for her growing outspokenness on issues was her increasing comfort in the role of first lady. Deeply concerned about the environment, she was clear from her first years in the role on the need for strong environmental policies. This sometimes put her at odds with major Republican Party donors, but her husband's support for her was unaffected. On one occasion, Bill recalled, Jay Van Andel, cofounder of the Amway Corporation, referred to Helen's position on cleanup and women's issues and said "something to the effect of, 'Can't you keep your wife under control?' I had no intention whatsoever of telling Helen what she could think or do or say," Milliken recalled.[28]

Another factor in Helen's growing public leadership on women's issues was what she called "the second great education of my life," her awakening to and study of legal inequalities between women and men in the United States.[29]

Both Helen and Bill credited their daughter, Elaine, with stimulating them to consider women's rights more deeply. Elaine and her mother recalled the commencement speech by feminist Gloria Steinem at Elaine's 1971 graduation from Smith College. Elaine told a reporter years later that "both mother and I thought her ideas were pretty radical."[30] Building on her undergraduate degree in political science, Elaine enrolled at the University of Michigan law school and became determined to reform laws that discriminated against women.

Helen said her daughter's experience in law school changed her perspective. "Elaine talked about how she was treated differently than the men by some of the professors. I had personally never felt oppressed, but I began to see how things weren't as equal as I thought."[31]

The Millikens' other child, Bill Jr., noted that Helen had come from a background in which "income production and decision making was left to the husband." He recalled that Elaine "started wagging her finger and working on her mother" during the governor's second term, adding that Elaine's advocacy was a "key element" in his mother's awakening.[32]

While serving as a member of the Women's Task Force on Rape at the Law School, Elaine helped redraft state laws to provide stronger punishments for offenders and more protection for women during the process of rape prosecution. Before graduating in 1975, she cofounded a legal aid program for indigent women known as Feminist Legal Services, attracting statewide publicity.

As Elaine explained it, the organization was "especially interested in cases involving feminist issues." She said, "All cases we handle at Feminist Legal Services help the one client, and many affect us all as women."[33]

More Than a First Lady

Helen credits her daughter with causing her to look more deeply at women's issues. "She started jogging her mother," Helen said. "It was an awakening. Once the window gets open, it's never closed. How far we've come, but how far we have yet to go."[34]

The year her daughter graduated from law school, 1975, Helen joined the National Organization for Women (NOW), the nation's leading feminist organization. This new involvement continued her education. "I had no idea that women in other states, especially the South, had far fewer rights than women in Michigan." But Helen also said that a friend's injury during an illegal abortion in the late 1960s had caused her to rethink the issue of reproductive choice. "That was very traumatic. I saw the injustice of it."[35]

A prime cause of both mother and daughter was ratification of the Equal Rights Amendment (ERA) to the U.S. Constitution. Designed to bar any discrimination on account of gender, the amendment had a history dating back to 1923, when it was offered by Alice Paul at the seventy-fifth observance of the Woman's Rights Convention of 1848 at Seneca Falls, New York.[36] Revised by Paul decades later, the proposed ERA won the official support of both the Republican and Democratic Parties in the 1940s. But it wasn't until 1972 that Congress approved the amendment and sent it to the states for ratification, placing a seven-year deadline on the process.[37]

Ratification by 38 states was needed to incorporate the amendment into the Constitution. Twenty-two ratified it within a year of its submission to the states by Congress, but in the next three years, only 12 more did so, bringing the total to 34. An anti-ERA movement, led by Eagle Forum founder Phyllis Schlafly, was gaining strength.

> Anti-ERA organizers claimed that the ERA would deny woman's right to be supported by her husband, privacy rights would be overturned, women would be sent into combat, and abortion rights and homosexual marriages would be upheld. Opponents surfaced from other traditional sectors as well. States'-rights advocates said the ERA was a federal power grab, and business interests such as the insurance industry opposed a measure they believed would cost them money. Opposition to the ERA was also organized by fundamentalist religious groups.[38]

When the seven-year ratification deadline passed in 1979, Congress granted a three-year extension until 1982. But in 1980 the Republican Party officially abandoned its support of the ERA. That didn't deter Helen Milliken from strongly advocating its adoption.

In an extraordinary evolution of activism, Michigan's first lady went from a foot soldier for equal rights to a leading national spokeswoman for the ERA. In 1979, as feminists lobbied Congress for the three-year ratification extension, Helen became the national cochair of ERAmerica, sharing the post with Sharon Percy Rockefeller, the wife of West Virginia's Democratic governor, among others. On her own behalf and as cochair, Helen made high-visibility lobbying visits to lawmakers. She had previously typically spoken out privately, mostly through correspondence, such as a 1975 request to a Michigan congressman to oppose an amendment barring federal funds for abortion services and referrals for poor women. Helen characterized the amendment as "denial of a basic health service that should be freely available to any woman, regardless of financial or social status."[39]

Now she was out in the open. She marched in an ERA ratification rally in Chicago, lobbied members of the Florida Senate for that state's ratification, and frequently shuttled to Washington, DC. "It was exhilarating," she said. "It was doing something you really believe should be done."[40]

In a speech to the Oakland County National Organization for Women, she described a "curious coalition" of anti-ERA forces, including church groups, the insurance industry, the Ku Klux Klan, and the Daughters of the American Revolution. Calling the ERA "the heart of the women's movement—one of the greatest phenomena of our time," she added that "none of the horror stories" offered by opponents had come to pass in the 15 states that had already written equal rights for women into their constitutions.[41]

Becoming an activist meant creating some enemies. Helen and Elly Peterson, the former Michigan Republican Party chairperson who was also a cochair of ERAmerica, attempted in 1979 to meet with the head of the Mormon church to discuss its opposition to the constitutional amendment. A representative of the church snubbed them both, saying, "there is nothing that could be gained by such a meeting." A week earlier, former governor Romney, a Mormon, had said the cause of ERA ratification had attracted "moral perverts" who would benefit from the amendment, thus implicitly condemning his successor's spouse.[42]

The first lady's independence was never more clear than when she skipped the opening ceremonies of the 1980 Republican National Convention, which her husband had lured to Detroit, to join a protest march against a party platform women's rights plank that did not include support for the ERA. "Without the equal rights amendment," she told her fellow marchers, "we are kidding ourselves if we think that small little privileges, small steps toward righting a particular law, token women in token jobs, means we have achieved our goal of equality."[43]

Two days later, the governor's wife and 14 other ERA supporters met for more than an hour with the presumptive Republican Presidential nominee, Ronald Reagan, unsuccessfully seeking to reverse his opposition to the ERA. Helen Milliken took issue with Reagan's argument that the ERA would undermine laws that provided special protection for women.

"We told him that kind of legislation is discriminatory rather than protective," she told a reporter.[44]

Helen's pro-choice stance attracted both strong criticism and strong support among citizens. An example of the former is an exchange of letters between the governor's wife and a Warren businessman in 1981.[45] The man reacted to a *Detroit News* article detailing Helen's pro-choice position by writing a letter to the paper (and enclosing a copy to Helen) pointing out the contrast between an article on child abuse and on the same page Helen's attempt to "justify killing unborn babies."

> Now if a woman who didn't like her baby, after she saw it, killed it and disposed of it, would she be justified in claiming it was a personal problem? Would it be appropriate for her to state, as did Mrs. Milliken about abortion, "I feel so strongly that it's got to be left up to a woman, her doctor, and her God"?

Helen was unflinching in her reply.

> Perhaps another reader seeing the two articles together might surmise, "Some of these children's deaths would never have taken place if a woman—especially a poor woman—had not felt forced to bear

a child she did not want, did not need, could not afford, and would never nurture."[46]

At the same time, Helen's outspoken defense of reproductive rights won her fans. "[A] bright spot is knowing you are a strong, outspoken, pro-choice, pro-woman advocate," wrote a Battle Creek woman. "I'm proud that I live in a state where the woman whose husband is governor, is articulate and sensitive to the plight of women."[47]

Her ERA position also aroused passions. After a *Flint Journal* article quoted Helen in support of the constitutional amendment in 1979, a reader wrote to her, "This finalizes my decision on whom to vote for in the next election for governor. Due to this and Governor Milliken's stand on the abortion issue, I will be voting against your husband." Helen retorted, "I agree with you that ignorance and superstition are the bane of most women. Else they would have joined hands long ago to work for the equal justice under the law that the proposed 27th Amendment to the Constitution envisions."[48] To another critic she wrote that "it is because of my children and their children that I am supporting the Equal Rights Amendment. For two centuries women have been second class citizens in this great country and it is time we let women into the Constitution. There has been great distortion and misleading propaganda concerning the Equal Rights Amendment."[49]

Although her husband had declared his support for a woman's right to choose whether to have an abortion in the late 1960s, Helen was perceived by many as a strong voice in the governor's ear to hold the line against attempts to undermine that right after the U.S. Supreme Court issued its controversial *Roe v. Wade* decision in 1973. Particularly after Congress limited Medicaid funding for abortions for low-income women in 1977, the abortion battle shifted to the states. Year after year Michigan legislative majorities enacted bans on state funding for elective abortions for Medicaid recipients, and year after year the governor vetoed them, touching off both legal and rhetorical battles. The governor in 1978 charged lawmakers favoring an abortion ban with perpetuating "a cruel hoax on the poor by holding them hostage and jeopardizing other medical services" when they tacked the abortion funding ban into a larger Medicaid funding line item, triggering a gubernatorial veto of the entire Medicaid budget. He based his veto on the argument that "to restrict Medicaid abortions is to discriminate unjustly against poor women because more affluent women are able to pay for abortions." The Michigan Catholic Conference retorted that those "who favor abortions for poor women believe that destroying unborn children is somehow beneficial to society. The killing of any innocent human being can never be considered beneficial."[50] In all, Milliken vetoed bans on state funding for elective abortions for Medicaid recipients 10 times, and each veto was sustained.[51]

A clue to Helen Milliken's role in her husband's staunch defense of abortion rights was her more outspoken role in defense of reproductive rights for women after he left office. In 1987, she told a reporter, "If a woman cannot determine how many children she will have and when she will have them, all the other rights she may have are of limited value."[52]

As the ERA ratification drive faltered and the nation began to turn to the right, Helen found herself warning that the previous decades' gains in rights for women were in danger. In a speech to the Michigan Students for Reproductive Freedom in East Lansing, she told the young activists that control over their bodies was "the most essential of women's rights." Attacking a proposed Constitutional amendment to prohibit abortion, she said it could also undermine birth control and would be "government intervention in that private part of women's lives at a time when officials are saying they want less government involvement."[53] In an opinion column in the *Detroit News* in November 1981, she wrote:

> In the two centuries after the founding of the nation, women gradually gained the right to own property, to get an education, and to vote. The latter required 72 years of unmitigated struggle, culminating in the passage of the 19th Amendment. Some of the arguments that were used against suffrage have a strangely familiar ring: that women really didn't want it; that it would break up the family; that woman's place was in the home . . . Those same arguments are used against the Equal Rights Amendment.[54]

Once the pleasing and politically innocuous wife of Bill the politician, Helen had become a political figure in her own right. Reaction was divided. "Helen Milliken has incredible courage," said Democrat Martha Griffiths, who was elected to serve as lieutenant governor when

Milliken left office. "It's remarkable that a woman in her position had such deep moral convictions that she spoke out. And she's had an enormous impact on young women."[55] But Elaine Donnelly, an anti-ERA leader, criticized Helen for using "her prestige to gain high visibility for her convictions. She never agreed to debate the issues with us. She didn't play fair."[56]

Her growing identification as a feminist did not deprive fashion reporters of their interest in the more conventional side of the first lady. Even as late as 1981, just months before her husband announced his political retirement, a reporter for the *Traverse City Record-Eagle* observed that Helen was "not immune to the lure of color and design in personal attire . . . The result is pleasingly effective. Her clothes are a good example of the 'less is more' principle, especially in accessories. She prefers the simple rather than the elaborate."[57]

Helen's most vivid memories as first lady included three trips to China, two of them as an official representative of the state. On the first, with American Women for International Understanding in 1975, she was struck by the drabness and uniformity of garb—both men and women typically wore the "Mao outfit" of plain jackets and pants— and by the sight of a generally well-fed, friendly populace. "It was culture shock, it was a part of the world you never really knew existed," she said.[58]

"It was astounding to realize that Chinese women have come from slavery in their society to near equality in just over two decades," she told a reporter on her return. "Their status was so far down the ladder, they were non-entities . . . Today, many women are doctors and scientists. They work equally with men in almost all jobs and professions. They control their own destinies in terms of choosing their own marriage partners and limiting the number of children they have through family planning." But, Helen noted, their political progress was "somewhat slower." Women had generally risen no higher than "vice-chairperson" in most cities.[59]

The final trip to China, in 1982, came less than three weeks after she had undergone a mastectomy for breast cancer, illustrating her remarkable resiliency. Obliged to deal with the state's continuing budget difficulties, her husband was unable to make the official visit to Michigan's sister state, Sichuan. An aide and friend, Holly Angell, said Helen was courageous in making the long journey. "She was a remarkable traveling companion under the circumstances, gracious, curious and wonderfully witty. The Chinese took to her immediately. I always admired her—even more so after traveling with her in China."[60]

Had her activism ever bothered her husband? Helen admitted that some of her political activities "have made his job more difficult. I think most men have had moments of being disconcerted by the women's movement. But for the most part he has been very supportive. He understands how I feel and he supports the ERA."[61]

As Bill prepared to leave office, the inevitable media retrospectives on his political career and legacy had room to consider Helen's. "From a reserved, almost shy woman who, for fear of rocking her husband's political boat, seemed to measure her words with an eyedropper, Mrs. Milliken has become downright outspoken. And she speaks out on controversial matters—most notably in favor of abortion rights, sex education in schools and the Equal Rights Amendment . . . The Helen Milliken who leaves Lansing in a few weeks is a woman fully in bloom, not the tightly furled bud who arrived. But she has kept the best part of her old interests, too, and they continue to sustain her."[62] The *Detroit News* named her a Michiganian of the Year in 1982.

After her husband retired from public office, Helen continued to participate in public life. She served on the boards of the Michigan Land Use Institute, the Nature Conservancy, the Dennos Museum, and Planned Parenthood. She was also a longtime member of the Women's Resource Center of Traverse City, which provides services to victims of domestic abuse. In the 1990s, the organization named its 27-bed shelter for abuse victims Helen's House.

How significant was her expansion of the traditional sphere of interest of a governor's wife? By the mid-1970s, it was not unusual for the spouses of chief executives to take public positions on controversial issues, especially equal rights for women. A 1977 *Detroit News* article on political spouses convening for the National Governors' Conference in Detroit noted that several had addressed the ERA and other issues. Carolyn Hunt, the wife of North Carolina governor James B. Hunt, said she had "worked hard" to win ratification of the ERA by that state and had also addressed the high rate of illiteracy there.[63] Donna Lou Askew, the wife of Florida governor Reubin Askew, had spoken out forcefully—and only—on the ERA, supporting ratification, but "maybe I was too outspoken." On the other hand, Beth Bowen, the wife of Indiana governor Otis Bowen, said she wasn't publicly "involved with issues because I'm not the elected official." And Muriel Shapp, the wife of governor Milton Shapp of Pennsylvania, said she was "not an official member of my husband's party—he's very capable of being governor and doesn't need me to cut ribbons at the openings of supermarkets."[64] On balance, it is fair to say that Helen Milliken was among an emerging cadre of governors' wives who believed it their right and responsibility to address issues beyond the safe topics of the arts and beautification. But perhaps the most remarkable fact about her advocacy was the personal distance she had traveled in terms of consciousness and forthrightness. Thinking back on her first visit to a governors' meeting in 1969, she recalled, "That was a wholly new world for me. I was really nervous about it. I remember a man in our security detail saying, 'Don't worry, it's going to be all right. You're going to fit right in.'"[65]

Her emergence as a confident public figure inspired many other women. "Helen Milliken meant a lot to me as I was discovering my own political ambitions," said Lana Pollack, who won the state Senate seat from the Ann Arbor area in 1982 and served three four-year terms. "I think it's hard for a man to understand what it's like to grow up without heroes you can identify with—without role models. Helen made it possible for women of my generation to imagine ourselves as powerful leaders without having to compromise our femininity. She was graceful, but she took no guff. It was a beautiful and inspiring combination."[66]

The program for a 1995 Michigan "Women of Courage" banquet may best capture the feeling among many in Michigan for Helen Milliken's legacy. Featured on the same page as Rosa Parks, the revered "mother of the modern civil rights movement," who refused to surrender her seat on a Montgomery, Alabama, bus in 1955 and then moved to Michigan, Helen was celebrated for her work on the arts and women's issues.

> Independent, committed, and principled, Ms. Milliken has never sought, but has never shrunk from controversy. When her commitment to equality conflicted with her political loyalties, she clearly chose the former. Her choice, her service and her spirit have enriched the lives of countless . . . Michigan citizens.[67]

10

THE PRIVATE MILLIKEN

Two months after Governor William G. Milliken announced his decision to retire as governor, the senior editor of *Monthly Detroit* magazine, Hillel Levin, authored an article entitled "Milliken: The Man You Never Knew."[1] Levin said, "It's amazing how little we have seen of Milliken . . . When Milliken leaves office next year, he'll be as much of a mystery as he was fourteen years before, when he first became governor."

Levin's observation rang surprisingly true of a governor who was known for his accessibility and openness to the public and the news media. Although radiating comfort and security in his political persona, Milliken actually fiercely guarded his privacy and bared his soul to few. The result, Levin noted, was that before Milliken had announced his decision to retire his likely move "had remained virtually unknown. In any other administration, a cadre of insiders would have swarmed over Lansing ready to break the news."[2]

That wasn't the Milliken way. In his later years as governor, his closest counselors tended to be his wife and the two chief architects of his political success, Chief of Staff George Weeks and Appointments Director Joyce Braithwaite. To others on the staff, his cabinet, and the Capitol world of legislators, reporters, and constituent groups, he typically presented a formal front that inspired both respect and distance. But from their memories come a few clues to the inner Milliken.

"He's the gold standard of politicians," said Christine Hollister, then Christine Fedewa, who served as Milliken's consumer protection adviser among other roles.[3] "I put him on a pedestal."

Hollister remembers the only time she saw Milliken angry. The governor had discovered that responses to letters his office had received were being long delayed. "He called everyone that was around into his office that day," she said. "He raised his voice—it's one of the few times I ever heard him speak that way. He said, 'I want these letters done on time.' He felt very strongly about getting people an answer from their government."[4]

Although rare, glimpses of the Milliken temper remain in the memory of outside observers as well. Joseph Tuchinsky, a consumer advocate, attended a meeting in the governor's conference room just after the 1974 election in which the Michigan Citizens Lobby had successfully championed a ballot proposal repealing the state's 4 percent sales tax on food and prescription drugs. Milliken had opposed the initiative, arguing that it would simply require tax hikes in other areas to support needed government programs.

After a 15-minute wait in the conference room, Tuchinsky remembers, "Milliken came in angry. He just tore into [a representative of the Citizens Lobby]. He said the proposal had left a big hole in his budget and there was no choice but to raise income taxes to make up for it. He thought it was dishonest of the Citizens Lobby, that there would be no net savings."[5]

Tuchinsky said Milliken's anger "put a damper on the meeting. I was surprised at his outburst. He eventually calmed down and we had a constructive dialogue."

Harry H. Whiteley, a Milliken appointee who served six times as chairperson of the Natural Resources Commission, said one of his fellow panel members criticized the Department of Natural Resources director at the time as being "like a rat to a rat hole," implying that the agency head quickly relayed what went on at commission meetings to the governor. "I remember so well sitting with the governor in his office and hearing him say, 'This is reprehensible,' and he was mad and showed it," Whiteley said. "He asked me if I had the culprit's phone number, which I did, and on the spot he called this individual and dressed him down, but in an unabusive way, a trait to be admired."[6]

Milliken could flay legislators, too, on occasion. Although known for his determination to accommodate all views, to consult with legislative leaders of both parties and both houses in so-called quadrant meetings, and to seek compromise, Milliken's patience wasn't infinite. Late one night, as lawmakers debated Milliken's proposal to reform the state's business levies and create something called the single business tax, Republican members of the Senate balked. Senator Jack Toepp of Cadillac, according to one observer, protested that Milliken had lavished more attention on the majority Democratic caucus than his own. He insisted that the governor should come and make his case personally to the Republicans.[7]

So a call was placed to the Governor's Mansion and in about twenty minutes the always tanned and fit Governor arrived at the back door of the Capitol, his State Police security detail in tow. Surprisingly, he was still wearing his pajama top beneath an overcoat, the labels of which flapped open, revealing the criss-cross pattern of his PJ top, as he purposefully strode the Capitol corridor toward [Republican leader Robert] Davis' office. What was also surprising was the dark scowl that he wore in place of his usual million dollar smile . . . He slammed the heavy door behind him and the muffled roar of a very unhappy Governor could be heard. About ten minutes later he exited the office and returned to his car . . . The Republican Caucus was hushed, even somber, after he left. They returned to the Senate floor in little groups of three and four on the back "Senators Use Only" elevator.

Shortly after, Secretary of the Senate Beryl Kenyon started the voice roll call, and the single business tax legislation was on Governor Milliken's desk a few days later.[8]

On another occasion, the governor thought he had a commitment from Senator Thomas Guastello, a Macomb County Democrat, to support a temporary income tax increase to relieve the state's deep budget crisis. Milliken watched from the Senate floor as the vote was taken. When Guastello voted against the increase, one witness said, "Milliken stormed into the Senate chambers. He was in his shirt sleeves and breathin' fire. Marched up to Guastello and gave him an ear full."[9] After a recess and additional negotiating between Milliken and the senators, the tax increase was approved.

WILLIAM G. MILLIKEN

When Milliken learned that a member of the House GOP caucus might miss a key vote on transportation issues because ostensibly he had scheduled a speech in his district, Milliken said within earshot of others, "If he walks out, tell me, and I'll go tackle him, literally."[10] When another Republican legislator who had voted against Milliken saw him in a Capitol hallway later, Milliken said he was sorry that they hadn't agreed. A reporter quoted the rest of the exchange as: "'So am I, governor, but you remember my position,' replied the legislator. 'Yes . . . I will,' replied Milliken, in a rather icy tone."[11]

Shortly after taking office in 1969, Milliken let it be known that he was not a pushover. When state highways director Henrik Stafseth publicly criticized the Milliken proposal to spend $1.6 million in transportation money on a State Police task force, newspapers reported that the governor was "taking stern action to insure that his appointees reflect executive office positions in public statements . . . What apparently disturbs Milliken is the fear that his administration will appear divided and that he cannot control appointees who serve at the pleasure of the governor . . . One source said Milliken feels that 'government should operate with some degree of agreement.'"[12]

Milliken himself acknowledged that his nice-guy image was misleading if it led some observers to think he lacked a temper. In conversational notes taken by his longtime aide George Weeks after Milliken left office, he said, "Some people suggest that I seldom, if ever, lose my temper. In all candor, that is not the correct assessment. I do become angry. I do become frustrated. I do, especially when a trust has been betrayed, find it very difficult to forgive that betrayal . . . But I do not believe in public anger and the expression of it."[13]

Indeed, Milliken projected, even to those who worked most closely with him on a day-to-day basis, a polite, pleasant character. "He is unchanging, sensitive, gentle and pleasant, and infuses the whole staff with enthusiasm," his longtime personal secretary, Phyllis Dell, told a reporter in 1970.[14] In private, the assessments were remarkably similar. Nancy Dockter, who served as his personal secretary during most of his last eight years in office, called him "dignified and controlled . . . very gubernatorial. He had the highest moral standards and integrity." She said when he announced his decision to retire in December 1981, "I was sad because I loved working for him. I thought he was a very good governor and these were tough times."[15]

Billie Harrison (at the time Billie Lilley), a special assistant to Milliken who coordinated policy-making, said Milliken "was always civil. I think I only heard him swear two or three times. He could become impatient or annoyed, and he might disagree with something you had done, but it was always privately handled."[16] She said his politeness and kindness were not to be confused with weakness. "He's really one of the nicest men in the world, but when he was determined to do something, and usually it was something he thought was important for the state, he pursued it," she said.

Milliken's combination of pleasant manners and guardedness, it should be said, enabled many to see the man as they wanted to see him. Even after close observation, he remained essentially unknowable. He walked through life and the governorship still projecting the image of the sweet-tempered all-American high school class president.

Dockter, his secretary, remembered that a typical Milliken day at the office began at about 8 A.M., sometimes after he had indulged in his morning swim at the State Police facility in East Lansing. He frequently ate lunch alone in his personal office, preferring a formal table setting on a tray. After lunch, he would take a short nap in a lounge chair tucked away inside an alcove. Alternatively, he would ask several aides to join him in lunching at Bill Knapp's, an East Lansing branch of a restaurant franchise with a low-cost, conventional menu of sandwiches, salads, and soups, or at Michigan State University's Kellogg Center. At either location, he would sometimes have sport with aides by remarking how much he would enjoy a chocolate sundae for dessert. When the waitress came to take their dessert order, the story goes, Milliken would watch his aides, one by one, order sundaes to stay in line with the boss. The governor would sometimes then say he was too full to have dessert, smiling at his aides.[17]

He would leave the Capitol close to 5 P.M. whenever possible, taking paperwork home. On weekend trips to Traverse City, he would take an exceptionally large pile, including as many as 40 to 60 pieces of correspondence, returning on the following Monday "with replies noted," said Phyllis Dell.[18] "He was very disciplined in turning things around. He took a pile of work home every night and on weekends . . . He was adamant that everyone should get a response to their letters and notes."[19]

To relieve the pressures of his office, Milliken increasingly turned to exercise. An active skier since childhood, he took up jogging in the 1970s. Michael D. Moore, later the director of the Department of Natural Resources, participated in the Governor's Conference on Forestry at Houghton in 1980. He said "it was a great eye-opener to watch the sitting Governor run around the track at the Michigan Tech indoor athletic facilities with his State Police bodyguard keeping time alongside . . . It was clear Bill Milliken was dedicated to his exercise regime."[20]

Milliken's personal staff learned that the governor's compassionate side sometimes required them to attempt to shield him. A former employee of the Milliken family, down on his luck, occasionally journeyed to Lansing to ask for the governor's help. Once the man rode a bus from Traverse City to Lansing to see the governor. When his presence was announced, Milliken said, "I'll see him." The man asked for a loan and bus fare back to Traverse City. Milliken gave him both and had a state trooper deliver him to the bus station.[21]

Several incidents illustrating the governor's sensitivity won him plaudits in the news media. In November 1971, *The Eccentric,* a newspaper published in the Detroit suburb of Birmingham, reported that a 69-year-old Romanian woman unable to speak English had boarded a plane from Bucharest to New York with a note on a pink card bearing her name and saying she had a brother in Bloomfield Hills, Michigan. A flight attendant on the plane knew that Milliken was also a passenger and showed the card to him. After having his picture taken with the woman, Maria Magdas, Milliken visited her five additional times on the flight. Upon their arrival in New York, Milliken arranged for a wheelchair and ensured that her relatives had found her before he departed. The day after her late-night arrival in Detroit, Milliken called to check on her. "I was so impressed," said her brother, John Popp. "As busy as that man was, he managed to call. He deserves a lot of credit. We are very grateful."[22]

The governor's compassion also influenced his executive decisions. He frequently used his constitutional powers to exercise clemency toward prisoners in state institutions. "Subsequent governors have worried about the political implications if you pardoned or commuted the sentences of too many people," said Peter Ellsworth, Milliken's assistant legal adviser beginning in 1974 and chief legal adviser in 1978–79. "Milliken had a political side, but he didn't think of this part of his job politically. He was criticized at the time for being too lenient."[23]

Ellsworth said Milliken was particularly active in the area of commutation, averaging about a dozen a year. In addition, the governor several times exercised a rarely used (and since abolished) power to deny an extradition request from another state when he believed the Michigan resident involved had been rehabilitated. "He was a very compassionate guy, that entered into it, but it was really a philosophy of rehabilitation. He believed in giving people second chances."[24] In a notable case in which Indiana sought extradition of a convicted murderer who had fled to Michigan, begun a new law-abiding life, and been stopped in Eaton County, west of Lansing, on a traffic offense, Milliken balked. "He said he wanted to meet with the man one on one," Ellsworth said. "It drove the security people nuts. They were going to leave him alone with a convicted murderer? But they did. He met with the governor for 70 or 75 minutes in his office. When the man left, the governor walked out of his office and said, 'I'm not granting the [extradition] request.'" Milliken's belief in rehabilitation was not always borne out in fact. One recipient of clemency in 1970 (a commutation recommended by the state parole board) apparently went on to commit multiple murders.[25]

Perhaps more than any other single impression, the governor's emphasis on a high ethical standard in his performance of the duties of his office impressed his aides and many followers. William McLaughlin, at the time chairman of the State Republican Party, remembered dining with the governor and his wife in a private room at the Grand Hotel on Mackinac Island on August 8, 1974, the night President Richard M. Nixon announced his plan to resign from office the next day in order to head off impeachment proceedings.[26] When the governor's party emerged from the dining room and walked into the lobby of the hotel, it encountered hundreds of guests and visitors who had watched Nixon's speech on televisions placed there for the occasion by hotel's owner, Dan Musser.

When Bill and Helen came out, there was silence for a moment, then a quiet round of applause that swept through the group, including the media [reporters] that were there. It was because of the contrast between what Nixon had done and the integrity of Bill

Milliken. Here was a guy—and this was much of his magic at the polls—people might not agree with him on the issues, but they *trusted* him.[27]

James Phelps, at the time Milliken's education adviser, said he once advised the governor to veto a special appropriation to provide free paperback books to schoolchildren as a way of encouraging them to read. Placed in a larger bill by State senator Charles Zollar of Benton Harbor, the appropriation, Phelps thought, would lead to more such riders by legislators. Milliken did not veto the money. Phelps learned later that Milliken had soon thereafter returned $15,000 in campaign contributions made to his cause by a distributor who would benefit from the book giveaway. "I cost [Milliken's campaign] $15,000," Phelps said, by making the governor aware of the clause in the bill and the appearance of impropriety that might result if the contribution was linked to it.[28]

Milliken hoped to legislate stronger ethical standards in government, too. Responding to the 18-month-long Watergate controversy that ultimately toppled Nixon, the governor sent a special message on ethics and election reform to the legislature on October 25, 1973. "My own view from long and close association with politicians," he wrote, "is that most are honorable people, committed to the public good. The measures that I am proposing are designed to protect against the abuses of a few, abuses which erode public confidence and subvert the electoral process . . . This has been all too painfully evident this year."[29]

The sweeping package proposed by Milliken included, for the first time in state and local races, public disclosure and auditing of campaign contributions and caps on the maximum contribution that could be made to candidates, disclosure by candidates for statewide office and the legislature of financial holdings and sources of income, registration of lobbyists and reporting of their expenditures made to influence policy and legislation, strengthening of the state's open meetings law for government bodies, and creation of a board of ethics to police potential conflicts of interest by state employees.[30]

The most controversial of the measures within Milliken's Republican Party may have been the limitation on contributions that an individual could make to a campaign. Craig Ruff, an aide who worked on the ethics package for Milliken, later toiled in the 1974 campaign. "I

The Private Milliken

153

had to contend with these Republican types, who'd say, 'I'll write a $50,000 check.' I'd have to tell them, 'No, $1,700 is the most I can take.' Then they'd say, 'How about if each person in my immediate family gives that amount?' I'd have to say, 'That's probably not a good idea.'" But, while it created difficulties for Milliken's campaign funding, Ruff pointed out, "1974 was a Republican debacle nationally, and Milliken survived it."[31]

One of the few exceptions to Milliken's unblemished public record was an imbroglio over the hiring of a "girlfriend" of Detroit Recorder's Court judge James Del Rio by the governor's administration, allegedly in exchange for the African American judge's support of Milliken in the 1970 election. The *Detroit Free Press* reported in April 1973 that 27-year-old Glenda McGuire had been given a job with a salary of $18,462 a year and was "doing practically nothing as a member of Gov. Milliken's executive staff."[32] The newspaper reported that the administration had hired McGuire on the recommendation of Don Gordon, then Milliken's chief of staff, who had met with Del Rio shortly before the 1970 balloting. Del Rio, a Democrat, had shortly thereafter issued a campaign newsletter praising Milliken. The implication was that McGuire's job was a payoff to Del Rio for his support. McGuire, who was supposedly doing urban research but could not describe any completed work projects to the *Free Press,* became a front-page embarrassment to the governor but even more so to John T. Dempsey, the Milliken adviser who had been directed to hire her. While Milliken distanced himself from the McGuire case, Dempsey was left to defend her state employment but could offer no specific evidence that she was working for her salary. McGuire was terminated from state employment not long after, and the governor managed to come out of the incident untarnished. "Gordon got the blame, Dempsey got the heat, and Milliken got editorial praise for acting forthrightly to clean up mistakes others had supposedly made," reporters observed.[33]

A trait of Milliken's that received little notice in public reports but was evident to those at close hand was a mischievous sense of humor. Apparently because it contrasted with his serious, sober image, Milliken's humor never excited comment in the news media, but it was evident to some reporters. Tim Skubick, who started work as a Capitol correspondent around the time Milliken became governor, told of several occasions when the governor made sport of the Capitol news corps or Skubick personally. Once he followed Milliken as he left the Capitol to press the governor for a statement on whether he supported Michigan Department of Agriculture director B. Dale Ball, who was defying Milliken on a proposal to lower the standard for allowable amounts of PBBs in food. As Skubick recalled it, he challenged the governor to say whether he was "100 percent supportive" of Ball. Halting on the back steps of the Capitol, not far from his state car, Milliken handed his briefcase to the accompanying state trooper, smiled, and said, "Tim Skubick, there are some days when I'd like to throw you over this rail."[34]

Aide Billie Harrison said Milliken "didn't get credit for his sense of humor." Once he was greeting a line of Boy Scouts entering his office when she joined the end of the line. "He was never looking down to the end of the line," she said. "You got his undivided attention." When she reached the governor, who hadn't noticed her until that moment, she introduced herself. "I'm Billie Lilly, assistant to the governor. He laughed and laughed."[35]

Joyce Braithwaite noted that on one occasion, as she and Milliken were standing in line greeting hundreds of guests at a Bill's Birthday Beefsteak, the annual fund-raiser for the governor, Milliken noted the appearance of a Detroit area woman whom Braithwaite detested. "I'm sure you won't mind," he whispered to his aide, "if I excuse myself from the line for a few minutes. You can just keep chatting, I'll be back in about half an hour."[36]

When Milliken phoned Grand Rapids attorney and angler Hilary Snell to offer him an appointment to the state Natural Resources Commission, the governor reported to Braithwaite: "He wants a few days to think it over." When Braithwaite questioned that, Milliken quipped, "Actually he grabbed it quicker than a trout grabs a fly."[37]

The Milliken policy process was far-reaching and deliberate. As the gubernatorial years passed, Milliken's annual State of the State message, a published document that accompanied a January speech to the legislature, became an exercise in seeking the best ideas from state agencies and a comprehensive agenda of almost every issue lawmakers would have to tackle in the ensuing 12 months. Billie Harrison said the process began in October of the preceding year with a memo to directors of cabinet agencies and staff requesting ideas and text for the message.[38] Harrison would take the ideas and suggested text and seek advice and reactions from the governor's top advisers. She would organize meetings, often in November and December, which the governor, senior aides, and department heads would attend. Harrison would summarize the proposals before the meeting in a memorandum, and Milliken would indicate yes or no on every issue after hearing the back-and-forth on dozens of proposals. In later years, his chief wordsmith, Bob Berg, would then craft the message the governor delivered. "There were no surprises in the State of the State. If it appeared in the message, he knew it was going to be there," Harrison said.

She added, "He had a very strong interest in policy. He didn't make decisions off the top of his head. His decisions were well-considered. And he was willing to stick his neck out."[39]

Longtime environmental policy aide Bill Rustem commented that in contrast to his successors, who often gave thematic State of the State messages focused on a single issue or a small set of issues, Milliken "wanted to give a comprehensive view of the state. Milliken had a position on almost everything in the legislative process. The entire executive branch was involved in setting policy. Everyone in the governor's office was involved in the policy process."[40]

If policy was paramount, politics was not forgotten. While the governor won praise for his statesmanlike approach to issues, his two top aides for most of his years in the executive office expressed other sides of his personality and took care of the sometimes nasty business of reelection. The outspoken, respected, and sometimes feared appointments director, Joyce Braithwaite, frequently said the things Milliken wouldn't, or couldn't, to protect his political flanks.

In one notable incident, Braithwaite publicly scolded one of the governor's least favorite senators, western Upper Peninsula Democrat Joe Mack. Mack attempted to remove a $4,370 pay raise for Braithwaite from an appropriations bill—ostensibly because she had ignored his recommendations for gubernatorial appointments—and called her "Joycie-girl" and "just some secretary" on the floor of the Senate.[41] In a retort made via a letter copied to the *Detroit Free Press,* Braithwaite wrote, "Thank you for making my holiday season so much brighter by providing the vehicle by which great numbers of people could learn quickly that you and I are not friends . . . The real embarrassment would come only if anyone thought I had any kind of a relationship with the most reprehensible, scurrilous, least respected person in the building and the poorest excuse for a public servant ever to occupy an office in this state . . . You, sir, are proof positive of an observation once made by an unknown sage: 'There are more horses' asses in the world than there are horses.'"[42] Pressed by reporters to say whether he agreed with his aide's assessment of Mack, Milliken said, "I think the behavior of Joe Mack is outrageous."[43]

Braithwaite was equally quick to defend the governor when he was accused, on occasion, of not being strong enough in defense of the rights of women or other constituencies. When a local officer of the National Organization for Women criticized the governor for appointing a man rather than a woman to fill a judicial vacancy in the Ingham County Probate Court, Braithwaite said, "I have no time for those who merely wish to talk about advancing women without giving endless hours to make the action match the words. I'm throwing down the gauntlet on this. Strong women will pick it up—weak women will whine and criticize."[44] Her staunch defense of the governor was personal. "I had the opportunity to be associated with Governor Milliken who is so sincerely committed to equal rights for women that he allowed me to climb in his administration as far as I was capable of climbing."

The rhetoric was not pure bluster. Close Capitol observers credited Braithwaite with "having one of the best political minds in Michigan," suggesting that she, along with Chief of Staff Weeks and state GOP chairperson William McLaughlin, had engineered President Gerald Ford's significant margin of victory in the May 1976 Michigan presidential primary. "She is the governor's liaison with local GOP organizations and is playing an important role as Milliken branches out nationally," said Booth Newspapers Lansing bureau chief Robert H. Longstaff. "She is involved in the governor's effort to give moderate Republicans a stronger voice in the party . . . Ms. Braithwaite has consistently run the busiest and probably the best shop in the governor's office."[45]

Although most of Milliken's appointees were subdued and plunged themselves into the work of state government, another besides Braithwaite added a touch of color to the administration. Peter Fletcher, a University of Michigan graduate and Republican National Committee member from Ypsilanti, won headlines while he was transportation commission chairman for adorning the corner of the state highway map that contained a slice of Ohio with fictitious towns named Goblu and Beatosu.[46] The flamboyant Fletcher shunned his expense reimbursements for official duties, issued frequent quips to reporters, and caused a furor when Milliken appointed the former Wolverine to serve on the Board of Trustees of archrival Michigan State University. But the appointment was no accident.

Milliken's office had collected almost 200 names of people interested in the Board of Trustees appointment, Fletcher said. But in the middle of a meeting with his staff Milliken suddenly said with a smile, "I know who I'm going to appoint—Peter Fletcher."[47] When his staff gently pointed out that Fletcher's affiliation with the University of Michigan would provoke protest, Milliken said, "I've learned that my most controversial appointments are my most successful." Fletcher weathered a brief storm of criticism and continued to make headlines while on the MSU board, decrying the school's search for a "pigskin messiah" to elevate its reputation through a winning football program.[48]

Weeks was closer in temperament and style to Milliken. Low-key and friendly, he defused tensions that might have plagued the governor. Popular with reporters, he helped reinforce the governor's instincts for openness in dealing with them, a lasting benefit to Milliken's news coverage. In a practice considerably different from his immediate successors under other governors, Weeks erected few barriers to direct conversations between members of the executive office staff and reporters rather than channeling all media contact through himself.

"Openness was his natural inclination," said Weeks. "But having covered the Capitol myself, and knowing so many reporters, it made sense to be open. He had good individual relationships with most reporters."[49]

Reporters saw the governor's accessibility as "a reflection of Milliken's temperament. He was a gentleman, rarely resorting to profanity. He was disarming in nature and believed—rightly or wrongly—that decency would prevail at the end of the day," said Tim Jones, then a *Detroit Free Press* correspondent.[50]

Weeks's credibility with reporters was bolstered by their understanding that he participated in most of the high-priority meetings and decisions in the executive office and had virtually instant access to the governor. When he moved from the position of press secretary to executive secretary (later renamed chief of staff), his critical role in the governor's processes was confirmed.

"The key member of Milliken's court is George C. Weeks, 44, the chief of staff," observed the *Detroit Free Press* in 1977. "As such, Weeks is the governor's point man in the jungle of state government and politics. More than anyone other than the governor, Weeks influences both broad general policy and the politics of the Milliken Administration . . . Weeks is in robust good health and works 60 to 80 hours a week. He sees more, hears and knows more, and like a slow but irresistible force has enormous influence on the affairs of the state . . . yet he is unprepossessing, calm and collected, easy-going, restrained, low key, and affably deceptive."[51]

In the same article, reporters Remer Tyson and Hugh McDiarmid raved about the governor's ability to inspire loyalty among his aides. "These people reflect Milliken and his methods, exuding a mood of congeniality and informality that disguises the deliberateness and the sharp-edged flint underneath the administration . . . Like a professional football team, each member of Milliken's palace guard knows his or her assignment and accepts that the collective goal is to protect and glorify the quarterback."[52]

A measure of that devotion was the decision by several key aides to cosign a last-minute loan to the Milliken campaign in 1970. With the Milliken candidacy teetering on the edge of victory or defeat, the finance chairman, John Stahlin, asked aides Braithwaite, Dempsey, and others to put their personal finances on the line for the governor, a legal loan at the time. They did. Milliken's subsequent victory saved them from economic hardship.[53]

Patrick Babcock, who served in several roles in Milliken's cabinet, including director of the Departments of Mental Health and Labor and the Office of Services to the Aging, said one reason for the loyalty was that it was a two-way street. "That was one of his greatest assets, his support of his staff. It could also be a liability when he supported some people too long that weren't serving him well anymore, but basically it was a fine quality."[54] Babcock long appreciated Milliken's defense of him after he taped a television campaign commercial for a Democratic candidate for the legislature. Senate Republican leader Robert Vander-Laan was outraged that a key adviser to a GOP governor was openly Democratic. "[Milliken's] statement was to the effect that he hadn't asked me how I voted when he hired me, and he didn't expect me to change just because I had joined his administration."[55]

Indeed, Milliken's appointments were frequently surprising by latter-day standards of partisanship. Dr. Maurice Reizen, who became the state health department director in 1970, applied for the vacancy in the job and at interviews with Milliken and his staff was not asked his political affiliation. "At best, I was an independent," said the Democratic-leaning Reizen. "I was never asked about my political beliefs. He just wanted to know how I would go about doing the job."[56]

Once appointed, Milliken's department heads were often left to use their best judgment. Reizen said that in 11 years as health director under Milliken "he called me twice to look into questions for constituents." In one such case, Milliken called Reizen on to look into a friend's complaint about a regulatory decision denying a septic drain permit in wet soils. Reizen did so and said, "I determined my people had done the right thing. All [Milliken] said was, 'Thank you, Dr. Reizen.'"[57] Such unfaltering support for his appointees led many of them, in the words of one political insider, to "take a lot of bullets" for the governor.

Milliken valued this trait in his aides. Two of them, John Stahlin and Stanley Pratt, served for long spans as volunteers within the executive office, troubleshooting for Milliken. Although not party to the key decisions of Milliken's administration, Stahlin handled the sometimes unpleasant assignment of raising campaign cash and dispensing hard-boiled political advice, while Pratt roamed the administration as a counselor looking out for the governor's best interests. "He had a wonderful quality that I appreciated and it was loyalty," Milliken recalled.[58] In a fashion reminiscent of Braithwaite's outspokenness, Stahlin also expressed a side of the governor's personality of which Milliken rarely gave signs. "He was an old-line politician. He was blunt and could be rather crude. He was fun to be around," said the governor.

Stahlin defined his loyalty to Milliken differently. In 1970, he told a reporter that as a state senator he had found out "how smutty and crooked things could be in public life." He then said of Milliken, "He wouldn't do a damn thing crooked, or barter anything for promises. How many guys are there that come along like that? I tell you, it's just a pleasure to be around trying to help out."[59]

Pratt, a former newspaper publisher whose wife, Ann, was the granddaughter of former governor Chase Osborn, with whom Milliken had corresponded in his youth, watched for problem areas in the administration and helped address them by relieving the governor of the unpleasant task. It was he who delivered the bad news to at least one member of Milliken's cabinet that it would be in everyone's best interest if the agency director resigned.[60]

Other longtime aides spoke in glowing terms of the governor for decades afterward. Said Peter Fletcher: "He represents all of the major qualities you seek in a superior public servant: a genuine gentleman, great integrity and a clear vision of the paramount need to serve the public good through responsible public pursuits . . . [He had] an impeccable standard of integrity, eschewing selfish, narrow interests."[61]

"He had a way of charging up your batteries," said Noble Kheder, who was Milliken's final director of the Department of Social Services. "You'd see him in an elevator at the Capitol and he'd touch you on the shoulder and say, 'I want you to know how much I appreciate the job you're doing.'"[62] Kheder also remarked on Milliken's graciousness when the governor asked him to take over the DSS. "He asked me if I would take the job, as if I was doing him a favor," said Kheder.[63]

The governor dispensed his political charm in a bipartisan fashion. Leo Lalonde, a Democratic state representative from Macomb County, encountered Milliken personally for the first time at a Lansing event in 1980 attended by local government officials from Lalonde's district. Spying Milliken sitting at the head table in a large meeting room making notes on his prepared speech before the luncheon began, Lalonde approached the governor and introduced himself. He then asked Milliken if he would come to his table and meet the officials from Lalonde's district. "He not only did that, but he acted like he and I were old friends," Lalonde said. "That really impressed my guys." As the governor departed, Lalonde said, "Thanks, Bill." He learned later from the governor's aides that "no one calls him Bill."[64]

Lalonde years later asked Milliken to send a personal note to former House Democratic Speaker William Ryan, then in a nursing home. Milliken quickly obliged, penning a warm note in which he said, "I think I have never known anyone in public life who stood more for principle and who was [more] willing, always, to put partisanship aside for the sake of what was right and decent and good for all the people of Michigan."[65]

Milliken's need for privacy and his formal political persona were foremost in the memories of some close observers. Dennis Cawthorne, who served as House Republican leader at a time when the GOP held the minority in the lower chamber in the 1970s, called Milliken "essentially a loner. His idea of a good time would have been getting in a car and driving 500 miles by himself." Cawthorne noted that while the governor maintained cordial relations with Republican leaders he did not invite them to the governor's summer residence on Mackinac Island. Remembering Milliken's straightlaced style, Cawthorne added that "the only thing approaching an off-color joke I ever heard him say was, 'what's the difference between a cactus and a caucus? With the caucus, the pricks are inside.'"[66]

Milliken's reserve and deceptively rigid sense of self-control may have protected him from the wear and tear of politics, but there was also a personal price. Son Bill Jr., who drove his father to annual late winter stays in Arizona in the 1990s and the early years of the new century, said that the trips enabled him to understand his parent better. "We've really gotten to know each other. There's been lots of thoughtful time to do simple things together that we didn't do before."[67]

Bill also remembers the reaction when he gave his father driving gloves and a gift certificate to race car driver Bobby Rayhall's driving school at Watkins Glen, New York. "Oh, that's really thoughtful of you," Bill quoted his father as saying, and added, "That's Millikenese for it'll be a cold day in hell before I use this gift." But surprisingly, over a month later, the retired governor phoned his son and asked him to make the arrangements for him to attend the driving school. He did and said he enjoyed it.

The governor's unassuming style and subtle sense of humor never left him. Years after Milliken left office, a state employee took a ferry to Mackinac Island for a meeting. Since the boat was full, the man took the last seat in the last row. Thinking the man beside him looked familiar but sure that a man of importance would not be riding alone in steerage on the ferry, he turned to him and said, "Did anyone ever tell you that you look like Governor Milliken?"

"Yes, they have," the man said.

A few minutes later, the state employee asked the man, "Well, are you related to the governor?"

"Yes, I am," the man said.

Only after a few more minutes passed did Milliken end the suspense and introduce himself. The other passenger "still is embarrassed by this but gets a good laugh out of Milliken's sense of humor," a friend reported in 2004.[68]

Curiously, for all the warmth that characterized descriptions of Milliken by aides and friends, the image of the retired governor traveling alone and almost unnoticed on the ferry to his beloved retirement home on Mackinac Island also conveys a sense of his nature and legacy. He kept his counsel closely from beginning to end. The public man was respected and revered. The private Milliken was never completely known.

II

REPUBLICAN RELATIONS
AND STRAINS

R EPUBLICAN POLITICS characterized the male line of the Milliken family for three generations. But any suggestion that they were typical Republicans is contradicted by history. After William Milliken's retirement from the governor's office, heirs to leadership of the Republican Party would brand him out of the mainstream of Republican thought. In doing so, they were only echoing, with a harsher tinge, the observations of those who had watched his father perform in Traverse City and the Michigan Senate.

Viewed in the broad context of Republican Party history, the tension between the views of Milliken father and son, on the one hand, and the generally dominant conservative faction of the party on the other illustrates both a long-term struggle and the brief ascendance of the moderates in the 1960s and 1970s.

Michigan political commentator William Ballenger, who served in Milliken's cabinet, points out that former president Theodore Roosevelt ran and won in the presidential election in Michigan as the progressive candidate of the Bull Moose Party in 1912. This "shows you that Michigan has long been fertile ground for Milliken- (or Romney-) style Republicanism."[1] But that brand of Republican thinking was often more revered outside the conservative party ranks than on the inside.

Milliken Republicanism started out unremarkably. Contemporaries remembered William Milliken's grandfather, James W., as "a staunch Republican" and credited his leadership of the Grand Traverse County party with increasing the Republican majority there. Although he "completed a very successful term as state senator . . . nothing could induce him to accept another political office. He was thoroughly wedded to the calling of his choice, and the halls of legislation could not inveigle him away from his business."[2]

A 1971 retrospective on Milliken's father, James, noted, "Those who remember him best say the father often voted with the Democrats."[3] Jack Green, who covered the senior Milliken for the Associated Press, dubbed him "very progressive and liberal. He used to irritate some [Republican] party people because of his 'far out' ideas." A former *Detroit Times* reporter, Don Gardner, said James Milliken had been "very forward thinking when it came to social legislation. You might even say he was to the left of any Democrat then in the Senate." On the other hand, Doug Graham, a former Lansing correspondent for United Press International, while acknowledging that James Milliken was "a rather decided liberal," observed that he "would be horrified to be identified as a Democrat."[4]

James Milliken identified himself strongly with an activist approach to government, including programs that benefited his district. A scrapbook kept by the Milliken family details James Milliken's support for the promotion of northern Michigan tourism, expanded funding for the state hospital in Traverse City, and increased gasoline taxes to pay for better roads. It also includes news articles on his effort to end secret legislative committee meetings and votes. "We are here on a public trust. I think we should be on the record all of the time," he said.[5] He briefly considered running for lieutenant governor in 1946 but instead completed two more state Senate terms.

Where the son departed from the father, it seemed to some, was in grasping the pragmatism required of a successful politician. Graham said the elder Milliken had been "dedicated more to idealism than to practical realities of politics." James Milliken's pet cause, establishment of a single-house, or unicameral, legislature, had gone nowhere in a Capitol whose elective jobs would have been substantially reduced. Asked whether he supported a unicameral legislature, William Milliken as governor replied, "It does deserve some study. There are, I realize, strong arguments on the side of checks and balances. I haven't made a final judgment, although I don't think it is a panacea."[6]

Longtime state Democratic Party leader Neil Staebler remarked in his political memoir that he had tried to induce the "intelligent, principled" Milliken to enter politics as a Democrat and "he almost made the move, but in the end decided that he could not split with his father, who was a Republican member of the State Senate."[7] Milliken has no memory of having spoken to Staebler before entering politics, but the impression persists in many Democratic circles that William Milliken was a Democrat in disguise.

At the time when William Milliken emerged on the state political scene, the Michigan Republican Party was modernizing, throwing off its image as an auxiliary of the Michigan business community, even as state Democrats continued to align themselves largely with organized labor. State Senator Milliken's defiance of the so-called conservative Neanderthals meshed nicely with George Romney's good-government rhetoric in his 1962 campaign for governor. In fact, some credited Milliken's 1961 Traverse City Pact, the manifesto of moderate senators that he helped engineer, with providing the basis for Romney's gubernatorial program.[8] But Romney deserves credit for advancing the idea of a free-thinking Republican. Candidate Romney said in 1962:

> For some considerable period of time, it has been my conviction that any government bearing the brand of any single clique or class, and thus deriving its strength primarily from one faction or special-interest group, is doomed to eventual failure . . . such actions and policies, designed for the benefit of the dominating group, must—of sheer necessity—bring harm and hardship to those members of the community who live and have their being outside the border of the privileged circle.[9]

The appeal of such a platform spanned a wide range of voters. It was especially attractive to moderate voters living in the fast-growing suburbs of Detroit and other urban centers. Suggesting that his chief allegiance was to issues rather than party dogma, Romney was able to wear a Republican mantle for GOP loyalists yet project a kind of independence to the general population. In a famous remark, Romney's 1966

Democratic opponent, Zolton Ferency, joked that "I called Romney a Republican and was accused of conducting a smear campaign."[10]

Milliken learned from the Romney playbook but also followed his own moderate inclinations. From the earliest days of his activism in the Grand Traverse County Republican Party in the early 1950s, Milliken identified himself as moderate, said Robert Griffin, a friend from Traverse City who represented the area in the U.S. House of Representatives from 1955 to 1966 and represented the state in the U.S. Senate from 1966 to 1978. "Bill Milliken was always very interested in the party and in moving it in what he thought was the right direction, a middle-of-the-road philosophy," Griffin said. "But you couldn't be an ideologue and win in those days. You couldn't win on Republican votes alone. You had to attract a large bloc of independents."[11]

Doing so left Romney, and later Milliken, vulnerable to attacks from the right wing of their own party. As early as 1970, when it could be argued that Milliken's moderation was the chief reason for his narrow victory in his first gubernatorial election campaign, the right wing of the Michigan GOP nibbled at his heels. Under the leadership of State senator Robert Huber from the conservative Oakland County suburb of Troy, who narrowly lost that year in the U.S. Senate party primary to Lenore Romney, the conservatives challenged Milliken's alleged assertion that they had no alternative but to support his course as the lesser of two evils. "The Republican party is suffering with a kind of political schizophrenia," remarked Capitol correspondent Robert Longstaff, "split between liberalism of the kind that helped them win elections and conservatism which demands support for President Nixon and his policies."[12] The conservatives, he added, disliked Romney's "alleged liberal approach to the solution of problems. In Milliken they feel they have another Romney, a bit younger and more liberal."[13]

Milliken survived that dissension in election campaigns and continued to suggest that the party needed to move to the center. After a stinging midterm rebuke of President Richard Nixon's conservative thrust in 1970, Milliken extended his efforts to the national party.

Milliken is trying to convince party leaders that the GOP approach has been too doctrinaire in the past, and that the secret in a 1972 victory lies in convincing the independent voters in this country that they should vote for the GOP . . . He has told other governors that a sort of political consumerism has cropped up in the nation. Result is a whole generation of voters who care more for results than they do for promises and slogans. He believes that blacks, young persons and the laboring man can no longer be counted on as Democrats, no more than farmers and professional and business persons can be regarded as Republicans.[14]

From the start, Milliken found himself differing with more conservative Republican figures on the national scene. At a 1969 National Governors' Conference, California governor Ronald Reagan sent a note to Milliken and Massachusetts Republican governor Frank Sargent saying that he wanted to introduce the two new chief executives to reporters. When the time came, Reagan prefaced the introduction by calling for the use of the National Guard to quell antiwar and racial justice protests on university campuses. "It became apparent that [Reagan] wanted to do more than introduce us, he wanted us to support his position on the National Guard. I hadn't given much previous thought to that question. I said to the reporters that I could not think of anything that was more provocative and inflammatory. Sargent agreed fully. Reagan had figured these two neophytes would follow his lead," Milliken said.[15]

Milliken's 1970 victory, coming against the backdrop of a Democratic sweep of most other top Michigan posts and a repudiation of the Nixon law-and-order strategy, positioned the young governor as a national figure. "The national administration may not be excited about [Milliken's] low-key approach to a number of issues, but he is a man to be reckoned with . . . He is the kind of Republican who is aware of the shifting tides of our restless times and is trying to come up with new answers for old problems."[16]

The Nixon-Milliken relationship was never close, but the men were not above using each other for political purposes. As he faced a tough election campaign in 1970, Milliken traveled to Washington to demonstrate his influence with the Republican president. He emerged after a 45-minute White House meeting with Nixon proclaiming that he had won pledges of millions of dollars in federal aid to combat high unemployment. "Milliken apparently wanted to demonstrate that he is held in high regard by the Nixon Administration," the *Detroit News* observed. "The President responded by giving him the red carpet treatment."[17]

At one point, Milliken's staff suspected Nixon of wanting to use the governor as a stalking horse for his strategy to appeal to white voters by opposing cross-district busing for purposes of school integration. In 1972, Nixon dispatched his domestic adviser, John Ehrlichman, to meet with Milliken on educational policy. According to Milliken aide James Phelps, Ehrlichman was "very pleasant, very smooth and congenial," but it wasn't clear what the meeting was about. When Ehrlichman left, Milliken asked his aide to stay and asked him what he thought the presidential aide had been after. "Nixon wants you to be his surrogate, opposing cross-district busing," Phelps said. "That's what I thought," Milliken replied. "No, thank you."[18]

Milliken's relationship with Vice President Spiro T. Agnew was even more complicated. The governor disapproved of Agnew's strident rhetorical assaults on Vietnam War protesters and the administration's apparent abandonment of African American voters and the cities. Before a 1970 governors' meeting in Idaho that Agnew attended, Milliken organized a "quiet, informal movement among liberal governors" to try to steer Nixon away from a tough line on law and order and toward a more progressive, inclusive agenda that would appeal to urban dwellers, minority groups, and young voters.[19] "That's not an anti-Nixon tack," Milliken told a reporter. "I know from Michigan's point of view, we can win if we broaden our base. It's got to be a total commitment that comes shining through."[20]

The private session that Agnew held with GOP governors in Idaho was not a success. Milliken termed Agnew's scathing, take-no-prisoners rhetoric with the Republican governors "incredible." Tom McCall, the Republican governor of Oregon, described Agnew's remarks as "a dirty rotten bigoted little speech." As Milliken recalled it, Agnew challenged McCall on the quote the next day. "McCall jumped up and said, 'Mr. Vice President, I didn't say that. I didn't use the word '*little*.'"[21] Milliken shared the sentiments. But he ultimately refrained from further open dissension. By late 1971, the *Detroit Free Press* could publish a photo of Milliken and Kentucky governor Louie Nunn applauding Agnew after a speech with the lead sentence in an accompanying article "Spiro is still very much the hero of Republican governors."[22]

At times before the Watergate scandal that eventually destroyed Nixon's presidency, Milliken evinced a measure of enthusiasm for the Nixon-Agnew ticket. After a June 1972 governors' conference that Agnew attended on behalf of the Nixon administration, Milliken wrote him a warm note of thanks: "You not only established your supremacy on the tennis court. You also helped Republican governors establish a point that is becoming increasingly apparent across the country: We are more united behind the President, his programs, and his Vice-President than ever before . . . Those of us in the [Republican Governors' Association] have high personal respect for you, and we are gratified for all that you have done to improve relations between the governors and the administration."[23] Agnew thanked him a few weeks later, saying, "the confidence which you and the other Governors of the Republican Governors' Association have placed in this Administration evidences both the cooperative spirit and determination so necessary for the success of the President and his programs."[24] Nixon wrote Milliken several times in 1971 and 1972 to thank him for his outspoken support of the Republican ticket in the 1972 reelection campaign, which Nixon and Agnew won in a landslide.

The erupting Watergate scandal changed all that. By the fall of 1973, Congress and the news media were battering Nixon over disclosures that persons associated with his reelection effort had burglarized the Democratic National Committee headquarters at the Watergate Hotel in Washington and that others in the campaign or administration had launched a "dirty tricks" initiative to embarrass partisan foes and critics. Worry in the GOP grew that the scandal might cause lasting damage to the party. On November 20, 1973, Milliken and other Republican governors met in private with Nixon in Memphis. Milliken relayed the exchange to aide George Weeks, who recorded the governor's thoughts in notes.

> It was a totally candid discussion by a troubled President [Milliken said] . . . He said he was keenly aware of the problems that Watergate was causing for Governors and others . . . The President insisted he had no knowledge of the Watergate cover-up, saying, "Apart from the morality of it, I'm not that stupid . . . when the facts are known, I know we'll be all right . . . in the last four weeks I probably have gone through more than any of you have gone

through in four years . . . I'm working my damn butt off." He spoke with great feeling and emotion.[25]

Milliken suggested that Nixon "go public through an open-ended, unlimited meeting with a representative press group, taking any and all questions, discussing them until full disclosure is accomplished." Nixon was noncommittal.

Nixon had already shed Agnew. Resigning in October 1973 after an indictment on charges of receiving kickbacks as Maryland governor and in his vice presidential office, Agnew had returned to private life. Surprising Capitol Hill, Nixon had nominated Gerald Ford, a 25-year veteran of the U.S. House from East Grand Rapids, Michigan, to replace Agnew as vice president. Well liked in the House, Ford had breezed through his confirmation and become vice president.

For Milliken, this created an unusual dynamic. Although he was not a close friend of Ford's, the two had known each other for decades and shared an easygoing persona. At the same time, Ford moved more toward the center as vice president, occupying ground congenial to Milliken. Additionally, a Michigan man in the vice presidency offered Milliken's state new prestige and influence with Nixon, whose own future had been blackened by the relentless scandal.

Michigan was also key in measuring voter response to Nixon in light of the allegations of his misconduct. In the February 18, 1974, special election to replace Ford in the U.S. House, Democrat Richard VanderVeen upset the Republican candidate, Robert VanderLaan, with 53 percent of the vote. VanderVeen had made a centerpiece of his campaign Nixon's "moral fitness to govern." Michigan Republican Party chairman William McLaughlin said, "Few were still living who could remember when a non-Republican had last held that seat. I was embarrassed. We had lost the Vice President's seat." McLaughlin told a reporter, "Watergate killed us."[26] When national Republican officials criticized McLaughlin for the remark, the party chairperson talked to Milliken and said that he had spoken the truth and would understand if Milliken differed with his assessment. "He did not say that he did," McLaughlin remembered.[27]

Next on tap was an April 16 special election to fill the congressional seat of Republican James Harvey, whom Nixon had appointed to a federal judgeship. Harvey's Eighth District comprised a large part of

Michigan's Thumb, reaching from Saginaw and Bay City east. Early polls showed that Democratic candidate Robert Traxler, a state representative, had a small but surprising lead over the GOP candidates in the heavily Republican district. James Sparling, Harvey's chief of staff, won the Republican primary, setting up what the White House decided would be a test of Nixon's popularity. But Republicans on the ground in Michigan did not want such a test.

"I believed that if we kept the focus on issues other than Watergate and Sparling ran hard against Traxler, keeping him on the defensive and away from Watergate, we had a chance . . . For the first time in months, I was pumped," said McLaughlin.[28]

But in a meeting with Sparling, the Michigan GOP chief learned that the candidate had invited Nixon to campaign for him in the Eighth District. This set up exactly what Milliken's camp did not want—a referendum on Watergate. Milliken did his best to distance himself from the increasingly unpopular Nixon. National political journalist Jack W. Germond wrote:

> Two days later the Nixon visit fulfilled all the predictions of political disaster—and one witnessed by an entourage of more than two hundred from the national and international press. The president was greeted at the Saginaw airport by Governor William G. Milliken, a popular moderate Republican who then found it necessary to flee to Toronto for a meeting on water pollution problems that simply could not wait . . . [Nixon] was viewed by small clutches of people along the road while the television cameras focused on the empty spaces. If Republicans in Congress needed hard evidence that Richard Nixon was poison, it was right there, first in the reports on the trip fiasco and then in the narrow defeat Sparling suffered a week later when, significantly, Republican turnout ran well below the norm.[29]

When Nixon resigned under pressure on August 9, 1974, Republicans across the nation shuddered, including Milliken and his political team. But after carefully distancing himself from Nixon in the crucial months leading up to the president's demise, as well as continuing to appeal to moderates and independents, Milliken won reelection by a larger margin than he had racked up in 1970. Still, the devastation of the party in national and state races put it in a deep hole. "The GOP has a pinhead for a base and we're kidding ourselves if we think it can be turned around in anything like two or three years," said Michigan GOP chairperson McLaughlin.[30]

In the Republican ruins of Watergate, Milliken renewed his call for a more inclusive party, winning national attention. A 1976 *Time* magazine article heralded Milliken as one of several party leaders with "drive and imagination" who had demonstrated "what can be accomplished in the face of Democratic majorities." *Time* described Milliken as a fiscal conservative with close ties to the business community who "makes frequent forays into ethnic areas and appoints blacks, Hispanics and members of other minorities to state posts."[31] Milliken was well regarded by other observers. A staffer at the National Governors' Association listed Iowa governor Robert Ray, Washington governor Dan Evans, and Milliken as "the three best governors of the 1970s."[32]

That year's presidential campaign put Milliken to a special test. Struggling to fend off the insurgent conservative Ronald Reagan, President Gerald Ford badly needed a home-state win in the Michigan GOP primary election in May. Trailing Reagan in the delegate count at the time, Ford was perceived by Milliken and his aides to be in trouble in Michigan as well. Out of a determination to keep alive the hopes of the more moderate Republican faction, as well as to deliver the state to his friend, Milliken went to work.[33] Milliken lobbied Ford's campaign manager, Rogers Morton, for an intense last-minute drive by the president and his organization in the days leading up to the May 18 primary. Included was a "massive" get-out-the-vote operation and a two-day whistle-stop tour conceived by party worker Jerry Roe. Milliken dispatched Republican Party chair McLaughlin and his own top political aide, Joyce Braithwaite, to bring the election home for Ford. They did. Ford won by more than 325,000 votes, defeating Reagan soundly by a 65 to 35 percent margin. Milliken received much of the credit for rescuing Ford's candidacy. The *Washington Star* said, "Ford's victory was also a testament to the effective support of the Michigan campaign organization led by Governor Milliken and State Chairman William McLaughlin."[34]

Milliken was tapped to deliver the nominating speech for the president at the GOP convention in Kansas City. Ford "has demonstrated to all the world, that government can be conducted openly, honestly and successfully," Milliken said. "He has shown that the historic American principle of government by the consent of the governed is workable in this modern age of incredibly complex problems . . . President Ford has united this country, and as our candidate, he will unite this party."[35] The *Flint Journal* said, "Milliken acquitted himself and Ford well. The governor is hardly an old-school orator, and he doesn't bring tears to the eyes of his audience, but his calm approach to things usually gets over his point."[36]

Milliken supported Ford strongly throughout the fall campaign, even though he was at first taken aback by the president's selection of Robert Dole as his running mate. In 1971, Milliken had chided Dole for an attack on Senator Edmund Muskie of Maine, telling fellow governors that Dole was using "sledgehammer tactics" harmful to the party as a whole.[37] Milliken had personally written Dole in 1971 that the party could not succeed by "following the doctrinaire, rigid, negative approach that we Republicans too often take."[38] After Ford tapped Dole, Milliken said blandly, "Senator Dole is an excellent campaigner and speaker, and he brings geographical balance to the ticket."[39] But Dole's role as "hatchet man" for the national ticket was blamed by some observers for costing Ford re-election by a narrow margin.[40] Meanwhile, Milliken helped home state man Ford carry Michigan in the election, giving the President a critical but insufficient 25 electoral votes.

When Republicans struggled in the 1976 election, Milliken organized a meeting the following year of "several like-minded, middle-road Republicans" on Mackinac Island to discuss forming an organization that could coalesce GOP moderates to counter the influence of conservative groups within the party. "Milliken is an ideal leader for such a movement," columnists Jack W. Germond and Jules Witcover wrote, "because he is notoriously modest about his own political ambitions."[41] The two journalists predicted difficulty: "The moderates, by their very nature, are never able to find issues to inspire that type of zeal. Milliken may have the best of intentions, but it will be a hard road."

Michigan's 1980 Republican presidential primary tested Milliken's command of the state party again. This time he sought to promote the candidacy of a moderate, George H. W. Bush, over Reagan, who had surged ahead in the battle for the 1980 GOP presidential nomination.

The desire to help was based on more than politics. The Millikens and Bushes had become friends when George Bush had served as the Republican national chairman during the Nixon era. A 1973 letter from "Geo." to "Bill and Helen" after a visit to Traverse City by the Bushes thanked them for "the tennis, the food, the super-considerate hospitality" and concluded, "We're friends Hooray! And thanks!"[42] The Millikens twice visited the Bushes at their compound in Kennebunkport, Maine. Years later the former governor described Bush as a "very decent man, a very honest man" and described their friendship through the 1980s as close.[43] Milliken devoted himself to the Bush presidential candidacy in 1979 and 1980. His team's successful all-out effort to deliver Michigan for Bush in the 1980 Michigan primary gave Milliken's friend stature sufficient to qualify him as Reagan's ultimate choice for a running mate.

It could be argued that Milliken was instrumental in the rise of the Bush family to the White House in 1988 and 2000, for without the pivotal 1980 Michigan primary victory the father might not have rated the second place on the GOP national ticket that year and George W. Bush might never have come near the White House. In 2004, Helen teased the former governor in front of a reporter: "I keep telling him, 'Bill, George Bush, Jr. is all your fault.'"[44]

Despite his misgivings about Reagan, Milliken campaigned with his party's nominee in 1980. After Reagan's election, rumors circulated that the new president wanted Milliken to run for the U.S. Senate in 1982. The *Detroit News* quoted an unnamed presidential aide as saying, "The president is sure Bill Milliken would win his primary and is a good bet to blow Riegle out because of his demonstrated ability over the last decade to convincingly win statewide races."[45] But, according to Milliken and aide Weeks, the governor never seriously considered making the Senate run. Years later Milliken would speak with disapproval of Reagan's antichoice views and steep cuts in social programs.

Although it never came to pass, the close friendship between Bush and Milliken led Washington journalist David Broder to speculate that if he was elected president in 1988 Bush would name the former governor to a top post. "I would be willing to bet anything that he'd be invited into the cabinet," Broder said while in Traverse City. "If Bush could have had his druthers eight years ago, I know Bill Milliken would have been the person he'd have asked to run as his vice-presidential candidate. There was a real bond between those two men—you couldn't spend any time with George and Barbara Bush without knowing how they felt about the Millikens."[46] Milliken said in 2003 he might have accepted an appointment from Bush.[47]

The bond was tested and then ruptured in the 1980s. To earn the vice presidential slot on the national Republican ticket in 1980, the elder Bush repudiated his longtime pro-choice stand and said he now supported abortion restrictions, which appalled both Millikens. But they did not openly differ with Bush until the latter's 1988 campaign for president. Trailing Democratic nominee Michael Dukakis as the two men came out of their respective party conventions, Bush launched a series of successful attacks on the liberal Democrat. One particularly outraged Milliken. Bush dubbed Dukakis "a card-carrying member of the ACLU [American Civil Liberties Union]," implying that he was disloyal to American values of faith and moderation. Milliken retorted publicly that he, too, had an ACLU card and was proud of the organization's defense of civil liberties. "I didn't hear anything from him after that," Milliken said.[48] In 2003, former treasury secretary James Baker, on a visit to Michigan, tried to connect the elder Bush and Milliken on the phone but allegedly couldn't track down the former president.[49]

Milliken had no use, either, for the second Bush to take the presidency. In 2003, he belittled the advisers with whom George W. Bush had surrounded himself, including Defense Secretary Donald Rumsfeld. The younger Bush's Pentagon chief had served in the U.S. House in the 1960s and 1970s. Milliken remembers a visit in the 1960s: "Rumsfeld, Bob Griffin, I, and our wives were riding in the Washington area, with Rumsfeld driving. He ran a red light. Bob said, 'Don, do you know what you just did?' He said, 'Yes, but we have total immunity.'"[50]

The price of moderation included a reputation for being largely unable to transform voter support for himself into a mandate for Republicans. "As a partisan political leader, he's proved only average in his ability to translate his own rapport with voters into support for other Republican candidates and his moderate views and policies," Susan Martin of the *Detroit News* noted in 1980.[51] James Hill, a moderate Republican and onetime aide to Senator Bob Griffin, said, "Milliken was well-liked but his brand of moderate Republicanism was

Growing domestic tension over the Vietnam War in the late 1960s and early 1970s triggered frequent protests when Milliken, initially a supporter of Richard Nixon, spoke in public. (Photograph courtesy of George Weeks.)

Milliken's two election contests with Democrat Sander Levin in 1970 and 1974 were closely fought races whose intensity belied the gentlemanly demeanor of both candidates. In this 1970 meeting they trade verbal jabs as Helen Milliken observes. After Milliken's retirement and Levin's election to the U.S. House of Representatives, the two former foes became friends. (Photograph from the Milliken family collection.)

The Milliken grin disarmed many political foes. On key votes, his earnest pleas to lawmakers to do what he thought was in the best interest of the state turned more than a few around. (Photograph courtesy of George Weeks.)

Milliken's concern about equal rights for all citizens and his personal interest in state aid for troubled urban areas won him friends in the African American community. (Photograph courtesy of George Weeks.)

As first lady of Michigan, Helen Milliken was a quiet but unmistakable voice for protection of Michigan's natural beauty. Many credit her with reinforcing the governor's instincts on environmental protection issues. (Photograph courtesy of George Weeks.)

Milliken with the conservative Republican pillars of western Michigan: Jay Van Andel and Richard DeVos, founders of the Amway Corporation, and their wives. Milliken resisted pressure from Amway to block tough controls on phosphorus in laundry detergents. The state rule was credited with helping reduce algae outbreaks in the Great Lakes. (Photograph courtesy of George Weeks.)

An opponent of the state lottery, Milliken accepted the verdict of voters, who approved it. Here he marks the first $1 billion in sales of daily game tickets in 1981. (Photograph courtesy of George Weeks.)

Milliken and Detroit mayor Coleman Young, a Democrat, were the most unlikely of political allies and personal friends. But the two men teamed up to bring state aid to Detroit, including an "equity package" that poured millions of dollars into the city to compensate it for spending on institutions such as the Detroit Institute of Arts that benefit the whole state.

In her latter years as First Lady, Helen Milliken spoke out for adoption of the Equal Rights Amendment to the Constitution and other feminist causes, winning both fierce critics and adoring admirers. She had come a long way from her youth in a conservative Republican family in Colorado. (Photograph courtesy of George Weeks.)

Governor and Mrs. Milliken pay their respects to Pope John Paul II, who visited Detroit in 1979. (Photograph courtesy of George Weeks.)

Milliken maintained a regular schedule of physical exercise, running and swimming throughout his nearly 14 years as governor. One of his favorite jogging trails was at the tip of the Old Mission Peninsula not far from his home, where he could gather his thoughts and renew his energies in the quiet of nature. (Photograph courtesy of George Weeks.)

The governor couldn't always run alone. Here a state trooper assigned to his security team follows him at a respectful distance as Milliken runs along a canal adjoining the Potomac River on a business trip to Washington, DC. (Photograph courtesy of George Weeks.)

In 1980, Milliken's conservation aide, Bill Rustem, managed to lure the governor and his wife to a remote cabin on Craig Lake in Michigan's Upper Peninsula. There the entourage fished, enjoyed the sighting of bald eagles, and sat before a hearth in the evening enjoying informal conversations. (Photograph from the Milliken family collection.)

The PBB food contamination episode troubled Milliken's administration from 1973 on. When the chemical flame retardant PBB was accidentally mixed with cattle feed, the resulting poisoning forced the state to condemn and bury thousands of afflicted cattle and other farm animals in specially designed landfills. Critics charged that Milliken was too slow to take action to stop the contamination, but his aides said he responded as aggressively as possible given the uncertainty of the sources and effects of the contamination. (Photograph courtesy of the State Archives of Michigan.)

At the annual Mackinac Island leadership conference in May 2005, Milliken sounded his lifelong theme of civility and moderation in a time of increasing incivility in politics. He told the audience, "150 years ago Lincoln told a nation that 'a house divided against itself cannot stand.' In the twenty-first century, a Michigan divided against itself likewise cannot stand." He won a standing ovation. (Photograph by David Trumpie, used by permission.)

more personality than ideology and his moderate views in the party dimmed quickly after he left office."[52]

The moderate governor became increasingly unpopular with his own party. Before he announced his retirement in late 1981, Republican conservatives announced that they would seek to "purge the state GOP of its leader," Milliken, "because he behaves like a Democrat and 'does not belong philosophically within the Republican Party.'"[53] Meeting organizer Norm Hughes said that the conservatives would "be prepared to do whatever they could to retire" Milliken if he did not voluntarily retire, citing his positions on abortion, economics, and taxes.

After leaving office in 1982, Milliken saw his point of view become first a minority perspective and then almost invisible within the Michigan Republican Party. Referring to noted conservatives of the time, he said, "The Dick Durants, the Robert Hubers, the Kirby Holmeses had always been there. After I left, they were suddenly free to take over the party." Milliken also credited the growing strength of the anti-abortion movement, which found its home in the GOP, with driving the party away from the center.[54]

Disapproving of the rightward turn, Milliken refrained from endorsing Republican nominees for governor of Michigan in the first five elections after his retirement, with the exception of African American William Lucas in 1986. Although he did not endorse Democrat Jennifer Granholm when she successfully sought the office in 2002, he publicly condemned a television advertisement by Republican nominee Richard Posthumus that appeared to pit Detroit against the rest of the state. He called the ad "morally wrong and politically stupid," echoing a comment he had made in the 1970s about the GOP's shunning of urban and minority voters. In a statement sent to numerous media outlets, Milliken added, "As a life-long Republican who has worked many years to bring a wide spectrum of people together under our party's umbrella, I am embarrassed by some aspects of the campaign now being waged by my party in the race for governor . . . I worked very hard to try and bring this state together, and this really runs contrary to everything I tried to accomplish."[55]

In 2004, Milliken openly broke with his party over the candidacy of George W. Bush for reelection as president. In a statement widely noted by state and national news media, Milliken endorsed Democrat John Kerry.

My Republican Party is a broad-based party, that seeks to bring a wide spectrum of people under its umbrella and that seeks to protect and provide opportunity for the most vulnerable among us. Sadly, that is not the Republican Party that I see at the national level today . . .

This president has pursued policies pandering to the extreme right wing across a wide variety of issues and has exacerbated the polarization and the strident, uncivil tone of much of what passes for political discourse in this country today . . .

The truth is that President George W. Bush does not speak for me or for many other moderate Republicans on a very broad cross section of issues . . . Sen. John Kerry, on the other hand, has put forth a coherent, responsible platform of progressive initiatives that I believe would serve this country well.[56]

Kerry personally thanked Milliken for the endorsement in a phone call. *Detroit Free Press* outdoor writer Eric Sharp pointed out the environmental implications of a vote for Kerry versus a vote for Bush. "I called Milliken in Traverse City to talk about [the endorsement]," Sharp wrote, "and one thing I asked was what advice he would give voters who are also outdoors types. The response from Milliken, who describes himself as a committed Republican, was instantaneous: 'I can't understand how any thinking, responsible person can ignore the environmental damage done by this administration.' As a hunter and angler, and someone who depends on those activities for his living, neither can I."[57]

A spokesperson for Bush's Michigan campaign, John Truscott, who had also worked for Governor John Engler, brushed off the governor's endorsement. "He isn't part of any organization, and people who are likely to follow him already have their minds made up one way or another," Truscott said. "What Governor Milliken doesn't realize is that times have changed and what we need is a very strong leader as president to keep us safe."[58]

The downfall of the moderate Republicans may, in part, have been the result of their temperament. In a 1978 column speculating on why Milliken and other moderate GOP governors, "a wholesome species," did so poorly in presidential politics, David Broder wrote, "Part of the answer is that they are cursed with the most belittling label in the lexicon of political journalism. They are moderates. Their speeches may inform, but they rarely inspire or inflame. Even their political appetites are limited. They do not get excited, and they fail to excite."[59]

Milliken never contemplated leaving the GOP, not even in retirement. When New York mayor John Lindsay abandoned the Republicans for the Democratic Party in 1971, Milliken said, "I am convinced that the Republican Party is broad enough for the Lindsays—and for the Buckleys. It's far better to work within your party for the things in which you believe, than to switch parties for political expediency."[60] Milliken said that party switchers like Lindsay could never go back and were never completely trusted by their new party, thus ending their effectiveness. (A rare exception was Michigan's own Donald Riegle, who switched from a GOP member of the U.S. House delegation to the Democratic Party and won three terms in the Senate in his new incarnation. Milliken at one time scorned Riegle for his "overriding ambition.")[61]

Asked whether moderate Republicanism had any future two decades after Milliken left office, former state party chairperson Elly Peterson, who had helped build the pragmatic Michigan GOP of the 1960s and 1970s, replied that "moderate Republicans are no longer wanted in the party. Republicans are closely controlled by fundamentalists . . . 'Moderate Republican' to me means open arms to any and all voters, no stringent rules of 'think as we think or leave,' and an open mind on new issues of the day."[62]

Even during his gubernatorial years, Milliken was not representative of his state party, said Jerry Roe, long active in the Michigan GOP. "The party was a lot more conservative than Milliken," Roe said. When county party chairs descended on Lansing to meet with Roe, he said, "They would say things like, 'If that goddamned Milliken doesn't shape up—' Then they'd go to a reception with the governor and tell him they loved him."[63]

Milliken traced the party's rightward march to its Presidential success in 1980. "I have to say that Ronald Reagan was the beginning of the downward sweep of the [Republican] Party. His influence is felt to this day," he lamented in 2003.[64]

Although his politics were out of favor in the Michigan Republican Party, former supporters and ticket splitters occasionally issued pleas for a return of the Milliken moderation. "Former Gov. William Milliken represents how Republicans used to be," said a Grosse Pointe letter writer to the *Detroit Free Press*. "Many people still vote Republican because they expect they will be getting someone with Milliken's principles and integrity—someone who will do the right thing regardless of pressure. Where are the Republicans who should be providing leadership? When I see a Republican of Milliken's quality, I will gladly vote Republican again."[65]

12

THE PERILOUS CAMPAIGN

A S 1974 BEGAN, Governor William G. Milliken had a number of reasons to be optimistic about his chances to win a
second full term as governor that November. He had signed into law a
school aid formula regarded as a breakthrough in promoting equal educational opportunity. He had continued to build a commendable
record on clean air and water issues. He had delivered $500 million in
tax cuts, largely by increasing the state personal income tax exemption.
The Middle East oil embargo in the autumn of 1973 had sent a shock
through the state's auto-dependent economy, but the international
roots of the problem and Milliken's empathy and emergency action to
help the unemployed removed some of the sting. Milliken continued
to be personally popular with a majority of registered voters.

The only cloud on the horizon lay in the direction of Washington,
DC, and it was called the Watergate scandal.

As the year dawned, the Nixon White House was in crisis. In what
quickly came to be known as the Saturday Night Massacre, the president in October 1973 had fired independent prosecutor Archibald Cox
and triggered the resignations of Attorney General Eliot Richardson
and Deputy Attorney General William Ruckelshaus, a turning point in
Nixon's descent toward resignation. Emboldened, the U.S. Congress
and prosecutors continued to pursue evidence implicating top aides of

the president in the expanding web of scandal. Even many Republicans were beginning to turn against him. Said Michigan GOP chief William McLaughlin: "The thing that kicked the slats out was the Saturday Night Massacre. The phone didn't stop ringing for days and all the calls seemed to start, 'I'm a life long Republican and I voted for him but I want to know how we can impeach Nixon.'"[1]

As national head of the Republican Party, Nixon endangered the reelection chances not only of GOP members of Congress but also of Republican governors. To claim four more years in office, Milliken would again have to distance himself from his party while running as its titular state head. As never before, the Milliken approach to statewide victory, cobbling together a majority by expanding beyond the Republican voting base, would be critical.

At the end of January, Milliken was still officially uncommitted to seeking a second full term. In a letter to his father-in-law, he said, "Shortly I will be making the decision about running again. While I lean in the direction of doing it, it is an appalling thought to contemplate the months of campaigning which would lie ahead. We'll keep you informed of our thinking."[2]

But during the same month a friend of Milliken's, Robert Teeter, the president of Market Opinion Research, a Republican polling firm, asked former U.S. Environmental Protection Agency official A. James Barnes to audition for the role of managing the governor's reelection campaign. A Michigan native, Barnes had interviewed for a staff position the previous autumn and recorded this impression of Milliken.

> He is one of those rare individuals who in the first few moments after you meet him, you conclude that he is a very special human being. He had a particularly warm smile and gracious manner that put me immediately at ease. He was also someone who seemed completely comfortable with himself—he knew who he was and what his values were—there was no need for any pretense . . . I left the interview even more impressed and believing that it would be a privilege to be able to work with him.[3]

Barnes ultimately signed on as campaign manager. A former associate of both Richardson and Ruckelshaus in the nation's capital, Barnes was able to reinforce the public perception of Milliken as an honest man who was independent of the ethical lapses that appeared to characterize Nixon's administration. In a sense, Nixon's failings underscored Milliken's virtues. The campaign adopted the slogan "What Michigan needs is a good honest governor—and it has one."[4] Strikingly, Nixon's negative was Milliken's positive. In a year in which personal character would define electoral outcomes, Milliken seemed better positioned than many of his peers to survive the Watergate winds.

On March 7, Milliken announced his bid for reelection with a simple, six-paragraph statement that began: "I believe I have been a good Governor, with a good record of accomplishment . . . Although I will not formally be a candidate until petitions are actually filed, I wanted at this early time to be candid about my intentions rather than being coy and going through the usual prolonged build-up ritual. This is no year to be a play actor in politics or any form of public life."[5]

One of the few difficult decisions Milliken would have to face early in the campaign was the choice of a successor to Lieutenant Governor James H. Brickley as a running mate. A respected member of the Milliken team during the governor's first full term, Brickley had decided to leave the ticket and would ultimately assume the presidency of Eastern Michigan University. Although there was speculation that Brickley had wanted assurances Milliken would step down in 1978 and pave the way for the lieutenant governor's candidacy for chief executive, relations between the two men remained (and would always remain) cordial. Not long after announcing his decision to leave the job of lieutenant governor, Brickley gave his boss an enthusiastic reelection endorsement, saying, "Those of us who have been privileged to work with Governor Milliken have seen him reject politically expedient methods that would have advanced his personal career at the cost of his program. He has faced the issues honestly. He has used factual and substantive approaches—and fortunately he has been successful in writing a commendable public record."[6]

Milliken needed to find someone who was compatible with his moderate views and could balance his Traverse City roots with a southeastern Michigan, or at least an urban, background. In a move that would have significant unintended repercussions for his campaign, the governor settled on state Representative James Damman of vote-rich, Republican Troy in Oakland County, north of Detroit. "I asked him to run with me . . . because he seemed to be a bright young man and he provided some geographic balance to the ticket," Milliken said three decades later. "It was not one of the outstanding decisions I made."[7]

In fact, it was a fateful choice that ultimately put Milliken's own political survival at risk.

But in the meantime, the Nixon drama had to play itself out in Washington. When U.S. senator Barry Goldwater and House minority leader James Rhodes, until then Nixon backers, told the president in early August that he could count on only a few votes against conviction on impeachment counts in the Senate, the die was cast. Nixon announced his resignation on August 8, 1974, to take effect the following day. Suddenly the complexion of the campaign changed. Gerald Ford, the Michigan man with a blight-free reputation, took over. It appeared that Milliken's ethical nature might be a less important selling point than previously thought, said campaign manager Jim Barnes. "By Labor Day, the issue of integrity in government (the Governor's strong suit) had dropped way down on the list of voter concerns and the race turned into a typical Michigan horse race with economic issues at the forefront. The governor's lead in the polls largely disappeared."[8]

For the second time, Milliken's Democratic opponent in the race was Sander Levin, a state senator from Oakland County who had trounced former Detroit mayor Jerome Cavanagh in the August primary. The men knew each other well and years later said they respected each other, but the debate grew unusually sharp for a Milliken campaign.

In a September appearance before the annual meeting of the Michigan Municipal League in Detroit, Milliken derided Levin as a candidate "whose approach is to pile promise upon promise until [he has] constructed a gigantic mortgage on the future . . . Promises, promises. People are tired of it. What they need is progress."[9]

Milliken was particularly incensed by Levin's endorsement of a proposal on the statewide ballot to exempt food and prescription drugs from the state's sales tax. Milliken charged that at the same time Levin was proposing the loss of $200 million annually in state tax revenues he was making huge spending promises "for the cities, for the schools, for the health systems of Michigan. Where will he get the money? I'd appreciate an answer, but I don't really expect one."[10]

Levin remembered the issue differently in 2005. "I believe that the years immediately after the campaign showed that the position I took—that we could afford the sales tax exemption on food and prescription drugs—was right. I took my position in favor of it, and then a week or two later I came out with the detailed information to back it up. They were all over me in the meantime."[11]

In preparing for a debate with Levin that fall, Milliken was asked by aides how he would respond if the sales tax exemption ballot proposal came up. "I'll say I'm still thinking about it," he declared, agreeing with his advisers that it was imprudent to oppose the idea openly. But he couldn't contain himself when Levin spoke warmly of the proposal during his opening remarks. Milliken denounced Levin's position as irresponsible. "On the way home, he said, 'What have I done?'" said aide James Phelps. "But he didn't really regret it. He thought the proposal really was irresponsible."[12]

Despite the national Democratic tide, which had been reinforced by revulsion inspired by President Ford's pardon of Nixon on September 8, Milliken seemed to be in decent position to win reelection in late October. A *Detroit News* survey had him leading Levin by a margin of 47 to 41 percent among likely voters on October 2. But in the event of a high turnout, the newspaper reported, he was trailing by two points. The governor's campaign, now guided principally by political aide Joyce Braithwaite and state Republican Party chairperson William McLaughlin, swung into higher gear. McLaughlin visited campaign headquarters in 22 of the state's 83 counties in a one-week period, pushing volunteers to increase their canvassing and phone calling. "Apathy is still great but work is proceeding methodically," he reported to Milliken.[13]

McLaughlin fired back at once against a Democratic Party advertisement in the *Detroit Free Press* that linked him to Nixon. Below the ad's headline—"They were together on inflation, unemployment and the economy"—it read: "Governor Milliken is the leader of the Republican Party in Michigan. He was the leader while Richard Nixon was mismanaging the White House."[14] McLaughlin condemned the ad as misleading and irresponsible. It was one of the few times in the campaign that the Democrats tried to link Milliken to Nixon directly.

Late in October, the Milliken campaign faced its greatest challenge. On October 31, less than a week before the election, the *Detroit Free Press* broke the news that Milliken's running mate, James Damman, while a local official, had participated in drafting a development plan for Troy while the firm in which he was a partner was buying land that would inflate in value if the plan was approved. The headline of the story in the year of Watergate was far from what the campaign wanted: "Damman Involved in Land-Buy Scheme."[15] Joe Stroud, the newspaper's editorial page editor, said Damman had engaged in "subterfuge, profiteering and abuse of power." McLaughlin wondered whether this was "to be a different shade of Watergate at home."[16] As the *New York Times* later said, "Mr. Milliken's chances of re-election seemed in extra jeopardy for a time."[17]

Milliken gathered his top political advisers around him at the governor's residence—but not Damman. Included were top aides Braithwaite and Weeks, GOP chairperson McLaughlin, campaign manager Barnes, and several others. McLaughlin found the four-hour meeting difficult.

> I remember little about the meeting except for the cool leadership of Bill Milliken. At one time or another, most of us were of the opinion that Damman should be dropped from the ticket. The Governor was never of that mind and reasoned, correctly, that we should do nothing in haste. Earlier in the day, he had asked [attorney Lawrence] Lindemer to investigate facts on his behalf. This wise decision probably came at the suggestion of Braithwaite. Lindemer had done much of the investigation by the time we arrived.
>
> By the time we broke up at about 11 p.m., we all agreed with the Governor that we would be cautious, wait for Lindemer's investigation to be completed and say as little as possible. . . . Only Milliken and Lindemer were talking to [Damman]. It was my understanding he was asked to keep a low profile.[18]

The running mate did not do so. In a series of statements to reporters, Damman avowed his innocence and rejected calls that he step aside. "I don't back away from a fight and I have nothing to run away from or be ashamed of in this matter," he told one reporter. McLaughlin was incensed to see a photograph of Damman in a dark shirt, seated at his kitchen table on the front page of the *Free Press*. "It hit me that he looked like a criminal. Not what we needed. I was so mad that I have never forgotten it. While everyone else was running around trying to save him, he did this. I thought it unforgivable."[19]

The governor wanted to dispatch attorneys Lindemer and David Dykhouse, a longtime Milliken legal adviser, to meet with *Free Press* reporters and explain their findings. Damman's candidacy hung by a thread and was based on whether he had possessed inside information about the Troy master plan or had simply capitalized on publicly available data. Lindemer had determined that there was no clear breach of law on the part of Damman.

According to a later account published in the *Columbia Journalism Review* (CJR), Milliken called Stroud at home on Friday evening, November 1, and asked whether the two attorneys could meet with reporters Remer Tyson and Dave Anderson, who had coordinated the investigation of Damman. Stroud said he didn't have jurisdiction over the News Department and referred Milliken to Kurt Luedtke, the executive editor. Lindemer spoke to Luedtke, who agreed to meet with Milliken's representatives the next day. Stroud also decided to attend the Saturday morning meeting in Detroit.[20]

What ensued caused significant internal tension at the newspaper—and helped protect Milliken from the controversy. Milliken's representatives, Lindemer and Dykhouse, began the meeting by saying they needed to have all the information at the newspaper's disposal so that the governor could make a decision on whether to dump Damman from the ticket, as Stroud's editorial had suggested. Milliken had scheduled a news conference for later that day—the final Saturday before the balloting—in order to announce the choice. The reporters replied that they had published everything they knew in the October 31 article, and Stroud said he had based his editorial on what the reporters had written. It was a critical admission. Luedtke told the CJR that once Milliken's attorneys knew the paper had printed everything it knew, "they knew they had the story coldcocked."[21]

Lindemer and Dykhouse set out to rebut the story. They pointed out, among other things, that Damman had taken his seat on the Troy City Commission two weeks after the adoption of the Troy master plan on March 31, 1969, and that his land investment company had acquired most of its holdings after the master plan became final. This seemed to weaken significantly the newspaper's case that Damman had a conflict of interest.[22] Reporters Tyson and Anderson did not directly attempt to defend the original allegation—in part because they didn't understand the meeting to be a forum for doing so. Instead, they thought the meeting was "to be that of a press conference: Listen to the visitors' story, record it for the next day's paper, and leave."[23] But editor Luedtke believed their failure to rebut the facts presented by Lindemer and Dykhouse had seriously undermined the validity of the newspaper's allegation.

In a second meeting begun immediately after the first among Lindemer, Dykhouse, *Free Press* editorial page editor Stroud and his second-in-command, David Cooper, Milliken's men persuaded Stroud to back down on his call for Damman to step aside. The "highly emotional" meeting, in which Lindemer was said to have broken into tears, delivered all that Milliken could have asked. At his news conference, the CJR later said, he was "highly selective," capitalizing on ambiguities in the *Free Press* article. The governor said all land purchases made by Damman's partnership "within the boundaries of the City Center Plan were made after that plan became public knowledge."[24] What Milliken didn't say—and may not have known—was that a separate study had come before the Troy City Commission after Damman became a member involving the potential downzoning of land his company owned and that the commission had rejected the downzoning, averting a potential financial loss to Damman's firm. The *Free Press* would not confirm this on its news pages until November 20.

On the Sunday before the election, *Free Press* editor Stroud officially backed down on his earlier editorial, saying that his earlier conclusion was "not in our judgment supported by the facts at hand." In the article covering Milliken's defense of Damman, Luedtke inserted a note, saying, "At this time, we have no evidence that Damman actually used his knowledge or his influence for personal profit. If our stories implied otherwise, that implication—so far as we know—is inaccurate."[25]

The *Free Press* reporters were outraged, feeling that they had been undercut by the newspaper's management. "One reporter got so angry after the Sunday 'skinback' that he rammed his fist into the wall, breaking a knucklebone. A macabre joke circulated in the newsroom was that 'the editorial writers had better ride the elevator using the buddy system,'" the CJR said.

The newspaper's de facto retraction of its editorial and the news article, which had portrayed Damman as an "albatross" from which Milliken would have to free himself, probably worked to the incumbent's benefit beyond simply removing a negative; some voters may have felt that the highly ethical Milliken had been sabotaged by last-minute reporting that turned out to be unfounded. But, as the CJR observed, one reason for the eleventh-hour story was that Damman had refused to release his financial records to the reporters until very late in the campaign. Meanwhile, Milliken was not above using his warm personal relationship with *Free Press* editor Stroud to suggest that the newspaper had been off-base and to urge the extraordinary hearing Milliken's aides received the Saturday before the election. One of the lessons the CJR cited for journalists was: "Never turn your back on a politician wearing an albatross."[26]

Freed from the taint of a potentially corrupt running mate, Milliken won the following Tuesday by a 114,000-vote margin over Levin, garnering 52.2 percent of the vote. Democratic secretary of state Richard Austin won reelection by 1,025,000 votes and Democratic attorney general Frank Kelley by a million. Defeated for a second time by Milliken, Levin, accompanied by his wife, swallowed the bitter pill with grace, going to the governor's headquarters to shake his hand. "We did have a respect for each other after those campaigns," Levin said.[27]

Coming in the midst of a maelstrom for Republicans statewide and nationally, Milliken's was "an immense personal victory," the *Detroit News* said. Voters had rejected his stand on ballot questions regarding the sales tax exemption for food and prescription drugs (which they approved) and a $1.1 billion mass transit bond (which they rejected) "and battered the candidates of his party—but they did so after they voted for the man at the top of the ticket—Bill Milliken . . . Milliken's successful re-election campaign will propel him onto the national political stage from which so many familiar figures were swept in yesterday's elections," the *News* added.[28] Stroud of the *Free Press* called the win "a remarkable personal achievement. The people have shown great confidence in him."[29]

In its next-day postmortem on the election, the *News* quoted some of nearly 100 voters it had interviewed as they emerged from polling places in the Detroit metropolitan area. "I voted for Milliken because he's the best governor we've ever had," said Tiffany Bates of Warren.

All 20 voters interviewed in Bloomfield Hills' First Precinct said they voted for Milliken. Each said the charges against Damman, Milliken's running mate, had no influence at all on their vote . . . Evidence in nearly every precinct studied by *The News* indicated that Milliken was virtually immune from the charges that swirled about his running mates and his party.[30]

But Milliken was not undamaged. When the *Free Press* essentially reaffirmed its original charges with new and more damning facts on November 20, the issue became whether to permit Damman to take the oath of office on the following New Year's Day. For a time, Milliken was mum on that subject.[31] The relationship he and Damman might have forged as they worked together in the Capitol was permanently undermined. Although Damman was ultimately cleared of any statutory wrongdoing, he never emerged as a force in state politics again.

Both Milliken and his aides never forgave Damman for the near-disastrous embarrassment. Milliken later said that his running mate "should have disclosed the allegations at the time I asked him to run." Braithwaite remembers joining Weeks at the breakfast at which the offer of the lieutenant governorship was informally tendered. Noting that Damman at the time seemed a sound choice because "he had good manners, a moderate voting record, and a personality that seemed like [Milliken's]," she said that, over breakfast, "Innumerable times I asked the same question I always asked. Any skeletons in your closet? Anything that someone could make to look like a skeleton? Anything public or private that someone could whip up that would be embarrassing to you or us?" The answer from Damman, she said, was negative.[32] By the time of the next gubernatorial campaign in 1978, "Milliken stopped communicating with Damman and quietly and surgically removed him from consideration."[33] Milliken said of Damman, "He was never able to fit into my administration. It may have been my fault. I could have done better."[34]

Indeed, he and his team could have. By failing to investigate Damman's background more thoroughly, they had put Milliken's impeccable personal reputation at risk in the climactic year of the Watergate corruption scandal. But Milliken and his aides had also shown an extraordinary deftness—even ruthlessness—first in pressuring the *Free Press* to essentially recant its reporting and editorial before the election, and, second, in ultimately cutting Damman loose, leaving him to drift through four years as lieutenant governor virtually on his own. For those who thought of Milliken as merely "a nice guy," his ability to survive politically in a national year of disaster for Republicans provided a lesson.

13

ONE MORE TIME

IN THE 1970s, Michigan's newspapers and radio and TV stations devoted considerable resources to coverage of the state Capitol. All three major Detroit television stations had Lansing bureaus with several reporters; by the late 1990s, the stations had eliminated them. The intensity of Lansing coverage meant that the most casual speculation about faraway political trends and candidacies could find newspaper space or television or radio time. By early 1976, only 16 months after his second reelection and more than two years before his next campaign, the future political plans of Governor William Milliken were a hot topic.

"Bill Milliken is giving serious consideration to running for governor again," reported Robert Longstaff of the Booth Newspapers' Lansing bureau in March 1976.[1] He added, "Now starting his eighth year as governor, Milliken has learned how to use some of the powers of the office to help him become an 'activist chief executive' . . . What it all means is that Milliken is enjoying being governor. He's comfortable with the job."

Longstaff cited as reasons to believe in Milliken's 1978 candidacy his increasing control over patronage, which gave him policy-making influence over state highways, natural resources management, and civil service practices. Although the state's 1963 Constitution has increased the powers of the governor, it left in place numerous boards and commissions whose members served staggered terms, prolonging the power of his predecessors and the independence—or defiance—of some key state agencies. "It just has taken him seven years to fill key slots in state government with officials who are intensely loyal to him," Longstaff wrote.[2]

Much closer to the decision time for a 1978 campaign, *Detroit Free Press* columnist Frank Angelo reported that Milliken was proud of his high level of personal approval in state opinion surveys. "It makes him feel pretty good since, he insists, that fact will help him when he's making his decision about the future," Angelo wrote.[3] Milliken was clearly pleasing to the columnist, who described him as "the sort of person who seems continually interested in people and what's happening around him. He listens. He asks questions. He probes and one is taken with his warmth and approach to life."

One reporter thought he saw a clue to Milliken's intentions in the late summer of 1977, when "a film crew hired by his press secretary . . . made a visit to a Ford assembly plant that looked like the start of a campaign."[4] Although the press secretary, Al Sandner, denied that the filming of Milliken shaking hands with auto workers and inspecting 1978 Ford Mustangs was intended for political use, speculation began to grow that Milliken was going to run for a third full term because, in part, he was "the mainstay in a state capital dominated by Democrats."[5]

But, although there was no reason to doubt Milliken's enjoyment of the job and his personal popularity, he was genuinely undecided about whether to seek an unprecedented third four-year term in the job—which, if completed, would make his nearly 14 years in office the longest of any Michigan chief executive, surpassing the 12 years that G. Mennen Williams had held the job. Williams's final two-year term had tarnished his reputation and delivered a fatal blow to his hopes for a presidential bid as he fought legislative Republicans to an impasse on the state budget, resulting in a payless payday for state employees.

Some of Milliken's aides wondered whether it was truly a good thing for one man and his team to run the state government for so long. "Any Administration gets old and tired after a while. You can run out of energies and ideas," said appointments director Joyce Braithwaite-Brickley a quarter century later. "There was some real hard thinking about what to do."[6] Milliken had never lost an election, and some wondered whether he should push his luck. Adding to the reasons for pondering a new role, Democrat Jimmy Carter took the presidency in 1976, significantly reducing the clout Milliken had enjoyed with Michiganian Gerald Ford in the White House. Michigan's economy was recovering from the steep slump of the 1975 recession, and Milliken had the opportunity to go out on a high note.

On the other hand, polling for the Republicans suggested that Milliken was still a favorite among Michigan voters. Milliken had beaten Democrat William Fitzgerald, a likely opponent, 56 to 32 percent in a hypothetical matchup and had a 63 percent approval rating with voters. The only discordant numbers were his 24 percent disapproval rating—optimal for most politicians but unusually high for Milliken—and a finding that 65 percent of voters disapproved of the state's handling of the PBB contamination crisis, with 23 percent blaming Milliken and 23 percent the chemical's manufacturers.[7]

The internal debate crystallized in October 1977 when Milliken and top aides George Weeks and Joyce Braithwaite took a side trip after a meeting of Republican governors in Franconia Notch, New Hampshire. Traveling through the mountains and meadows of New Hampshire on their way to Boston, they discussed Milliken's future, using as a basis a six-page memo dubbed "The Notch Manifesto" that Braithwaite and Weeks had authored at Milliken's request on the last night of the meeting.[8]

Largely penned by Braithwaite on a restaurant place mat, the manifesto outlined three courses for Milliken: run for reelection; run for a U.S. Senate seat about to be vacated, it appeared, by incumbent Republican Robert Griffin; or retire. It is likely, though, that only retirement or reelection were seriously considered. As Milliken himself repeatedly told reporters about seeking election to federal office, "I don't have the fever."[9]

The manifesto, which was discussed at length in a subsequent *Detroit Free Press* article, listed far more impressive reasons for running for reelection than for a Milliken retirement. Among the "pros" for reelection were "a good record on which to run," "unfinished business," "more national impact as [senior] Gov.," and "Lack of Dem heavyweight opponent at present." On the retirement ledger, positives included "new life" and the "opportunity for privacy," while "cons" were "too soon to quit (age and unfulfilled potential)," "Public and Party need your leadership," and the lack of specific alternative career options.[10]

While he mulled over his options, Republicans called on Milliken to run again—and since some of the voices belonged to his associates that was likely not a wholly spontaneous development. "The heart and soul of this party is still Bill Milliken," said longtime friend, state Republican Party chairperson William McLaughlin. Elford Cederburg, a U.S. representative, said Milliken's candidacy was essential because his victory would enable Republicans to block Democratic reapportionment plans for the legislature and the state's congressional seats after the 1980 census. House minority leader Dennis Cawthorne said Milliken should run because "the governor's office holds the key to all the patronage." And the *Detroit Free Press* said, "All this places pressure on Milliken not to turn his back on people who have supported him for more than a decade in Michigan politics and not to let his party down in time of crisis."[11]

Despite Milliken's lack of ambition to live on the Potomac, the Senate alternative wasn't entirely hypothetical. In April 1977, Robert Griffin had announced his retirement, and Milliken's longtime Traverse City ally wanted the governor to run, arguing that he would be the strongest candidate to serve as his replacement. But, just as he would four years later when he decided not to seek reelection to a fourth full term as governor, Milliken took a long walk at the tip of the Old Mission Peninsula with his West Highland terrier, Mac, on November 13, 1977. After an hour's hike, he returned home with a decision not to run for the Senate and to defer consideration of a reelection campaign. A dismayed Griffin began thinking about reversing his retirement decision.[12]

Milliken aide Braithwaite weighed in with a personal note as the Millikens headed off on a Caribbean vacation in January 1978: "I hope you understood my explanation that I feel this is a very personal decision of yours and something I did not feel I could or should interfere with. It should not be construed as either a dimming interest in your political future or a lack of belief in your ability to win. I do believe you could win, [though] I also believe the campaign would be the toughest and possibly the most bitter we've ever had."[13]

In early February 1978—a mere six months before the statewide primary election and nine months before the general election—Milliken decided to run again for office. According to the *Free Press,* the decision came over the dinner table with his wife at the governor's residence on Tuesday, February 7. By that account, the two said, "Shall we do this?

Finally, we said this can be done."[14] The news article gave no reason for Milliken's decision. Another, perhaps apocryphal, account suggests that Milliken was unwilling to relinquish the office to "the immature Democratic standard bearer to be," state senator William Fitzgerald. A brash lawmaker from the Detroit area, Fitzgerald had briefly headed the state Senate Democratic caucus, but he was not well liked by members of either party. Milliken, this account had it, had not wanted to run again and almost resented the necessity.[15]

The resolution of two more question marks on the 1978 ballot had differing overtones. Once he had decided to run, Milliken wanted to woo James H. Brickley, his former lieutenant governor, back to the number-two spot. Relations with his lieutenant governor since 1975, James Damman, had not warmed after the controversy over Damman's ethics in Troy on the eve of the 1974 election. Damman was never seriously considered to be Milliken's running mate for a second time.[16]

Brickley, who had become president of Eastern Michigan University, was a natural choice for a number of reasons. According to Keith Molin, who had managed Milliken's 1970 campaign (when Brickley had appeared on the ticket) and became a cabinet agency head under the governor, Milliken and Brickley shared "a common vision of what the role of government should be, a common agenda in terms of public policy, a common approach to problem solving, a common tendency to minimize partisanship" and "they trusted each other."[17] At a hastily arranged meeting at an Ann Arbor hotel on February 8, 1978, the two men conferred. "When they parted, another part of the ticket had slipped into place," the *Free Press* reported. While Milliken had promised nothing, the understanding was that Brickley would get the governor's support in a campaign to be his successor whenever Milliken chose to step down. Once Brickley made it clear he had no "skeletons" in his personal closet that would cause Milliken embarrassment, the announcement of Brickley as his running mate was assured.

The method of announcement displayed Milliken's impish sense of humor—and good judgment about how to make his selection a major news story. Before the news conference on February 10 at which Milliken would announce his candidacy and choice of a candidate for lieutenant governor, the governor's staff gave no clue as to who the latter would be. More than a quarter century later, Milliken enjoyed the memory of how he surprised Capitol reporters. So did one of the reporters, Tim Skubick.

> The usual drill when a ticket is announced is for the two candidates to walk in together. It makes a good picture and that's what we expected. Instead, Governor Milliken walked in alone. He couldn't contain his grin as he knew he had us right where he wanted us . . . still guessing who his choice would be.
>
> Milliken announced that he would leave the room and return with his running mate. Out the door he goes. He stayed out in the hallway for what seemed like five minutes. Back inside the news conference room reporters are going bonkers, names are still flying through the room when Milliken returns with . . . Jim Brickley.
>
> "I wish I would have had a camera to get the expression on your face, Tim," Milliken would reveal years after the fact. He had pulled it off. He called it one of the most rewarding moments of his political life. He had beaten us at our game. Nobody had guessed Brickley, but there he was back for another shot at being [lieutenant] governor.[18]

Milliken was delighted to get Brickley back. "He was a man of high integrity, great background and experience, genuineness and compassion. He had so many fine human and intellectual qualities. I felt extremely fortunate to persuade him to come back a second time to serve with me. As he once said, 'No one grows up dreaming of being Lieutenant Governor.'"[19] He said he considered Brickley his best appointment as governor.

There were unhappy faces in the Republican Party, however, when Milliken concurred with Griffin's decision to reverse course a few days later and run for a third term in the U.S. Senate. Although Milliken assumed the incumbent Griffin would be the strongest candidate, his return to the ticket forced U.S. representative Phil Ruppe, an Upper Peninsula Republican who had a sometimes tense relationship with Milliken, to drop his candidacy for the seat. Ultimately, Ruppe retired from Congress and Democrat Carl Levin defeated Griffin, in part by citing the Republican's earlier lack of interest in the Senate job. An aide to Ruppe, Paul Hillegonds—who would later become Speaker of the State House—said that he was "disgruntled at what amounted to an unusual power play by Milliken."[20] Milliken's management of party politics for the Senate seat revealed a rarely displayed streak of authoritarianism at odds with his nice-guy image.

The politically adroit and assertive Braithwaite was named Milliken's campaign manager, making her the second woman to run a Michigan gubernatorial campaign.[21] In effect, however, it was her second campaign in the role, as she had assumed many of the campaign manager's responsibilities in 1974 while never claiming the title. Although she didn't officially assume the post until late August, *Detroit Free Press* columnist Hugh McDiarmid said it was a formality: "At that time, she will become his campaign manager in title as well as fact. And it's about time."[22] McDiarmid described her credentials as unswerving loyalty to Milliken and a ribald sense of humor and passion for politics that contrasted nicely with Milliken's stately demeanor.

> Who else, in the prim and tidy world of Milliken, would leave a sign on her office door reading, "The person in this room is ready to be serviced?" Or hang from her bookcase the printed admonition, "Get out, goddammit, I'm making six judges today"?
>
> No wonder that William C. Marshall, the outspoken state AFL-CIO [American Federation of Labor–Congress of Industrial Organizations] president, once said of her, "I like old Joyce, even if she is the Dragon Lady."

As McDiarmid and others noted, Braithwaite also had a keen strategic mind and the ability to organize and discipline a major campaign.

At times, Milliken's campaign persona tested the credulity of reporters and columnists, who saw him as refined and above the fray. Tossing a baseball to a state trooper in front of wire service photographers in April 1978 as a staged warmup to throwing out the opening pitch for the Detroit Tigers the next day , Milliken generated an image that appeared in many of the state's daily newspapers. *Free Press* columnist McDiarmid mocked the photo opportunity as the campaign's effort to show "that Bill Milliken, despite occasional mutterings to the contrary, is no pansy, no fop, no popinjay masquerading as a man of the people."[23] Behind this calculation, he said, was a fear within the governor's circle of advisers that he was "walking a fine line of public acceptance." Voters, he speculated, might turn on Milliken if they began thinking of him as aloof from their concerns and ways of life.

One More Time

But Milliken's personal popularity, it seemed for most of the campaign, was never really at risk. The Democratic primary contest winner in the race for governor, Fitzgerald, accentuated Milliken's virtues of civility and calm. Fitzgerald's sniping at Milliken over the business climate, the PBB controversy, and alleged failures of leadership attracted unfavorable media attention. And Milliken felt free to fight back.

At the state GOP convention in Detroit that August, Milliken exploited one of Fitzgerald's chief weaknesses, his ousting by Democratic colleagues as head of the state Senate majority caucus in 1977. "I would ask you, senator," he taunted, "if you can't lead 38 people, can you really lead more than nine million people?" He said the campaign was "shaping up as a classic contrast between what is preached and what is practiced."[24]

Milliken also taunted Fitzgerald at a joint appearance before the Economic Club of Detroit in September. After joking that "I'm still a nice guy," Milliken said Fitzgerald was "dead wrong about some of the things you're saying about yourself, about me, and about Michigan." He pointed out that Fitzgerald had missed the final Senate votes on two economic development measures for which he claimed credit in his campaign literature. Milliken's team distributed a document to the Economic Club members entitled "Campaign Myths and Realities," indicting Fitzgerald's misrepresentations. Fitzgerald was left to play on Milliken's civility, complaining, "Pleasantness isn't enough to protect public health and safety or [encourage] economic growth."[25]

Milliken's strengths in addition to a winning personal image were considerable. Detroit mayor Coleman Young, a lifelong ardent Democrat, let it be known that Republican Milliken's generous treatment of the city should not go unrewarded at the polls, undermining a traditional base of Democratic votes in the governor's race. Even more extraordinary was the tacit backing of organized labor for Milliken's reelection. In a career unusual in its appeal to Democratic constituencies, Milliken's 1978 support from labor represents the pinnacle of his ability to disarm potential opponents.

Keith Molin, the Milliken's 1970 campaign manager, became his Department of Labor director in 1975. Molin's agency had just acquired responsibility for administration of the state's Occupational Safety and Health Act—a sore point with employers but a long-sought goal of organized labor—and the spending of millions of dollars of job-training money under the federal Comprehensive Employment and Training Act. This could have created sharp conflicts between labor and Milliken's administration, but Molin said the governor's "style became an asset," defusing tensions.

> At no time did he ever do anything other than counsel in the many strategy sessions and policy debates that became a major part of each day's deliberations. "Keith, I trust you'll find a way to be patient and insure that the ideas and concerns of labor, including labor and management, are heard and considered before a decision is made."[26]

Thus, Milliken won points as a Republican for simply listening to leaders that most Republicans would ignore. As early as his first gubernatorial candidacy in 1970, Milliken had demonstrated a rare ability to get along with labor leaders. August "Gus" Scholle, president of the state AFL-CIO at the time, called Milliken "a very nice guy. I respect him and I'm sorry he's in the Republican Party." Scholle did not say he would support Milliken but left no doubt he liked the man. Asked whether his union would back Democrat Sander Levin, an anonymous labor leader quoted in the same newspaper report said, "What's wrong with the man in the front office now?"[27] Communicating openly with labor leaders throughout his career in Lansing, Milliken had also voted or worked occasionally for labor's positions on critical issues, building a warm relationship.

Milliken's best friend in organized labor turned out to be William Marshall, who became head of the state AFL-CIO after Scholle. Marshall and Braithwaite initially clashed over Marshall's desire to get an appointment from Milliken to a Democratic seat on the state Transportation Commission. Braithwaite took umbrage at some remarks Marshall made about women and dismissed him as a "loud, uncivilized labor boss."[28]

He was that and more. Tim Skubick said of Marshall, "If you called central casting to send over a typical labor union leader, you'd get Billy Boy, as I called him." But Skubick also noted that Marshall had risen from being a bus driver in the South and had experienced segregation from the front of the bus, later becoming a champion "of the little person, black or white, in the back."[29]

The relationship between the Milliken camp and Marshall warmed. In 1977, Braithwaite convinced Republican Party chairperson William McLaughlin to invite Marshall, a member of the Democratic National Committee, to speak at the state Republican Leadership Conference on Mackinac Island. The appearance of a labor chief at the GOP meeting was unprecedented in its 22-year history. Braithwaite and Marshall "made quite a production" out of Marshall's appearance. Wearing a three-piece gray sharkskin suit and joking that if he was going to appear among Republican bankers and loan sharks he ought to look like one, Marshall invited Republicans to woo labor votes.

"All Democrats are not necessarily pro-labor, nor are all Republicans anti-labor," Marshall said. Milliken and Marshall were "beaming as they left the luncheon," despite a few murmurs from audience members that they did not need to hear from a Democrat.[30]

"After a very shaky start, Bill Marshall and I became the closest of friends," Braithwaite said. "In 1978, Bill was more appalled than I was at the candidacy of Bill Fitzgerald."[31]

Marshall and labor did little to assist Fitzgerald. Capitol reporter Skubick guessed that "Marshall voted for Milliken and maybe even helped him raise some cash quietly behind the scenes."[32] The Teamsters Union and some AFL-CIO chiefs in fact produced an election eve tabloid headlined, "Milliken: Labor's Best Choice." Although Marshall made a show of denouncing the tabloid and Democratic Secretary of State Richard Austin launched an inquiry into an alleged disbursement of cash from the Milliken campaign to the Teamsters to pay for the tabloid—a probe that ended inconclusively—Milliken appointed Marshall to the state Transportation Commission in April 1979.[33]

Women's groups, which were typically in the Democratic corner, shunned the anti-abortion Fitzgerald in favor of the pro-choice Milliken. An organization, Democratic Women for Milliken, was formed to back the incumbent. Fitzgerald had outraged the activists by saying he supported a cutoff of state funds for elective abortions for disadvantaged women, even if it jeopardized all health care services for the poor. "There's nothing wrong with Bill Fitzgerald having strong religious convictions against abortion," said one female union official. "We can respect that, but what we can't respect is his making political hay at the expense of poor welfare mothers in Michigan."[34] Fitzgerald's choice of Olivia Maynard, a pro-choice Democratic Party official from Flint, as his running mate failed to win over the activists. Buttons began to sprout with the slogan "I'm a Democrat, but . . ."

Abandoned by many of his traditional allies, Fitzgerald became increasingly strident. Trailing badly in the polls, he resorted to the conventional tactic of accusing Milliken of ducking debates "because I'd eat him alive."[35] Milliken, meanwhile, took the traditional posture of an incumbent ahead in the polls by agreeing to one televised debate and several "joint appearances" with Fitzgerald. These failed to produce a breakthrough for the Democrat.

Going down to the wire, Fitzgerald decided to use the issue that put Milliken in the most unfavorable light—PBB contamination. Angry constituents had hung the governor and Attorney General Frank Kelley in effigy when Milliken visited the site of a burial pit for PBB-contaminated cows in Mio the previous May. And surveys continued to show voter concern about the issue.

Fitzgerald's campaign produced an ad based on animal studies showing that mice fed large amounts of the chemical had produced offspring with defects, including some born with their brains outside their skulls. "Want to know the truth about PBB in Michigan?" asked the commercial's narrator. "Then listen to the people who know." Three voices then listed "symptoms" of PBB contamination, including "loss of hair, memory loss, blindness, liver cancer, birth defects, the brain developing outside of the head, and genetic mutations." A fourth voice then concluded, "95 percent of the people in Michigan have been contaminated with PBB. Everybody is going to get a case of this stuff before it's all over."[36] A significant problem with the ad was that no such problems had yet been documented in humans, and animal tests are not always indicative of human health risks.

The response to the ad was sharp but not in the way Fitzgerald had hoped. Campaign manager Braithwaite said that on the day the ad debuted, she "called the top of our campaign team into my office at the headquarters and said, 'Make a mark today on your calendars. This race is over.' It was. All the subsequent crap about the race closing was just that."[37] Milliken hammered the ad in a news release, calling it "a cruel hoax" and "reckless." He pointed out that as a state senator Fitzgerald had not supported Milliken's effort to toughen standards for PBB in food. "There is no research to justify your exceeding the bounds of decency and good taste and resorting to such disgraceful scare tactics," he said.[38] Further undermining Fitzgerald's case, the producer of the radio spot, Charles Guggenheim, told a reporter, "If the ad gives the impression that there were people born with their brains outside their heads . . . then perhaps the ad should be changed."[39]

The *Bay City Times* called it "the cheapest shot of the '78 political campaign," and the *Midland Daily News* called it "grossly misleading."[40] In an editorial entitled "His Own Worst Enemy?" the *Detroit News* said that Fitzgerald "had an issue but fumbled it. His hysterical ad victimized both the public and Gov. Milliken and gave the governor legitimate reason to write a devastating critique of the challenger's tactics."[41] Instead of undercutting Milliken, the advertisement reinforced the image of Fitzgerald as lacking the maturity and judgment needed in a governor.

There was one minor scare. Survey results released in mid-October 1978 by the *Detroit News* made it appear that the race was becoming closer, with Milliken up only 4 percent among likely voters, down from 12 percent in a previous poll. And among all voters, including those less likely to turn out, Milliken actually trailed by a margin of 47 to 45 percent, with 8 percent undecided.[42] The newspaper said the result showed a "dramatically tightening" race, which turned out not to be the case.

But both Milliken's internal polls and those of the *News* showed something remarkable. While continuing to fare relatively well for a Republican in southeastern Michigan, particularly in Democratic Wayne County, Milliken was increasingly unpopular in heavily Republican outstate Michigan. "The Governor was having problems outstate. It was different things in different places," said party chief McLaughlin. "In Grand Rapids, it was a gas tax increase. In Saugatuck and Holland, a new prison. Muskegon was down on him for support of state-funded abortions for the poor and throughout farm country, he was on the defensive over the PBB problem."[43]

Hillegonds, the moderate former Ruppe aide running in 1978 for the State House from the Saugatuck area—one of the most heavily Republican districts in the state—said his voters had by then "gone sour" on Milliken. "Increasingly the district was seeing him as, in their view, a Detroit Democrat," Hillegonds said.[44] After more than two full terms in office, the negatives of incumbency were starting to add up for Milliken in areas that had once reflexively supported him as a Republican.

In the end, the disenchantment of conservative Republicans with Milliken did nothing to detract from his 1978 victory. He smashed Fitzgerald by the greatest margin of his three gubernatorial wins, running up a margin of nearly 400,000 votes, winning more than 56 percent of the vote. At 8:02 P.M., just two minutes after the polls closed, NBC television projected Milliken as the winner, making this election night the shortest and least suspenseful of his career in statewide office. A minute later he received the news while dining with his campaign team at Detroit's London Chop House. Initially disbelieving after his two previous close contests, Milliken soon delighted in the win but had to wait until after midnight to declare victory because of a late concession by Fitzgerald.

Outraged by Fitzgerald's opposition to reproductive choice and other issues important to progressive women, many Democrats split their tickets that year to vote for Milliken. Said Lana Pollack, who later became a state senator, "Even though the top of our ticket went down in flames, there were no tears being shed at the Ann Arbor Democratic election night party in 1978. We'd just elected Dr. Ed Pierce, a home town favorite, as the first Democratic Senator to come out of this college town in any living memory. No one seemed to even notice that Democrat Bill Fitzgerald had lost until someone asked, 'Who'd you vote for, for governor?' I broke the awkward silence by saying, 'Milliken, I split my ticket.' A rapid ripple of 'me too' passed around our circle of Democrats, and then worked its way across the room—especially among the women. It was a combination of trust in Milliken and disgust with Fitzgerald, who'd been stupidly and openly sexist during the campaign."[45]

Even as Milliken scored a huge win, the candidate above him on the ticket, incumbent senator Griffin, lost by more than 100,000 votes to Carl Levin. The "dream ticket" described by the *Free Press* earlier in the year had yielded a major loss as well as Milliken's greatest victory. Ruppe blasted Milliken as "selfish" for not having campaigned aggressively enough for Griffin, a charge condemned by Milliken's aides, who said the Upper Peninsula Republican was angry because he had been bumped off the ticket.[46]

Most postelection reviews were more favorable. "Milliken's Quiet Style Wins the Day," ran a headline in the *Detroit News*.[47] J. F. ter-Horst, a longtime U.S. Capitol reporter and former news secretary for

President Gerald Ford, pointed out that Milliken had gotten 25 percent of the vote in some African American precincts in Detroit and 40 percent or more in some ethnic neighborhoods. "To beat President Carter in 1980, the Republican Party will need a candidate who, personally and politically, mirrors the same vote-getting qualities of quiet intellect, morality, public credibility and leadership skills as Milliken . . ." terHorst said.[48] That this assessment did not prove true does not detract from the compliment paid to Milliken's unique appeal to voters in a state then heavily Democratic.

Looking back on the campaign from the perspective of a quarter century, campaign manager Braithwaite-Brickley said self-deprecatingly, "1978 was a breeze, holding on to what we had and waiting for Fitzgerald to shoot himself in the butt, which he did even sooner than I expected . . . By 1978 we had King Bill, and any fool off the streets could have successfully managed that campaign." Millken's personal warmth and manners contrasted well with the "smarty-pants Fitzgerald," she said.[49]

Fitzgerald's assessment four years later, when Milliken retired, was that the longtime governor had failed to offer strong leadership on issues important to business and labor because he had been "so concerned about his political image." Like opponents Zolton Ferency and Sander Levin, however, Fitzgerald conceded that Milliken's brightness, competence, and civility had made him popular with voters.[50] Milliken had come off as especially appealing when compared to the abrasive Fitzgerald.

Yet even in victory there were signs of trouble. The same news pages that highlighted Milliken's win also reported on the passage of a statewide ballot proposition, Proposal E. Michigan voters approved it by more than 100,000 votes. Known as the Headlee amendment after one of its primary authors, insurance executive Richard Headlee of Farmington Hills, the constitutional change made it harder for both state and local governments to raise taxes. It was part of a nationwide trend in which voters in 12 of 16 states approved tax limitations and cuts.[51] The stage was now set for some of the most difficult budget choices of Milliken's career and a new era in the politics of a state and nation that for over 20 years had supported a steadily growing government.

14

MAKING PAINFUL CHOICES

GOVERNOR WILLIAM G. MILLIKEN took the oath of the state's highest elective office for the fourth time on January 1, 1979. The jubilation that had accompanied his first two inaugurals in 1971 and 1975 gave way to a more somber mood now. A Detroit newspaper reporter called the ceremony in front of the Capitol "frugal, solemn—at times even funereal."[1] Peter B. Fletcher, a longtime Milliken associate, told state agency chiefs in the front row of the audience to smile "and not look so solemn," the newspaper reported.

One reason for the dulled mood was petulance on the part of Democrats, who resented the manner in which Milliken had chosen to be sworn in. Instead of asking Michigan Supreme Court chief justice Thomas Giles Kavanagh, a Democrat, to administer the oath, he had turned to Detroit Common Pleas judge Jessie P. Slayton, an African American woman who had supported Milliken. "Democrats had complained privately that the inaugural program, which emphasized participation by a number of Detroit blacks, had been arranged for political advantage," the *Detroit Free Press* said.[2] That Milliken had such strong associations with African Americans and other constituencies typically associated with the Democrats frustrated his opponents. Democratic members of the Supreme Court and the Democratic secretary of state, Richard Austin, did not attend the ceremony.

Another reason for the tone of the inaugural was that it came at a time of changing attitudes in both Michigan and the progressive states about the size and scope of government and the burden of taxation. Michigan voters had not only reelected Milliken to a record third four-year term in November 1978 but had also voted to impose limits on state and local government taxes and spending through a constitutional amendment. Milliken sought to respond to that sentiment by citing "a new age of limits" in his address. "There is a growing realization in this country today that our physical resources are limited—that we live in a finite world with finite resources and we have a responsibility to use them carefully and wisely," he said.[3]

What none of the 450 or so people in the audience or Milliken knew was that Michigan was about to undergo its most punishing economic slump since the Great Depression. This was destined to be a near disaster for a state that had battled with a boom-and-bust economy pegged heavily to the fortunes of the domestic auto industry.

Millilken's first full term had begun with a "cash bind," in the words of one reporter. Just four years after the state's 1967 adoption of a 2.6 percent personal income tax, it was unable to match revenues with expenses, creating the prospect of $100 million in program cuts.[4] After months of impasse, in late 1971 Milliken and the legislature agreed on a 1 percent increase in the personal income tax as well as boosts in other levies.

The oil price shocks of the 1973 Middle East oil embargo delivered another blow to Milliken's stewardship of state government. As prices of gasoline at the pump tripled in late 1973 and 1974, American consumers turned to smaller, more fuel-efficient, and largely foreign made automobiles in record numbers, throwing tens of thousands of Michigan auto workers out of jobs and sending ripples of pain through the state's economy. Michigan's unemployment reached a record 549,000, a jobless rate of 12.5 percent, the highest of any major state.

In early 1975, the projected budget deficit—in a state constitutionally bound to produce balanced budgets—mushroomed from between $100 and $125 million to $180 million. Milliken sought to offer symbolic leadership by taking a 10 percent, or $4,200, pay cut for the remainder of the year, while withdrawing recommended pay hikes for more than 100 appointees to save another $400,000.[5]

As would happen in other budget crises and in other states, lawmakers and the governor tried to patch balanced budgets together with a variety of bookkeeping gimmicks as well as real cuts, hoping for a sudden recovery in the economy. In addition to across-the-board reductions equivalent to 4 percent in most state programs, Lansing decision makers talked about borrowing money from the $50 million Veterans Trust Fund and the $40 million Motor Vehicle Accident Fund. Falling personal and corporate tax revenues and swollen relief rolls dogged the state.

Struggling to protect the progressive government he had tried to build put a strain on Milliken. Education aide James Phelps remembered sitting in a Capitol conference room with his boss sometime in the mid-1970s when budget chief Gerald Miller entered the room and said, "Governor, we've just looked at the revenue estimates, and we have a deficit of $300 million." Phelps said Milliken's expression was first incredulous, then ashen, as he considered the cuts that would be necessary.[6]

But after that painful period state government continued to grow. From fiscal year 1971 to fiscal year 1976, the number of state employees rose from 47,286 to 57,856 or more than 22 percent. State general fund expenditures during the same time jumped from nearly $1.80 billion to $2.92 billion, or more than 65 percent. From 1976 to the state's peak in 1981, the size of state government grew by another 12,050 employees to 69,906, a five-year jump of almost 21 percent. And general fund spending rose another $1.9 billion to a 1980 peak of $4.77 billion, a four-year increase of 63 percent.[7] In good times, legislators and the governor used rising revenues to support new initiatives of a regulatory government; in bad times, they appropriated welfare payments and jobless benefits to support the social safety net.

The taxpayer outrage that had first manifested itself in California with the June 1978 landslide passage of Proposition 13—rolling back local property tax revenues by 53 percent—was not long in coming to Michigan.[8] Two competing tax limitation proposals appeared on the state's November 1978 ballot.

One seemed to articulate the gathering rage of middle-class taxpayers. Championed by Robert Tisch, the elected drain commissioner of Shiawassee County in 1976, the proposed Tisch Tax Limitation Amendment would have sharply rolled back both state and local taxes. "The Shiawassee drain commissioner quickly became a household word as he drove around the state in his 'Tischmobile,' which looked like the Flub-a-dub character on the old Howdy Doody kids show," said Capitol correspondent Tim Skubick. "The blue jeaned Bob Tisch was unpolished, unrefined, with an even greater tendency to pop off . . . a gangly, six foot something cusser from the back 40."[9] When he collected sufficient signatures to put his amendment on the ballot, startled Lansing policymakers scrambled to head it off with an alternative. One was waiting for them.

Authored by Richard Headlee, the conservative chief executive officer of the Alexander Hamilton Life Insurance Company in Bloomfield Hills, the alternative amendment was regarded as more moderate than Tisch's plan. It barred new so-called unfunded mandates, legal requirements on local governments that the legislature had imposed without providing revenues to pay for them; tied the growth of state spending to the rate of personal income growth; and capped tax revenues for both state and local governments.[10] Fighting to prevent the obliteration of the progressive programs for which he had fought since the 1960s, Milliken reluctantly endorsed the Headlee plan as the more responsible of the two alternatives. But it was clear his heart was not in it. "Apparently bowing to the inevitable," was how the *Detroit Free Press* described it.[11]

Defending his own efforts to limit spending and reform taxes, Milliken issued a "white paper" that downplayed the importance of the Headlee proposal while simultaneously endorsing it. But members of Milliken's own budget and tax policy team had privately opposed the measure; Milliken sided with his political advisers, who, in an election year, pointed out that most of his Democrat opponents and hundreds of other candidates for state office had endorsed the Headlee amendment. "Political leaders have an obligation to be responsive and not simply say, 'We know best,'" Milliken said, signaling his awareness of the growing nationwide tax revolt.[12] In November, voters approved Headlee by a margin of about 100,000 votes but rejected the Tisch proposal by more than 700,000.[13]

By the time Milliken began his third term, the "age of limits" to which he referred had become part of the state Constitution. It immediately changed some Lansing budgeting practices. It also gave long-term, high-visibility name recognition to a man who would bedevil Milliken's final term in office, Richard Headlee.

A Mormon—like Milliken's predecessor, George Romney, whom Headlee had supported in his 1967–68 campaign for the presidency—

Headlee would seek to become Milliken's successor. In the process, he aroused both fierce loyalty and animosity. After Headlee's death in 2004, conservative economist Patrick Anderson termed the tax fighter "a singular figure in Michigan history—one of a handful of people who remade Michigan in the latter half of the 20th Century." He added, "Limiting government was more than a slogan for Dick Headlee; it was a deeply-felt moral principle."[14] *Detroit Free Press* columnist and reporter Dawson Bell said Headlee was "a transformational figure in Michigan politics, involved in re-shaping the Republican Party from the moderate era of former Gov. William Milliken to the more conservative, tax averse generation that came to power in the 1990s."[15]

Moderates and progressives described Headlee's philosophy, and sometimes the man himself, in caustic terms. Although he would have choicer words for Headlee in 1982, in the long run Milliken's chief complaint about the Oakland County conservative was that he was unwilling to support a compassionate government. "Someone once said, 'Taxes pay for civilization.' The devices of government can be used to create opportunity, provide an orderly society in which people can feel safe in their town, and so much else. I see government in its broadest sense as a force for opportunity," Milliken said in summing up his vision of the public sector.[16]

Meanwhile, reporters loved Headlee, Skubick said. "He often engaged his mouth before he engaged his brain but he also spoke the truth as he saw it. Often his advisors cringed and wanted to sanitize his remarks. Headlee would not play along."[17] More flamboyant than the "Lansing politicians" he mocked, Headlee would stir Republican Party politics up as well in the final Milliken years.

The twin pressures of the Headlee amendment and a new petroleum price shock to the U.S. economy in late 1979 and 1980 turned the last years of the Milliken era into a seemingly endless round of budget cuts, forcing Milliken and the legislature to cut deeply into human services programs and other discretionary spending.

The recession that began in late 1979 worsened in 1980 and showed little sign of abating in 1981 and 1982. Reading Milliken's budget messages to the legislature during those three years suggests the scope of the state's fiscal problems. In 1980, Milliken noted that "our deteriorating economic situation this year also demanded a sharp modification in the budget development processes normally used. By mid-November, it was clear that the expenditure demands that I was initially inclined to support exceeded available revenues by at least $300 million . . . Indeed, the budget that I present to you today is the most constrained spending plan I have ever recommended."[18]

In 1981, Milliken noted that he had just signed the last of the year's spending bills, marking the end of "what for all of us was one of the most arduous and painful experiences we have ever shared . . . These actions were the result of economic forces largely beyond our control, and we can take no comfort from many of the choices we had to make . . . The decisions I asked you to support were as painful to propose as they were to accept."[19]

In 1982, Milliken optimistically predicted an economic recovery midway through the next fiscal year—one that didn't materialize. Looking back on the experience of the previous years, he said, "Never has Michigan's vulnerability to national economic fluctuations been so clearly demonstrated as in the past two years. Back-to-back national recessions have had a devastating effect on our economy, and have created depression-level unemployment in some parts of the state and substantial hardship for many Michigan families . . . Michigan's General Fund spending for the current fiscal year is 4.3 percent *below* what it was two years ago. At the same time, the federal budget, which has been described as extremely tight, is 24.2 percent *larger* now than it was two years ago."[20]

By the end of 1981, as he announced his decision to retire from office, the state's 12.5 percent unemployment rate and deep decline in revenues attracted the attention of the *Christian Science Monitor*.

> The cuts touch virtually every area in spending. Welfare benefits, for instance, are less than they were three years ago. And 20,000 Michigan residents have been removed from general assistance rolls altogether. All state park outdoor centers and most nature centers have been closed. Some 7,500 state workers have been let go through attrition and layoffs. In the state labor department alone, some 57 workers are currently adjusting to demotions and the lower salary scales that go with them.[21]

The newspaper reported that Milliken, ruling out tax increases to balance the budget, hoped the auto industry would rebound. Pointing

WILLIAM G. MILLIKEN

to his purchase of a compact car—a Mercury Lynx—Milliken said the craftsmanship that made the car would help rejuvenate the reputation of the auto industry. Milliken also predicted a change to a "less adversarial" stance in labor-management relations as a result of the state's near depression: "There will have to be more give and take. Unless we adjust and adapt to the new economic facts of life, we're not going to survive . . . Our auto industry isn't going to make it just doing business as usual."[22]

Instead of recovering, however, by early 1982 the state's economy had slumped further. In March, Milliken realized that despite $800 million in spending cuts already made for the fiscal year that was almost half over, the state still had a $400 million deficit. The new fiscal year, beginning October 1, would mark the onset of the government equivalent of balloon payments, as deferred expenses would have to be paid for, further inflating the deficit.

The difficulty of managing the state's finances was evident in a number of ways. Stephen Monsma, then a Democratic state senator from Grand Rapids, remembered Department of Management and Budget director Jerry Miller urging an appropriations committee to move the state's Medicaid program from a cash accounting basis, which violated standard accounting practices, to an accrual accounting basis. Monsma said:

> This would involve a one-time additional expenditure of, I think, one hundred million dollars or maybe even two hundred million. But Miller was persuasive and insistent, so the committee voted to go along with his urgings. But in the following weeks, and before the budget was finalized, the economic situation deteriorated and projected revenues were down. Therefore, a few weeks after having persuaded us to switch to accrual accounting for Medicaid, he came back to the committee and argued with equal passion and equal persuasiveness for going back to cash accounting! The committee meekly following his new recommendation and we went back to cash accounting, thereby "saving" over $100 million.[23]

Milliken remembers the winter of 1981–82 as one of the most difficult times of his tenure. "There were recommendations to cut very sharply in the areas of welfare and social services," he said later. He told

Making Painful Choices

George Weeks that the period was "clearly the most difficult, clearly the most painful, clearly the most wrenching time" of his 14 years in office.[24]

In a sober speech broadcast March 10, 1982, on statewide television and radio, Milliken laid out the grim facts.

> I am speaking to you because we face a crisis tonight in Michigan. It is a crisis that has been building for more than two years. And it is a crisis that, if not met forcefully and courageously, will cripple this state for years and years to come . . .
>
> The effects of the recession have included slumping auto sales that last month fell to the lowest level in 32 years, record high unemployment and welfare cases, record high interest rates which have increased state costs and jeopardized our economic recovery efforts, declining retail sales and other factors that have resulted in a sharp drop in anticipated revenue, and federal actions that have meant massive cuts in federal aid for Michigan . . .
>
> My duty as governor is to meet this crisis head-on, to prepare a responsible, realistic plan and then fight with all my resources to carry out that plan. During my State of the State message, after noting that so many other states had raised taxes in one way or another, I said, "I hope we again this year can avoid any general increases in taxes."
>
> We cannot. Hope has yielded to the reality of what the national economy has done to Michigan in the last two months.[25]

To address the budget crisis, Milliken proposed a mix of $450 million in new spending cuts and an increase of 0.7 percent in the state's personal income tax, boosting it from 4.6 to 5.3 percent. A portion of the increase would be earmarked to shore up the state's cash position and prevent the downgrading of its credit rating by Wall Street financiers. Beginning in 1983, a portion of the tax increase would be earmarked for roads, another for local schools, and the rest for state programs and further reinforcement of the state's cash flow.

A lame duck himself, Milliken was asking many legislators who would appear on the ballot in 1982 to cast a highly unpopular vote for higher taxes at the very time when many citizens were having trouble making ends meet. "Why is a governor who won't be in office after

December willing to swim upstream for an income tax increase?" asked the *Grand Rapids Press*. "Mostly because he believes sincerely that further budget cuts will be far more damaging to this state than a modest income tax hike."[26] The *Detroit Free Press* called Milliken's remedy "the unvarnished truth. The Legislature has to respond without blinking. There may be alternative answers. There are no easy alternative answers."[27]

A chorus of taxpayers and conservative legislators denounced Milliken's tax increase proposal. Democratic state senator Gilbert DiNello said he was "unalterably and vehemently opposed" to the income tax increase and called for additional budget cuts and more pay concessions from state employees. Referring to a vote in the state House on the tax increase just before Easter, DiNello called it "significant" that the vote came during "the very same time period that Judas betrayed Christ for 30 pieces of silver. History does indeed repeat itself, and Michiganians who pay income taxes were likewise betrayed by the power brokers in Lansing."[28] A letter writer to the *Detroit Free Press* blasted the "22 percent" increase in the income tax, urging the state to "balance its budget like a private individual who cuts his expenditures down to the level his income can support." House Republicans proposed $736.7 million in cuts they said would balance the budget without a tax increase, with steep reductions in revenue sharing to local governments, bigger cuts than Milliken proposed in aid to public schools, 10 days off without pay for all state employees, and large cutbacks in welfare.

Even moderate Republicans who were ordinarily allies of Milliken resented the shift from a posture of no tax increases. Representative Paul Henry of Grand Rapids said he would vote only for a temporary increase, and only after further cuts, and accused the governor of "serious misrepresentations" of the state's fiscal condition in the previous months. House Speaker Bobby Crim of Davison, a Democrat, said Michigan's "house of cards, financially, is just about to fall in on us. The governor is putting a finger in the dike, and I'm not sure it will do even that."[29]

To dramatize the urgency of the problem, Milliken announced on March 25 that he would work without pay for a week "in a symbolic show of commitment to solving the state's fiscal crisis," requiring the governor to sacrifice $1,346 of his annual salary. Democratic and Republican leaders in the legislature also gave up a week of pay and

Making Painful Choices

joined Milliken in asking state employees to make pay concessions. The governor said he would have to lay off 2,000 state employees in 1982 and 4,000 in 1983 if bargaining did not resume on the concessions.[30] Underscoring the state's fiscal problems, the March unemployment report from the federal government, released April 2, pegged Michigan's jobless rate at 16.1 percent, the highest percentage since the Department of Labor had begun collecting standardized data in 1970. The national rate was now 9 percent.[31]

While the legislature followed through on most of the cuts Milliken sought, tension over the income tax increase ran high in the election season. The governor trimmed the increase to a six-month temporary tax to meet opposition objections, but the 54 votes needed for passage were still not assured as the crucial session opened on April 8.[32] Democrats told Milliken's people that they would not support the temporary tax increase unless Republicans provided a respectable number of votes for it. The House, stalemated, ran an all-night session. Milliken personally lobbied for each vote needed to win passage.

Republican Edgar Geerlings of Muskegon, who had told Milliken he would support the tax increase but was now balking, left the House floor. The Milliken team turned to Paul Hillegonds, a moderate Republican House member from Allegan County, as the possible decisive GOP pro-tax vote. Hillegonds, who had bucked his constituents by adopting an anti-capital-punishment stance and supporting mandatory seat belt use, decided he could not further risk the wrath of his district. "This was one of the issues where I had to be representative of my district," he said.[33]

Still, Milliken, lobbying furiously for the income tax increase, asked to meet with Hillegonds in the early morning hours in the governor's Capitol office. The two men met privately. Milliken reminded Hillegonds that the state's bond rating was at risk if revenues were not found. "He said he wanted me to do the right thing, and he knew I knew what the right thing to do was." Hillegonds asked for 10 minutes to consider his position one last time.[34]

While outside the governor's office, Hillegonds encountered Republican Ralph Ostling, a Roscommon lawmaker with a secure seat who would vote for the increase. Ostling advised the promising young moderate not to support the increase and alienate his district. "He told me to go back and tell Milliken that I couldn't break the trust of my constituents." Hillegonds did so. When his second meeting with Milliken ended, the two men shook hands. "There were tears in his eyes, and there were tears in my eyes," Hillegonds said.[35]

Milliken worked on Republican members of the House from the Muskegon area. After Representative Mickey Knight initially opposed the tax increase, Milliken met with him. Knight asked Milliken to support a cross-lake ferry project of importance to Muskegon. According to the *Muskegon Chronicle,* "Knight got no promises, but Milliken's office did notify Muskegon County officials this morning that they would work on a last-ditch effort to get the Frankfort-based ferry *Viking* available for Muskegon-Milwaukee service this summer."[36] With that and other concessions, the Milliken team thought it had enough votes. Muskegon area Republicans, thinking they might be forced to run against each other in redrawn districts that fall, had made a pact to vote together either for or against the tax boost to avoid giving the others an advantage. All that was needed was the presence of Geerlings.

But he was no longer in the Capitol. "Come out, come out, wherever you are," said Matthew McNeely, a Detroit Democrat, who was presiding over the early morning session. House leaders sent State Police troopers, legislative aides, and others in search of Geerlings at about 5:30 A.M.

The manhunt turned up news that the Republican representative had retreated to his lodgings in Room 734 of the Plaza Hotel, across Capitol Avenue, to sleep. House minority leader William Bryant Jr. of Grosse Pointe Farms and Representative Donald Gilmer of Augusta, with the assistance of state troopers, entered Geerlings's room and tried to wake him. With television cameras and reporters in tow, Milliken crossed the street, entered the elevator, and rode to Geerlings's floor. As Milliken remembered it:

> I knocked on the door, and he opened it and was standing in his underwear. I felt sorry for him. I reminded him of his commitment, and he acknowledged it in front of the cameras. Within 10 or 15 minutes, he showed up on the House floor and cast the vote.[37]

Milliken's legislative liaison, Robert Law, called the scene "bizarre." By the time Geerlings dressed and returned to the House floor, the leadership had held the electronic voting board open for 38 minutes, a record. Tax opponents in the House had chanted, "Close the board." Although he kept his commitment to vote for the increase, Geerlings grumbled about being awakened. "I resent very much the unauthorized entry of a state police officer to jostle me out of bed. It was the principle. That I will deal with later. I think any citizen would resent that."[38]

The press singled out a Democratic representative, Patrick Harrington of Monroe, as the deciding vote in the nearly 22-hour session. Having earlier opposed the tax increase, Harrington reversed himself when Geerlings showed up to cast his vote. The fifty-fourth "aye" cast by Harrington would cost him his chance at a state Senate seat in November 1982.

Milliken's fight in the Senate was almost as painful. After adjourning for an Easter recess without acting on the tax increase, in defiance of Milliken's request, the Senate returned in late April and met for two weeks without passing the measure. On April 28, it rejected the six-month increase "in a startling repudiation of Gov. Milliken and legislative leadership," the *Detroit Free Press* said.[39] On May 6, Milliken announced that he had given up on the increase and directed budget chief Gerald Miller to recommend $312 million in new program cuts, bringing the fiscal year's total to $890 million out of a general fund budget of $4.6 billion. The cuts, Miller said, would damage colleges and universities and local governments.[40] Several days later Milliken renewed his push for the temporary tax increase, saying the alternative was "fiscal disaster."[41]

On May 11, the Senate finally passed the tax increase with two votes to spare, but only after members extracted further concessions from Milliken. They demanded another $50 million in state spending cuts and the elimination of an amusement tax hike the governor had proposed. Senator Thomas Guastello, a Saint Clair Shores Democrat, had conditioned his support for the tax increase on Milliken's consideration of cuts in consumer protection programs and "cooperation from interest groups concerning several of his personal goals, reportedly including a shot at the job of city attorney of Sterling Heights," reported the *Grand Rapids Press*.[42]

Milliken had finally prevailed. In the darkest hour of the state's deepest economic downturn since the Great Depression, he had managed to stitch together an emergency fiscal rescue package. But the cost was great. For one thing, it came too late to avert a lowering of the state's credit rating. On the same day that the Senate approved the tax boost, Moody's Investors Service reduced the state's rating from A to Baa, the lowest of any state.[43]

The victory was also a Pyrrhic one for Milliken's school of moderation, setting off a chain of events that would, over the remainder of the decade, lead to the rise of conservatives in his own party and ultimately to the dismantling of much of the progressive government he had championed. The tax increase was hugely unpopular. In the first days after Senate passage of the boost, Milliken's legislative unit received 44 calls from citizens against the increase, 5 in favor of it, and 73 letters in opposition, with only 10 in favor.[44] Because he was forced to settle for a temporary tax increase, the state's fiscal crisis would return again in 1983. Milliken's successor, Democrat James Blanchard, would raise taxes again, resulting in the loss of his party's control of the Senate. Voter anger over taxation would reach new highs in Michigan after Milliken left office.

As Milliken prepared to leave office at the end of 1982, state fiscal experts said the state had a $330 million deficit for the 1983 fiscal year.[45] Milliken toured hard-hit Detroit, taking up pleas from advocates for the homeless to convert a city building into a temporary shelter for up to 150 homeless Detroiters.[46] The human suffering in the state forced him to take an unusual action, declaring a "human emergency" on December 16, two weeks before the end of his term. Comparable to the emergency declarations governors had issued in the past after natural disasters, Milliken's declaration hinged on hunger and homelessness in the state. Milliken released a 40-point program prepared by a task force that called for using National Guard armories to store food for the hungry, setting aside $1 million in state money to help communities with severe hunger problems and identifying state-owned facilities that could be used as soup kitchens.[47] It was a humane response to the pain of the times, but a sad epitaph to his 14 years in office.

Milliken's policies on taxes and spending became a major problem for his handpicked successor in the 1982 Republican primary campaign for governor. Richard Headlee ran in a crowded field that included Milliken's choice as heir to the office, Lieutenant Governor James H. Brickley. Favored to win, Brickley defended the Milliken record of government management against fierce attacks by Headlee. While the conservative charged that state government had grown by 400 percent, or twice the rate of inflation, during the Milliken years, Brickley retorted that the state's average annual increase in spending under Milliken, adjusted for inflation, had been just 1.6 percent, less than the 15.6 annual increase under Romney and the 3.55 percent annual increase in California under Governor Ronald Reagan. "There's a notion out there that state government is the 'bad guy' in the governmental scheme of things—and it's just not so," Brickley said.[48]

But the impression persisted in the public mind that Milliken had contributed to a climate of high taxation and regulation, discouraging business investment and further worsening the economy. Although there is some truth to the judgment, Michigan's severe recessions of the 1970s and early 1980s were largely a result of global factors, including the rise of the international oil cartel. Even early in the twenty-first century, the state's economy continued to swing downward more dramatically than the national because of the state's continuing role as capital of the automotive industry and the effect of petroleum prices. And many of the rules promulgated and tax revenues raised under Milliken went to support quality of life factors that are now considered important to attracting business investment—including a clean environment, the arts, education, and good roads.

As he left office, two political scientists, writing in the *Detroit News,* characterized Milliken's last term as "a dead end. His legacy was not what he and many others hoped for as we lived through the prosperity of the 1970s. He had built the state public service to a professional level that few other states had achieved. And at the end it was coming apart. The governor and the rest of us deserved better. But life is not always just."[49]

The authors, Kenneth VerBurg and Charles Press, said Milliken's legacy, in addition to his personal decency and intelligence, was "his willingness to find answers to governmental problems by using professional expertise . . . one that did not make or promise political payoffs with state services." This raises the quality of programs, they said, but it can also lead to tunnel vision.

His inclination, we think, led him to accept readily, perhaps too readily at times, the views and advice of academics and near-academic types. This stance proved to be good politics. It made Milliken difficult to attack because what he proposed was "professional" rather than partisan wheeling and dealing. But it also was genuine—not just a calculated policy designed to perpetuate him in office.

This approach also lies at the root of his greatest failures. Milliken's receptiveness to the advice of professionals led him sometimes to accept too easily the fads of the day . . . Critics maintain that these efforts led not only to wasted effort but also to undesirable centralization of policy making in the hands of a few state administrators. And when professionals disagreed among themselves, as during the PBB poisonings or the present economic crisis, it led to delay in some critical decision making and even stalemate.[50]

Despite the final-year temporary tax increase, Milliken still left office on the first day of 1983 with the state facing a projected general fund deficit of $600 million, a whopping 13 percent of the general fund budget. But he wasn't alone in bequeathing a deficit. His successor, James Blanchard, left office in 1991 with a projected general fund deficit of $805 million, or 11 percent; John Engler left office in 2003 with a projected general fund deficit of $465 million, or 5 percent.[51] Even as resistance to taxes intensified, human needs and the demand for government services would outstrip them.

Another way to regard Milliken's difficult final years in office is to consider his heroic effort to straddle an ever-widening divide between antitax conservatives, mostly in his own party, and the lingering but dwindling majority in the state legislature that backed an activist state government. While trying to revive the state's business climate through cutbacks in regulation and workers' compensation costs, he sought also to preserve the state's commitment to numbers of jobless and homeless citizens that were unprecedented in the second half of the twentieth century. Although critics could justly question some of the individual cuts, tax increases, and program judgments, it is doubtful that any other leader of the time could have won agreement from a balky legislature on a politically volatile brew of steep spending cuts and tax boosts. Milliken had done his best at the eleventh hour. Others would have to decide where to take state government next.

15

BATTLING OVER THE
MILLIKEN LEGACY

GOVERNOR WILLIAM MILLIKEN concentrated his energies during his final year in office on keeping state government from bankruptcy. But he made no secret of his support for Lieutenant Governor James H. Brickley as his successor. Brickley faced two serious opponents in the August 1982 election, tax-cut champion Richard Headlee and Oakland County prosecutor L. Brooks Patterson. A third opponent, archconservative state senator Jack Welborn of Kalamazoo County, was not given much chance of prevailing.

The threat to Brickley seemed manageable. For one thing, both Headlee and Patterson, who had first won fame as an attorney suing to stop cross-district busing of suburban and urban students for racial balance, had an Oakland County and conservative base. It appeared reasonable to most pundits that the two right-wing candidates would carve up the conservative vote while Brickley would gain moderate Republicans and others who wanted to support a continuation of Milliken's governing style.

Milliken's decision to retire had touched off an even bigger scramble in the Democratic Party, with no less than eight serious contenders. They included a U.S. representative from Pleasant Ridge, James J. Blanchard, three state senators, gadfly Zolton Ferency, and William Fitzgerald, the defeated nominee from 1978. Seeing a serious opportunity to reclaim the governor's office for the first time in 20 years, most of the Democratic candidates vied for the all-important support of organized labor. That prize went to Blanchard. Although never a darling of the unions, Blanchard was regarded as the most credible candidate after he attracted favorable publicity over his role in engineering a congressional $1.5 billion federal bailout of the Chrysler Corporation, then Detroit's third-largest auto company. He was credited with saving tens of thousands of Michigan auto jobs. In the seven-way race, the 40-year-old Blanchard topped 50 percent of the vote on August 8, defeating his nearest rival by more than 250,000 votes and capturing the Democratic nomination.

In the Republican primary, the three conservative candidates repeatedly attacked Milliken. In late March, Welborn began broadcasting campaign commercials claiming that Milliken had "almost single-handedly destroyed our state . . . I'm really sorry that Bill Milliken quit. He took away our chance to fire him."[1]

In an April debate, two of the conservatives attacked Milliken's policies, forcing Brickley on the defensive. "I frankly think we need a no-nonsense businessman managing the biggest business in Michigan, which is the State of Michigan," Headlee said. Newspapers reported that Brickley spent much of the debate defending Milliken and the proposed income tax increase then before the legislature.[2]

Still, as the August 10 primary neared, Brickley was the favorite among Michigan political experts. The *Detroit News,* the state's leading, traditionally Republican newspaper, endorsed the lieutenant governor, saying that "he has the temperament of an effective leader. He has quiet confidence in his opinions and abilities. He knows what he wants to do, and his program seems firmly anchored to his personal convictions, regardless of whether his convictions are popular at the moment." In a swipe at Milliken, however, the *News* termed the governor's administration an era of "political accommodation" whose time had passed.[3] Significantly, a *News* analysis of the race on election eve said a loss by Brickley or Blanchard "would signal a profound upheaval in the philosophy and organization" of the two parties. "It is uncertain whether the wounds inflicted throughout the campaign will be readily healed. Several candidates refuse to commit themselves to support their party's nominee if they lose."[4]

On the Republican side of the ticket, primary election night delivered a stunning message. When all the votes were counted, Headlee had defeated Brickley by a small but clear margin of 26,000 votes. Just as dramatically, the conservative triumvirate of Headlee, Patterson, and Welborn outpolled the moderate Brickley with a total of nearly 450,000 votes to his 194,429. The *News* called it "another indication of the depth of Republican dissatisfaction with the Milliken administration." The newspaper pointed out that Democrat Blanchard "projects a moderate image that may have some appeal to suburban voters."[5]

In its news pages, the paper said surveys of voters as they left the polls "indicated Brickley was hurt more than helped by his association with Milliken, now blamed for Michigan's economic woes and recent tax increases." Brickley dismissed arguments that his defeat was a repudiation of moderation, blaming his loss instead on $500,000 of negative advertising aired and printed by his three opponents. But he was graceful in defeat, offering his support to Headlee. "One thing I've learned is to accept the will of the people," he said.[6]

The nomination of Blanchard and Headlee set up one of the most clear-cut ideological choices in a governor's race since the 1940s. As Capitol correspondent Tim Skubick put it colloquially, "Conservatives tagged Jamie [Blanchard] with being the handmaiden of organized labor, which turned out to be untrue. Democrats saw Headlee as a neonutso conservative who would move the state's social agenda back to the dark ages, which was only partially correct."[7]

Curiously, in a state with a near-depression level of unemployment the economy was only one of two top issues. As Skubick and other political observers noted with pleasure, Headlee was not a conventional politician. He spoke candidly and sometimes with devastating invective about his conservative political views. While that appealed to conservative voters, the trait likely cost him the governor's job—and all because one of the targets he chose to attack was the pro–Equal Rights Amendment position of Helen Milliken, the first lady of Michigan.

The angry, even intemperate debate about women's rights was set up by Blanchard's surprise choice of former U.S. representative Martha Griffiths as his running mate, who would become the first elected female lieutenant governor. As a member of the U.S. House in 1964, Griffiths had played a significant role in inserting the word *sex* in the Civil Rights Act to prohibit discrimination against women as well as racial and religious minorities. She had also sponsored the Equal Rights

Amendment in Congress. Like Blanchard (and the Millikens), she favored the amendment and professed to be in favor of women's reproductive rights. The Republican ticket of Headlee and former state Supreme Court justice Thomas Brennan opposed both ERA and abortion. The *Grand Rapids Press* saw this as a dramatic contrast.

> Whether the "gender gap" then will appear in Michigan in November will depend on whether the Headlee-Brennan team can change—or will even want to change—the perception which labels conservative Republicans [as unfavorable to women's concerns]. Gov. William Milliken, it should be noted, had no such problem . . . When [Griffiths] begins campaigning on equal rights, equal opportunity and equal pay issues, the opposition will not be able to dismiss her as a man-hating chick from the radical left of the women's movement. Her age, reputation and background guarantee that.[8]

A further warning to Headlee came from Helen Milliken herself. "There's a lot of soul searching going on . . . Republican women are looking very hard at the candidates on the two crucial issues of ERA and choice," she told the *Lansing State Journal.*[9] "Those of us who worked very hard in Michigan for ERA are not going to suddenly walk away from those issues and vote against them. Women are going to vote their consciences." In an election year, Helen Milliken was unafraid of speaking forthrightly on women's rights. In March, she had led a demonstration of 100 supporters of the right to abortion on the Capitol steps, urging opposition to proposed state and federal laws that would virtually ban abortion.[10]

Instead of seeking to reassure moderate Republican women that he would consider their views on both ERA and abortion, Headlee defiantly reaffirmed his opposition to both. He may have won respect for that from some, but his choice of words tended to infuriate rather than palliate women. Speaking to a small group of Republican women in mid-September 1982, he reportedly opened the meeting by saying, "Women are superior beings. They have more money because they live longer and they're pretty."[11] Headlee pointed out that he had a female campaign manager, a day care center for his campaign staff, and two female assistant vice presidents at his insurance company and that he allowed "flex time" for parents who needed to take care of family obligations. But the messenger drew more attention than the message. "It just isn't in his little world," an unidentified attendee at the meeting said about Headlee's concern for women's economic issues.

Political columnist Hugh McDiarmid said Headlee's problems with women voters included his practice of reminding audiences "repeatedly of his large family (a picture of the Headlees plus nine children and 16 grandchildren adorns his campaign literature) and that God, not man, created gender differences—reminders that, rightly or wrongly, conjure up for some women (and men) old, largely discredited 'barefoot and pregnant' images."[12] Calling Helen Milliken "the state's best-known Republican feminist," McDiarmid noted that in a public statement she had not ruled out voting for the Democratic ticket that included Griffiths. If she and other leading Republican women, such as former state party chairperson Elly Peterson, were not going to vote for Dick Headlee, McDiarmid advised, "it's time they said so . . . or said nothing."[13]

But it was Headlee who continued to say things that diverted reporters from economic issues to his views on women. A *Detroit News* gossip column reported that Headlee had left an audience of Republican women "steaming" over a remark that Blanchard and his wife had only one son while Headlee and his wife had nine. "So who doesn't like women?" he reportedly asked, drawing a retort from an unnamed female critic. "Can you believe that Headlee equates his reproductive powers with women's rights? What an insult," she said.[14]

By the end of September, the issue had begun to harden. Blanchard began actively touting his positions on so-called women's issues, and Headlee was forced to clarify repeatedly that he was not antifemale. But, while Blanchard emphasized the benefits of the ERA for helping stabilize single-parent families, Headlee continued to make gaffe after gaffe, denouncing the Republican Women's Task Force, which included Helen Milliken, as the "only nine women in the state who don't like me . . . These women are irrational . . . so obsessed with this they've become hardened. They don't even smile. They're unhappy." Headlee added that he felt women generally were superior educationally, culturally, and in many cases spiritually to men.[15]

Headlee reiterated his complaints about the governor's wife, criticizing "the carping, backbiting and whining" going on in the Republican ranks, and adding, "You never saw my wife out organizing 'Republicans for Fitzgerald' four years ago." Ellen Templin, the first vice chairman of the party, expressed her wish that Headlee "would stay away from that subject, because I think he's making it worse."[16]

Headlee refused to stay away from the subject. At an appearance in Kalamazoo, he joked, "I get criticized because I think that women are pretty. Maybe it's a hormonal imbalance." Referring to a graph showing the unemployment rate among minority city youth in Michigan at 80 percent, Headlee said he hoped a critic, Democratic state representative Mary Brown of Kalamazoo, would put "that graph on her mirror when she shaves every morning."[17]

The governor rarely spoke out during the campaign. When he did, he was not warm to Headlee. After the primary, he had responded unenthusiastically to Headlee's win and later cautioned the nominee to "stop pandering to prejudice or emotion" about Detroit. Although he agreed to appear with Headlee at the State Fair in Detroit in early September, he told reporters he still had "fundamental differences" with Headlee.[18]

Delighted with the way Headlee's views on women were playing with voters, the Blanchard campaign reached out to Republican women. Blanchard phoned several GOP women's leaders personally. Offering assurances that he would continue Milliken's policy of vetoing bans on state funds for elective abortions for women receiving Medicaid assistance, he was able to win the formal endorsement of about three dozen prominent women leaders from the party, the most important being Elly Peterson.

On October 5, Blanchard met privately with a group of 42 Republican women. He then attended a scheduled luncheon with 500 Democratic women, parading his female GOP supporters "like show-biz celebrities on opening night," said *Free Press* columnist McDiarmid. "The luncheon [reinforced] the widespread suspicion that Headlee, whose opposition to abortion and to adoption of a federal Equal Rights Amendment is deep and unwavering, makes him unusually vulnerable this year among women voters."[19]

In her comments about Headlee, former party chairperson Peterson underscored the other chief reason why she and the other women Republicans were backing Blanchard—a reason that the governor had offered as a Headlee problem. She said Headlee was trying to polarize

Michigan in an "unconscionable" attempt to pit most of the state against heavily African-American Detroit.[20]

The issue peaked in mid-October when a coalition of 28 feminist organizations calling itself Women's Assembly III gave Blanchard a score of 55 out of 60 on women's issues while Headlee scored a mere 9. Since Helen Milliken had cochaired the assembly, reporters speculated that she was close to formally endorsing Blanchard. The governor's office rushed to disassociate her from the ranking, pointing out that she had recently been hospitalized and "was not connected in any way with the release" of the results. "No one was authorized to speak on her behalf regarding the issue," the governor's statement said.[21]

Headlee was not mollified. He claimed never to have heard of Women's Assembly III, though Margaret Cooke, executive director of the Michigan Women's Commission, pointed out that he had sat through part of the assembly's debate.[22] Fuming over the continuing concentration of the campaign on the issue of women's rights as characterized by the feminist groups, Headlee characterized them himself, calling supporters of the Equal Rights Amendment "proponents of lesbian marriage, homosexual marriage, things of that nature, which I categorically resist and categorically reject as a basis for a sound society. [The ERA] has nothing to do with women's rights . . . It talks about sex." Some interpreted the remark to apply to Helen Milliken, who refrained from commenting. Headlee's later clarification of his statement, pointing to resolutions in the Women's Assembly III document as proof that the group supported gay rights, exempted some ERA supporters and assembly members from his charge but drew less attention than his initial comment.[23]

Although former Governor George Romney, a longtime ally of Headlee, defended him as being "utterly honest and frank" about the "blank check" that the ERA would give courts on matters of gender, he admitted the comments the nominee had made were "probably not too smart politically" and compared them to a notorious comment he had made about being "brainwashed" by U.S. military brass while on a presidential campaign tour of Vietnam in the 1960s. The furor over that comment had forced Romney to drop out of the race. Republican national committeewoman Ranny Riecker called Headlee's statement "shocking and disgusting," adding that his words showed a "total lack of understanding of what it's all about, what those women's groups are all about."[24] Marvin Stempien, a retired legislator who had authored the 1972 Michigan resolution ratifying the ERA, said Headlee's likening of the amendment to support for "lesbian marriage and homosexual marriage is outrageously insulting to my daughter, to my wife, and to me. Such repulsive, all inclusive statements are the natural result of the narrow minded, self-righteous thinking of political demagogues who think God listens only to them."[25]

Republican Philip Ruppe, who was running for the U.S. Senate, distanced himself from the gubernatorial nominee. He called the Women's Assembly a "fine, top-notch organization, composed of some of the best groups of women in the state of Michigan" and said he agreed with the assembly on the ERA.[26]

Significantly, William Milliken also spoke out in response to Headlee's remarks about the ERA. Responding to a survey showing Headlee 14 points behind Blanchard, Milliken expressed the opinion that "he's gotten himself involved in some other issues that have tended to turn attention away from the key issues of jobs and the economy." With a week to go before the election, he said the damage to Headlee was not irreparable but that it would be "difficult" for the Republican to take the election.[27] After disclosing that he had already cast his vote by absentee ballot, Milliken declined to tell a reporter which gubernatorial candidate he had supported. "I always believe in keeping my vote private," he said, touching off speculation that he had voted for the Democrat, Blanchard.

Editorial page editor Joe Stroud of the *Detroit Free Press* said in late October that Headlee's campaign "is well on its way to becoming a political classic . . . In the 14 years I have been in Michigan I have never seen such a mélange of bizarre social attitudes, self-righteousness, meanness and prejudice . . . He represents an incredible aberration in the history of the Michigan Republican Party."[28] Jane Myers, a columnist for the *Ann Arbor News,* wondered why Headlee "wants to be governor of a state in the grips of a serious economic depression requiring ingenuity of the first order, and he's talking about other people's sex lives."[29] But Headlee again affirmed his opposition to the Equal Rights Amendment at a Republican unity rally, saying, "95 percent of the women in this state are against a platform allowing the government to promote abortions for teenage minor children."[30]

Headlee wrapped up his campaign with a fierce attack on Mayor

Coleman Young of Detroit and Blanchard's alleged domination by the mayor—an ironic remark in light of the fact that the two Democrats would have a historic falling-out that would cost Blanchard reelection in 1990. But Young was unpopular among the largely white voting populations in the Detroit suburbs and rural Michigan, making an attack on him a likely vote generator for the Republicans. Accusing Young of corruption because of grand jury investigations into his administration, Headlee said Young wanted to be "mayor of Michigan." The mayor responded that Headlee had "an increasing and frequent penchant for putting his foot in his mouth."[31]

In his own closing campaign stops, Thomas Brennan, Headlee's running mate, issued a remarkable statement condemning his own party's incumbent governor and charging that Blanchard was too much like him: "They wanted a so-called nice guy who would not rock the boat, a candidate who looked like Milliken, who talked like Milliken, who thought like Milliken and who would be completely subservient to the same motley crew of union bosses, radical feminists and union hacks that [has] attached itself to the present executive office." The state, Brennan said, was "overburdened with the barnacles of 14 years of hobnobbing with self-styled business and labor leaders."[32] He told a columnist he had reacted out of outrage after learning that Milliken had refused to say whether he had voted for Headlee or Blanchard. "I have kept my mouth shut out of respect for him or his position, but this . . . was it." Brennan added, "Nice guys don't win ballgames." Columnist Hugh McDiarmid pointed out, "Except, of course, in 1970 and 1974 and . . ."[33]

Blanchard was consciously making an appeal to the moderate voters that Milliken had captured in the previous three statewide elections. Summing up the campaign at its end, political writer Susan Pollack said he "exhibited a measured, middle-of-the-road manner similar to that of Republican incumbent Gov. William G. Milliken," while Headlee had "railed against striking teachers, union bosses, feminists, utility companies and Detroit Mayor Coleman A. Young. His sharp criticism of Milliken during the GOP primary also sparked lingering antagonism within the party."[34]

The November 2 election delivered the governor's office to Blanchard by a clear but not overwhelming margin of 1,561,291 to 1,369,582 votes, about 53.2 to 46.8 percent. Headlee reacted angrily, grousing that "a governor that was sitting around sucking his thumb" during the campaign did him no good.[35] Milliken had his own pointed view: "The coalition sought by Mr. Headlee was not successful and therein lies a lesson for the Republican Party . . . It's really appalling that we've seen this kind of negative advertising in Michigan." Milliken had called Blanchard with congratulations and Headlee with condolences, but "Headlee did not come to the phone," an aide said.[36]

What did the election of Blanchard mean? The *Detroit News* called the elections a "disaster" for the state GOP and accused the Milliken wing of the party of "all but gloating over Richard Headlee's defeat, suggesting that the only way to run a Republican campaign in Michigan is to wrap yourself in 'positive' symbolism and say as little as possible that is 'divisive.'"[37] But the Milliken moderates saw it differently. Lieutenant Governor Brickley said Headlee had failed to realize that to win you needed coalitions in which "you take what you have and reach out for more. We had a candidate who seemed to draw the line."[38]

Independent observers placed the blame for Headlee's defeat squarely on his shoulders, saying he had run a polarizing campaign. And George Weeks, Milliken's executive secretary, told the *Grand Rapids Press* that a conservative who "didn't keep shooting himself in the foot and who would reach out to others" could win in Michigan. "A conservative this year, playing as Headlee did on the economy and jobs and without antagonizing blocs of voters, could have won," Weeks said.[39] Capitol columnist Robert Longstaff pointed out that Headlee had earned an edge in the parts of Michigan outside Detroit and its suburbs of only about 90,000 votes, short of Milliken's 120,000-vote margin in the close 1970 election. Detroit residents had been motivated to turn out in huge numbers because Headlee's attacks on Young made him appear "anti-black," while other voters had turned to Blanchard as the lesser of two evils given Headlee's strident rhetoric, Longstaff added.[40]

The Millikens weighed in themselves in December 1982 when they were interviewed, as they had been every year, for an *Evening with the Governor* program on statewide public television. "There's nothing, really, that I could have done to save Mr. Headlee from himself," Milliken told reporter Tim Skubick. "I found that Mr. Headlee, beginning with the primary campaign, focused . . . almost solely on the Milliken administration, attacking many of the things in which I deeply believe,

Battling over the Milliken Legacy

creating a situation" that divided the GOP, Milliken said.[41] When Skubick asked Helen Milliken whether feminists had damaged Headlee's campaign, she replied, "Frankly, I think that Mr. Headlee shot himself in the foot. We didn't."[42]

The enmity between Headlee and the Millikens continued for years. The summer after the election, Headlee again attacked Helen Milliken in the *Detroit Free Press*. Headlee acused the former governor's wife of supporting homosexual marriage. The former governor rose to the defense of his wife, telling *Detroit Free Press* columnist Hugh McDiarmid that Headlee "puts me in mind of an ass . . . I don't know how he can presume to be a credible candidate in the future . . . and you can quote me on that."[43] At the funeral of former governor George Romney in 1995, Headlee and the Millikens were seated next to each other. This time the former governor said Headlee "graciously" acknowledged that his previous remarks about Helen Milliken had been excessive.[44]

With the benefit of more than two decades of hindsight, it now appears that Blanchard's win postponed but did not prevent the conservative Republican takeover of the state government. With both Milliken and Headlee out of the picture, other conservatives rushed to fill the leadership void in the GOP. Although their nominee for governor, William Lucas, was trounced by Blanchard in 1986, that had more to do with the fact that Lucas was an African American and race was an issue in rural Republican Michigan than with approval of Blanchard. During the 1980s, conservative John Engler engineered a right-wing takeover of the GOP machinery, leading to his upset win over Blanchard in 1990. By the mid-1990s, the Republicans also controlled both houses of the legislature and were able to promote an agenda that was probusiness, antiregulatory, opposed to abortion rights, and socially conservative.

In effect, Blanchard's two wins were an extension of the Milliken legacy, victories won by a pro-choice, activist governor who operated in the style of the Traverse City man for a time. But by 1990 impatience with high property taxes, another economic recession, and the increasing coarseness of the tone of both Blanchard and Engler made the Democrat ripe for a surprise defeat. The Milliken legacy of moderation at the helm of state government would endure only eight years after his retirement.

The Milliken-to-Blanchard transition, given the convergence of the two men's political philosophies, should have been smooth. For the most part, it was, but under the surface there were strains.

For one thing, despite their shared moderation on issues, the two men differed significantly in personality. "Milliken was white collar educated at Yale. Blanchard picked up a blue collar sheep skin from Michigan State University," Tim Skubick wrote. "Milliken was a non-smoker. Blanchard was known to whip out a huge stogie when the spirit moved him. You'd never cuss around Milliken. Blanchard didn't mind. Blanchard loved sports. Milliken thought a red wing was found on a cardinal and never on the ice. Milliken was out the door headed for Traverse City on most Thursdays. Blanchard was just getting warmed up near the end of his week."[45]

Even more fundamentally, the two men and their staffs viewed the operation of state government differently. Milliken and his team liked to think of partisan politics as a necessary evil that occasionally interrupted the serious business of governing. Blanchard and his aides reveled in the personalities and power plays of politics.

Then, too, the governor-elect and his transition staff were insecure about entering office in the long shadow of Milliken. Democrats had no recent experience running the state and had to take a crash course in operating the huge state bureaucracy during a fiscal crisis. While distancing themselves from the economic woes that had materialized during Milliken's last term, they wanted to emulate the Milliken style of emphasizing coalitions and unity. It was not an easy feat for a governor-elect who had previously represented one-eighteenth of the state in the U.S. House.

Milliken did not put his responsibilities—governmental or political—on hold during November and December. In mid-December, he stunned Blanchard and his people by appointing two justices to fill vacancies on the Michigan Supreme Court. The appointment of his friend and lieutenant governor, James Brickley, to the court seat being vacated by Republican judge Mary Coleman on December 24, a week before Milliken left office, was undisputed and received warm praise. Brickley's thoughtful style, observers said, would make him an excellent justice.[46]

But the other appointment provoked Democratic anger. Justice Blair Moody Jr., a Democrat, had won reelection in the November 2 election but died shortly afterward. Milliken appointed a Republican state Court of Appeals judge, Dorothy Comstock Riley, not only to fill out the term that ended that December 31 but also serve the first two years of the term Moody had won in the November election. Riley had finished far behind Moody in the election, and her appointment would prevent Blanchard from putting a Democrat on the court upon taking office.

Blanchard complained of getting "a panic phone call" just minutes before Milliken announced the two appointments and said Milliken's staff had been discussing with his the constitutional issues involved before suddenly breaking off the talks.[47] Blanchard called the appointment of Riley "unfortunate and unwise" and accused Milliken of not being "statesmanlike." Responding to Blanchard's charge that the appointment would cause a constitutional crisis, Milliken replied that the crisis would come only if somebody attempted to displace Riley. An ally of Blanchard, Attorney General Frank Kelley, challenged the Milliken appointment early in 1984. After a bitter fight in which the Supreme Court justices themselves had to decide whether one of their own could serve, they ejected Riley from the court. Republicans were outraged. Riley successfully campaigned to get back on the court in the 1984 election, ousting one of the Democratic justices who had voted against her. She later became chief justice.

That was in the future, however. Milliken had the pleasure of swearing his friend Brickley into his post on the Supreme Court on December 27.[48] He also appointed an African American, Harold Hood of Detroit, to the Court of Appeals and Marianne Battani, to fill Hood's spot, on December 22. And after the Democratic state Senate rejected 69 of his pending nominees to state boards and commissions Milliken reappointed 18 of them when it was too late for the Senate to brush them aside a second time.[49]

Milliken's final "formal" full day in office, December 29, 1982, was a busy one. He signed more than 200 new laws, vetoing only a handful of the 211 bills presented to him. "I was doing this at home last night, and I got writer's cramp," he said. "When I look at all these bills, I don't feel too sentimental about leaving."[50] His aides sorted and packed 14 years' worth of records, while State Police troopers installed new locks on the doors to the governor's office and replaced Milliken's decal on the door with one reading "James J. Blanchard."

"Oh, I'll have mixed feelings when I walk out for the last time," Milliken said, "feelings of nostalgia in a way and feelings of anticipation of a new life. I'm going to miss some of the magnificent people I've worked with. There have been some exceptions, but I think we've had some superb public servants." A reporter observed that while Milliken's term had ended on a dark note economically "Milliken's personal popularity remains high."

> As he left the Capitol yesterday and opened his car door, a woman recognized him.
> 'Thank you, governor,' she said. 'You did a good job. We're going to miss you.'
> Milliken smiled, said thanks and was chauffeured away.[51]

16

NORTHERN CONSCIENCE

A FTER 22 YEARS in public office, in 1983 the longest-serving
governor in Michigan's history suddenly found himself a
private citizen. The transition was slightly bumpy in more ways than
one. As he prepared to leave office late in 1982, Milliken got behind the
wheel of a car, for the first time in years, on a trip to New York City. As
the state's chief executive, state troopers had chauffeured him. Unac-
customed to driving, Milliken cut off a taxi and incurred the wrath of
a New York cabbie, who had no idea he was scowling at a governor and
probably would not have cared if he had known.[1]

For a time, both the national and state news media kept an eye on
the former governor, who was now 60 years old. Less than three weeks
into his new regimen, a *New York Times* reporter looked Milliken up at
his new office overlooking the West Arm of Grand Traverse Bay. "I'm
just delighted to be out of the Governor's chair now," Milliken told the
Times, "just because there are times to move on, to turn a new corner
and begin a new life."[2]

Milliken still had his mind on public policy and the lessons of the
final years of his tenure. Recalling the steep unemployment and sharp
budget cuts that had characterized his final two years in office, Milliken
predicted that the midwestern states would have to restructure themselves if they were to recover. He recommended that primary schools
begin emphasizing computers to help prepare young people for emerg-

ing high-technology jobs, called for an end to the adversarial relationship between business and labor, and suggested that the Great Lakes states should emphasize their most abundant natural resource, water. "The Great Lakes [are] the world's largest collection of fresh water, and water will be for the Midwest almost like oil is to the OPEC countries," he said, referring to the Organization of the Petroleum Exporting Countries. "It is vital to life and agriculture and attracts industry and tourism." He dismissed the Sunbelt states, with their water scarcities, as "the Parched Belt." Milliken said he would promote awareness and protection of the lakes by serving as chairman of the board of the new Center for the Great Lakes in Chicago, funded by the Joyce Foundation. Milliken also accepted a seat on the Chrysler Corporation board in January 1983 and soon after joined the board of the Ford Foundation.

The former governor sounded an almost plaintive note, which would resound throughout his postpolitical years. "People can expect honesty and integrity, but not miracles," Milliken said of deteriorating public faith in government. "People now seem so eager to judge us by one single narrow issue like, say, abortion or taxes. Your stand dooms you forever in their eyes. But what about society's broader good?"[3]

Contrasting his new life with the old, the *New York Times* noted that the interview was "the only item on a neatly typed schedule that used to be so full of items it took two pages and a cluster of aides to whisper discreet reminders in his politically attuned ear."

Milliken deliberately refrained in most cases from commenting on the performance of his successor, the Democrat James Blanchard. Facing the same budget and economic woes that had tested Milliken in 1981 and 1982, Blanchard had proposed and won passage of—by one vote in the state Senate—a permanent income tax increase in the spring of 1983. Milliken publicly endorsed the plan as necessary to stave off harsh cuts in government services. But the resulting furor cost the Democrats control of the upper chamber of the legislature. Republicans successfully gathered petitions for recall elections for two protax Democratic senators from the Detroit suburbs in Macomb and Oakland Counties. The voters turned both men out and replaced them with Republican senators, giving Republicans a 20 to 18 edge in the Senate and making John Engler its majority leader. Blanchard soon began positioning himself as an advocate of phasing out the income tax boost and restraining the growth of government.

Northern Conscience

In the summer of 1983, before the recall elections, Milliken offered support for Blanchard's general fiscal policy. "We had reached the point where we could not make further major cuts without damaging our institutions in a very fundamental way for years and years to come . . . I'm not commenting on the specifics of what he did, what the percent increase was or what the further cuts were. I probably would have done that differently. But in the broad sense, he did what he had to do."[4]

While rarely offering personal praise or criticism directly about his successors, Milliken was less reluctant to express disdain for the rightward turn of the party and nation under President Ronald Reagan in the 1980s. "I have so many fundamental disagreements with him and I haven't had cause to change that," he said. "There's a whole litany of things I could talk about." He cited the Reagan foreign policy regarding Nicaragua and the president's nomination of conservative Robert Bork to the U.S. Supreme Court as examples.[5]

Responding to a question from a reporter from his native Traverse City about whether northern Michigan was paying for Detroit's problems, Milliken brushed the thought aside and said, "We are not an island. There are politicians who attempt to exploit the issue and divide the state. This is a very narrow activity which will hurt us in the long run. Detroit has its unique problems, but it has meant a great deal to the state . . . For northern Michigan, Detroit means tourists, people who make their living there and spend their vacation dollars here. It is a very parochial prejudice."[6]

As the years passed, Milliken clearly welcomed the persistent attention of reporters, taking pains to accommodate their requests. A 1985 profile carried by most of the Booth newspapers, a chain of large dailies in most of southern Michigan's urban centers outside Detroit, opened with the ex-governor leading a reporter on a cross-country ski trail at the end of the Old Mission Peninsula. Emerging onto a vista of the frozen bay, Milliken exclaimed, "Isn't this something!" Reporter Ted Roelofs observed, "Life after the governorship, clearly, fits Milliken just fine."[7]

A testament to the enduring loyalty of the Milliken executive office staff was a reunion organized by its alumni in November 1997, 15 years after he retired. "Renew old acquaintances and extend your warm personal regards to Governor and Mrs. Milliken," read the invitation.[8] More than 150 members of the governor's former staff attended the event in downtown Lansing. On another Lansing visit, when Milliken attended the unveiling of a portrait of his late friend and lieutenant governor James H. Brickley at the Michigan Supreme Court in 2003, Dale Arnold, a former deputy press secretary to Milliken, was astonished and delighted when Milliken tracked him down to complete a personal conversation after the two men had been separated in the crowd. "He was just always a believer in treating people nicely without being patronizing," Arnold said.[9]

Milliken continued to rack up favorable commentary—and dismissals from both conservative Republican voters and those now in charge of the Michigan Republican Party—more than two decades after leaving public office. In 2002, columnist Jack Lessenberry interviewed Milliken and said that he had "governed as if Abraham Lincoln was still the guiding spirit of the Republican Party." The impulse behind Lessenberry's column was Milliken's endorsement of a pro-choice moderate, Republican state senator Joe Schwarz of Battle Creek, for the 2002 Republican Party nomination for governor. Lieutenant Governor Richard Posthumus clobbered Schwarz by a margin of 81 to 19 percent in the primary election. "I don't care about that," Milliken told Lessenberry. "Sometimes you have to take a principled stand on the issues."[10] Milliken again backed Schwarz in 2004, when he ran for a U.S. House seat in south-central Lower Michigan being vacated by incumbent Nick Smith. Schwarz won a crowded Republican primary and was elected to the seat in the November balloting.

In another encomium, the editor of the *Traverse City Record-Eagle,* Bill Thomas, called Milliken "a Michigan treasure. A Michigan legend . . . He's from the old school. He believes politics and government can do good and it need not be in a world of rancor and polarization . . . There aren't many Bill Millikens around any more. That's too bad."[11]

Both Millikens lent their names to environmental causes in the 1980s and even more so in the 1990s. The Michigan United Conservation Clubs inducted Milliken into its Conservation Hall of Fame in 1997. Helen Milliken served on the board of the Michigan Land Use Institute, an organization devoted to improving public policy and practice in land conservation. The Michigan Environmental Council established the annual Helen and William G. Milliken Award in 1999, which honors a distinguished life and career of service to Michigan's environment.

Milliken was willing to do more than act the role of bland senior statesman. Time after time, and increasingly as the 1990s wore on, he emerged from his Traverse City retreat to speak out on the issues of the day. In 1998, he appeared in a television advertisement taped by supporters of a ballot proposal that would have legalized assisted suicide. The issue had particular currency in Michigan because that is where Dr. Jack Kevorkian practiced assisted suicide from 1990 to 1998, playing a role in more than 100 deaths. Dubbed "Dr. Death" by the news media, Kevorkian evaded successful prosecution until he was imprisoned following a second-degree murder conviction in 1999.

On this emotionally convulsive issue, Milliken spoke out for the right of individuals to determine the time of their own deaths without government involvement. "I believe citizens should be allowed to make end-of-life decisions according to their own religious and moral beliefs, not those of others or the state," he said in the advertisement.[12]

On the other side of the issue was Milliken's old nemesis, Right to Life of Michigan, which had fought him on the use of state funds to pay for elective abortions for women receiving Medicaid assistance, and a large coalition of religious and medical organizations. The opponents broadcast television advertisements of their own. One 60-second spot showed a scale, with the 11-page Proposal B on one side and weights representing the medical community, church leaders, the elderly, and the disabled on the other. A 30-second ad showed a match burning a copy of the Hippocratic oath. A third ad showed an elderly black man saying the proposal would harm minorities and the elderly.[13]

The issue became entangled with the gruesome image of the controversial Kevorkian appearing to relish the media attention accorded his assisted suicides. State senator William Van Regenmorter, a conservative Republican, called the proposal "an open invitation to Dr. Jack Kevorkian. This is his dream come true." Voters rejected the legalization of assisted suicide by a margin of 71 to 29 percent, over 1.2 million votes, turning it down in each of the state's 83 counties.[14]

In 2000, Milliken spoke out against another ballot proposal. Authored by local government associations, Proposal 2 called for amending the state constitution to require a two-thirds vote of the legislature, instead of a simple majority, before passage of any law that would limit or change the authority of municipalities and counties. It was a response to complaints by local governments that the state was preempting local authority in some areas.

WILLIAM G. MILLIKEN

In a letter published by the *Detroit Free Press,* Milliken cited civil rights and campaign finance disclosure laws as controversial reforms he had championed that might never have been enacted with the two-thirds requirement in place. He added, "Michigan's landmark environmental laws were adopted to end fouling of our air and water by both the private sector and by government, state and local. Those laws 'intervened' in local concerns, because of higher concerns for fairness, honesty and environmental health that did not and should not respect local boundaries . . . I shudder to think how nearly impossible it would have been to put together the kind of super-majority that Proposal 2 would require."[15] Voters rejected the proposal by a margin of better than two to one or more than a million votes.[16]

In 2000, Milliken attacked "the ugliness and innuendo" of advertisements supported by the state Republican Party that lambasted three Democratic candidates for the state Supreme Court as being weak on criminal law enforcement. The highly partisan, negative tone of the advertising—which Democrats matched—was not unusual for Michigan politics generally but had rarely been employed in judicial races. Milliken called on the three Republican incumbents running for the court to "disavow these scurrilous attacks on their opponents . . . [As governor], I would never have devised, condoned or tolerated such despicable and shameful tactics. Nor should the current leaders of the Republican Party." In response, Rusty Hills, the state party chairman, while saying he respected Milliken, refused to disavow the ads, saying they were based on the public record and "we're not about to unilaterally disarm and lose this election."[17]

The *Detroit Free Press* editorialized in sympathy with Milliken, although it pointed out that he could also have criticized the Democratic candidates for not disavowing attack ads on the Republican incumbents. "The Supreme Court, ostensibly the final, impartial arbiter of Michigan law, has been tainted, cheapened and forever politicized by the broadsides and distortions aimed at voters for the past several months," the newspaper said.[18] The Republican incumbents won reelection and held the party's 5–2 majority on the Supreme Court.

Milliken also lent his name to civil lawsuits and friend of the court briefs seeking to uphold laws he had signed or supported while serving as governor and legislator. In 2003, he signed on to a friend of the court brief asking the Supreme Court to uphold the authority of the legislature and governor to grant standing to any citizen to sue to prevent or halt "pollution, impairment or destruction" of the natural resources of the state. Milliken had signed the law granting such standing, the Michigan Environmental Protection Act, in July 1970. The Supreme Court did not directly rule on the constitutionality of the law, at least temporarily upholding citizen standing. Still, the court, which was dominated by conservative Republicans, including three appointed by Republican governor John Engler, seemed to signal its lack of confidence in that portion of the law.[19]

In August 2004, Milliken generated headlines by appearing as one of three plaintiffs in a lawsuit brought by the American Civil Liberties Union to halt the participation of the Michigan State Police in Matrix, an interstate crime and terrorism database. In 1980, Milliken had signed a state statute called the Interstate Law Enforcement Intelligence Organizations Act, a reaction to the disclosure that the State Police had engaged in surveillance of and maintained files on persons involved in the civil rights and antiwar movements of the 1960s and 1970s even though they had not been charged with or suspected of having committed a crime.

"I signed this act into law in order to protect the privacy of individual citizens and, at the same time, provide law enforcement agencies with the tools they need," Milliken said in a news release issued by the ACLU. "Nearly 25 years later, the technology has changed, but the privacy rights of Michigan citizens remain the same."[20] The Michigan State Police withdrew from the system in early 2005.[21]

Of all the issues on which Milliken spoke out, the most remarkable was his long-running effort to amend or repeal a law he himself had signed and had later come to regret. In fact, Milliken termed his initial approval of the law "a chief regret" of his career and one he was trying "in every way I can" to undo.[22]

In 1978, an election year, legislators had sent to Milliken a bill they said would reduce the state's worsening drug problem by cracking down on dealers. The so-called 650 Lifer Law imposed an extended mandatory term in prison without parole for anyone convicted of possessing 650 grams of hard drugs such as heroin and imposed other mandatory sentences. In Milliken's recollection, neither he nor anyone on his staff had serious doubts about whether he should sign the measure into law.[23]

But instead of leading to the capture of drug kingpins the law largely jailed "the younger 19- and 20-year-old people who had been runners or who maybe were addicts and were feeding their own habits," Milliken admitted to a reporter in 2004. As a result, he began to campaign for changes in the law, openly admitting his mistake in judgment.

I believed then that it was the right response to an insidious and growing drug problem. I have since come to realize that the provisions of this law have led to terrible injustices and that signing it in the first instance was a mistake—an overly punishing and cruel response which gave no discretion whatever to a sentencing judge, even for extenuating circumstances.[24]

Milliken cited cases like that of Karen Shook, a mother of three whose mandatory sentence of 20 years disturbed him. Heavily addicted to drugs, Shook introduced undercover officers to her supplier and was charged with delivery and conspiracy to deliver cocaine. By the time of her trial, Milliken said, she had completed substance abuse treatment, assisted police, and was genuinely remorseful, leading her arresting officer to request a lower sentence than the mandatory 10 years on each count. The dealer had received a 3-year sentence. When the judge attempted to impose a lower sentence, an appeals court reversed his decision and reimposed the full 20 years.

Milliken also cited the case of Timothy Allen Dick, who had been caught in possession of cocaine at Kalamazoo in 1978. Prosecuted under federal instead of state law, Dick served less than two and a half years in prison and upon his release launched an acting career that made him nationally famous as Tim Allen, star of the television series *Home Improvement*.[25]

By the late 1990s, Milliken said in a speech to the Federal Bar Association in Detroit that 220 inmates were serving life sentences in Michigan under the law, most of them addicts in need of treatment rather than major drug dealers. Milliken called the statute a "draconian 'one strike and you're out' hammer that falls most often on nonviolent offenders with no prior record."[26]

The admission by the former governor of his error in signing the drug lifer law won widespread notice. *Detroit Free Press* columnist Hugh McDiarmid applauded him for speaking out "loudly and courageously against a monstrous injustice" and suggested that lawmakers were reluctant to respond to his request because they feared being labeled "soft on crime."[27]

Milliken joined forces with an advocacy group, Families Against Mandatory Minimums (FAMM), which pressed for changes in the law. He gave speeches, authored newspaper columns, and corresponded with legislators to urge amendments. Milliken's appeal—and fiscal realities—contributed to a gradual change of heart on the part of lawmakers and Governor Engler. The swelling cost to taxpayers of imprisoning nonviolent drug offenders for life increased the pressure for reform. In 1998, 2000, and 2002, the legislature and governor agreed on reforms, loosening some of the mandatory sentencing clauses.[28]

In October 2003, FAMM gave Milliken its Justice Leadership Award. He spoke of the case of JeDonna Young, a then 24-year-old woman whose boyfriend had been targeted in a drug investigation. "Police saw the boyfriend hand her plastic shopping bags to put in the trunk of her car. JeDonna's boyfriend maintained until his death in prison that she did not know what was in the bags. She had no previous criminal record . . . The U.S. Sixth Circuit Court of Appeals . . . concluded that in her case, 'the tiger trap may have sprung on a sick kitten.'" Milliken said the 1998 reforms had made Young the first "650 Lifer" to win parole.[29]

Milliken's efforts did not stop with policy reform. He actively lobbied for early release of some prisoners. One of them was Michael Ward. Hearing of his conviction under the mandatory minimums law, Milliken wrote him and advocated for his early parole from prison. Twenty-six years after his arrest, Ward, now 53, was paroled and moved into his mother's house.[30]

It was not an easy campaign. The state parole board turned down Ward's parole several times. Milliken acknowledged that Ward "was not the easiest person to deal with. He was very intense. He probably was his own worst enemy, and I told him that. I said, 'Michael, you're going to have to lighten up if you ever want to get out of there.' He was so totally frustrated, so desperately wanting to be free, and I understood that."[31]

Ward wrote Milliken a letter of gratitude upon his release and told a reporter that Milliken's intervention was probably decisive in his early parole. "He made me feel at home. He made me feel comfortable. He made me feel someone cared," Ward said.

Milliken's efforts to amend the tough drug-sentencing laws displayed the same concern about fairness and giving lawbreakers a chance to reform themselves that he had put to practice as governor when he commuted the sentences of numerous state prison inmates. Milliken commuted the sentences of 94 prisoners; his successors Blanchard and Engler, commuted 6 and 14, respectively.[32] Admitting his error in signing the law was an unusual action even for a retired politician. It also suggested the same softheartedness that had made it difficult and sometimes impossible for him to discipline aides even when they performed incompetently or had plunged the governor into controversy. Milliken's kindness was not the product of a public relations machine.

Although he was feted by hundreds of well-wishers at a fund-raising dinner for a community college in 1988 in his hometown, Milliken rarely appeared at (or was invited to) Republican Party events. When he attended a Michigan Mainstream Republican Committee event in Dearborn in 1990, former aide turned newspaper columnist George Weeks noted that it was Milliken's first speech to a large party group since leaving office.[33] Milliken expressed his pro-choice views and endorsed pro-choice former state senator Dick Allen in the 10th Congressional District Republican primary. Weeks also noted that when Milliken checked into the Hyatt Regency Hotel after the speech the night clerk asked if he was related to Detroit area auto dealer Pat Milliken. "No. But I've certainly heard of him," Milliken replied.[34]

Detroiters more clearly and warmly remembered Milliken, however. At a dinner he hosted for newspaper editors, publishers, and reporters in 1986, Mayor Coleman Young took exception when the publisher of the *Arenac County Independent* said that Milliken's successor, James Blanchard, was not the traditional liberal politician that had been expected and was in the tradition of Milliken himself. "On behalf of Bill Milliken, I take offense at that comparison," Young retorted. After calling Milliken "a good friend," Young scoffed at a remark that Blanchard might grow into his job with time. "You don't grow balls. Either you got 'em or you don't," he retorted, adding that Blanchard had surrounded himself with "an Oakland County mafia" that was afraid to associate the governor with Detroit for fear of alienating white voters. Milliken had stood up for the city.[35] In 1988, Young declared a

William G. Milliken Day in the city, saying that the governor's administration had "developed a series of innovative programs which recognized the special needs of Michigan's urban areas and the stake which the state has in meeting those needs."[36]

In 1990, the year in which John Engler upset Blanchard in the governor's race, a disenchanted Young did little to turn out Detroit votes for the Democrat. Blanchard's 17,000-vote margin of defeat was small enough that a greater effort by Young—who felt Blanchard had treated him and the city disrespectfully—might have made the difference.

At Young's funeral in Detroit in December 1997, the former mayor's supporters and fans warmly welcomed Milliken. Delivering a eulogy for his unlikely friend, Milliken said that Young's "senses were sharp and clear from years of injustices that, sadly, seem to emanate too often from our human family . . . Coleman was not a perfect man—who among us can be? But he was a stand-out, a fierce warrior but with impeccable style, a courier bringing truth to places where truth was unwelcome."[37]

The retirement years included profound personal pain for both William and Helen Milliken. In 1993, while living and working as a consultant in Vermont, their daughter, Elaine Wallbank Milliken, became ill. Her parents cared for her in her final weeks at home in Traverse City. On October 6, 1993, Elaine died of cancer at the age of 45. She was interred on Mackinac Island. In a *Detroit News* account, the Millikens cited their daughter's "great compassion for people and dedication to the ideals of public service" in her career as a public defender in Detroit and chief counsel to the U.S. Senate Committee on Rules through 1986. Her brother, William Milliken Jr., called her a "very quiet and gentle person."[38]

The stoic public statements could not conceal the grief of the parents. The ex-governor, his eyes tearing, admitted to wishing he had spent more time with both of his children in their youth, when he was building his political career and frequently away from the home.[39]

A few years after her death, a former state official vacationing on Mackinac Island bicycled past the island cemetery. He saw Milliken sitting on a bench by the grave of his daughter, leaning forward as if silently communicating with her.

Milliken also battled a drinking problem almost twenty years after he left office. In the late 1990s, he said, he began "looking forward too much" to the cocktail hour.[40] His friends grew concerned. When he didn't initially respond to their suggestions that he curtail his drinking, Helen persuaded his friends to meet with the former governor and urge him to seek therapy.

He checked into a Minnesota clinic to break the habit, staying for more than three weeks. The regimen was successful. He did not drink alcoholic beverages again, while admitting he sometimes missed the relaxation they provided.[41] "Going to the clinic was a very fortunate development in my life," he said.[42]

The former governor and his wife both saw the time as a turning point. Helen Milliken said emphatically, "We're all human. People can benefit from learning from what we went through together."[43]

During the first 20 years of his retirement from public office, neither Democratic governor James Blanchard nor Republican governor John Engler tapped Milliken for advice in any official capacity. Blanchard at first seemed insecure in Milliken's shadow and deferential to his predecessor. In a speech to the Council of Great Lakes Governors in May 1983, Milliken jokingly (though perhaps with unconscious resentment) referred to a phone call the newly installed Blanchard had made to him from the official governor's residence on Mackinac Island. Milliken teased that he had been surprised to get a call from "my bedroom, in my house." Blanchard passed him a note that said, "Gov. Bill, If I hadn't known you are going to build a place on Mackinac Island . . . I would never have had the heart to call."[44]

Blanchard did call on Milliken twice to support his efforts to build on the former governor's Great Lakes legacy, first in 1985 to secure an endorsement of the proposed Great Lakes Charter, an interstate agreement to conserve water and prevent water exports to other regions and nations, and second in 1986, an election year, to award Milliken a Great Lakes Medal of Honor.

When Engler upset Blanchard in 1990, whatever small influence Milliken still had over state policy evaporated. Engler and Milliken had never been close, beginning with Engler's service in the state House of Representatives in 1970. Milliken's former aide, Joyce Braithwaite, described Engler as "arrogant" and lacking respect for both people and the role of government. Milliken, in retirement, put it more diplomatically with a backhanded compliment.

John Engler was the guy who worked to build the party in his own image. I've never known him to have a personal, passionate conviction, something in which he believes deeply. He sure was able, in a pragmatic way, to play various forces to his advantage. There's no question [that he was] a strong and forceful leader.[45]

Despite Engler's hiring of several former Milliken aides, including Gerald Miller, a former Department of Management and Budget chief, and Richard McLellan, a former legal adviser, the Republican openly spurned the Milliken model of governance. He disdained conciliation and deftly wielded his executive powers and influence to implement his programs. In 1993, stung by the defeat of an education finance reform proposal also backed by a traditional foe, the Michigan Education Association, Engler displayed the difference.

[I]nstead of implementing the Milliken strategy of consulting everyone to decide the next step, he reverted and retreated. He returned to his divide, attack and conquer mode. He went back to his bunker, locked the door, locked out all the folks he had coalesced with and drafted his own education blueprint that promptly divided this town.[46]

But it turned out that Engler didn't need to compromise, consult, or coalesce—or even to be liked—to remain in office. Putting the Democrats on the defensive, he was able to break the logjam on school finance reform that reached back to Milliken's first year in office. In the spring of 1994, Michigan voters backed his plan to cut and cap property taxes for schools and make up the difference with revenue from the state sales tax. Engler was able to run for reelection as a governor who had delivered property tax relief, and he easily bested his Democratic opponent that fall, former U.S. representative Howard Wolpe, though not before Wolpe asked Helen Milliken to be his Democratic running mate.

After defeating rival Debbie Stabenow in the August Democratic primary, Wolpe phoned Helen and requested a meeting with her to discuss a possible candidacy for lieutenant governor. The overture was "quite serious," she said. "I gave it some thought, but it didn't fit into the pattern of our lives at the time."[47] Her husband said he concurred in her decision not to join the ticket. "What he wanted and needed was the Milliken name," he said. Turning to her during an interview in early 2005, he said, "It would have been helpful to Howard Wolpe but not to you." Wolpe instead chose Stabenow as his running mate but lost in a landslide to Engler.

Engler won by an even bigger margin in 1998 against attorney Geoffrey Fieger, who had first come to prominence as the attorney representing Dr. Jack Kevorkian, the assisted suicide advocate.

Milliken's people had "mistrusted and sometimes scorned" Engler, said one commentator, and the conservative returned the feeling.[48] In his 12 years as governor he met Milliken only twice, once in the Capitol and once on Mackinac Island, and never for a substantive issue discussion. Milliken did acknowledge that Engler had been "gracious" on the Lansing visit, where the new governor showed off the remodeled Capitol.

After two decades of isolation from the executive office, Milliken found himself valuable to incoming Democratic governor Jennifer Granholm, the state's first female chief executive, in early 2003. She appointed him cochair, along with former Democratic attorney general Frank Kelley, of a 26-member council she created to recommend ways to conserve Michigan's undeveloped lands and promote urban redevelopment. *Lansing State Journal* columnist Chris Andrews predicted that the Milliken appointment would have the side benefit of appealing to "moderate Republicans whose votes often determine the winners and losers in Michigan elections" and observed that "out of necessity or style or both, [Granholm] is adopting the Milliken style of governing by tapping him to help lead the land-use commission."[49]

Tapping Milliken was a political calculation, but Granholm seemed genuinely respectful of his style and legacy. Although she had moved to Michigan with her family only after he left office, she called herself "completely a Bill Milliken fan."[50] She had been surprised in the mid-1980s to find friends remembering how Milliken had supported the state's urban centers. It was not something she associated with Republicans.

As an upstart candidate for attorney general on the Democratic ticket in 1998, Granholm secured the endorsement of both Helen Milliken and Joyce Braithwaite-Brickley, Milliken's former appointments chief. Granholm said she consulted with the former governor during her 2002 campaign for governor against Republican Richard Posthumus and also from time to time after taking office.

"His advice is always apt," she said. "He has been and still is a tremendous ally and guide for me in conducting affairs of state."[51]

But it was Milliken's approach to problem solving that she admired most and sought to emulate, the Democratic governor said. "You have to bring everyone into the solution to get anything done," she said. "If you're not concerned with who gets the credit, you can accomplish a lot." Granholm cited two direct Milliken inspirations: the revival in her first year in office of the so-called quadrant meetings of the four top legislative leaders and the governor; and the issuance of a special message to the legislature on clean water policy early in 2004. It was the first special message on an environmental topic from a governor since Milliken left office.[52]

Ironically—or fittingly, his conservative critics would say—in Lansing Milliken was more revered by the opposition party than by his own. Few Republican legislators, even after Granholm's election, openly connected themselves with the Milliken model. One of the few exceptions was State representative John Stewart, a moderate from Plymouth. Stewart displayed Milliken memorabilia in his office, including photographs of himself and the former governor; frequently corresponded with him; and sent the Millikens roses on their wedding anniversary.[53] He boasted of wearing a Milliken pin on his lapel during his first four years in the state House.

When she faced a large budget deficit in her first year in office, Granholm asked the legislature to defer a scheduled income tax rollback for Michigan business in order to close the revenue gap. Milliken wrote Stewart to encourage him to "pause" the tax rollback as "the least politically painful" option.

"I continue to believe we are fortunate to have you in government," Milliken wrote Stewart. "You are a man of good will with enlightened view and a civil approach to dealing with problems. There is a rigidity, a meanness, and a highly partisan spirit abroad that ill serves the public. You are also a credit to our party at a time when it is desperately in need of thoughtful and highly motivated people like you."[54]

Along with 14 other Republicans, Stewart supported Granholm's position and it became law. "I called [Milliken] and said the moderate

Republicans are back," Stewart said. He remembered having met Milliken in the 1960s at an inaugural event in Lansing when Stewart was a teenager: "What a gentleman . . . He was so polite to me." As governor, Stewart said, his most important characteristic was his ability "to get along with both sides of the aisle."[55]

More often, though, state legislative Republicans followed in the path mapped out for them by the successful Engler, who had initially won election and then reelection twice on a tax-cutting, antigovernment platform. At most, a handful of Republicans in both the House and Senate labeled themselves as moderates beginning in the mid-1990s. This signaled a change in the underlying tone and partisan identification of Michigan politics.

Not long after Milliken's 1982 retirement, a political scientist said, "The moderate views of partisans and independents alike stem largely from the pragmatic posture that seems to characterize Michigan voters. The great majority of Republicans, Democrats and Independents manifest medium or strongly positive feelings toward both liberals and conservatives, and classify themselves as moderate or middle-of-the-road in their issue orientation."[56]

The same analyst, however, seemed to imply that a watershed had been crossed in the 1982 election to succeed Milliken. Noting that G. Mennen Williams had campaigned for higher taxes and better services to the poor and Milliken for open housing and adequate aid to Detroit, "Blanchard and Headlee, by contrast, stood for election."[57] The implication was that professional campaign consultants and pollsters had taken command of campaigns, coining slogans and images to capture public sentiment rather than fashioning strong issue stands.

But this analysis was only half right. Headlee's surprising showings in both the Republican primary and the relatively narrow defeat by Blanchard in the general election suggested a rightward turn in the electorate not unlike that of the nation's voters in 1980 when they carried Ronald Reagan to the presidency. Blanchard was reelected in 1986 against a weak opponent. But his 1990 defeat, though also narrow, catapulted the conservative, tax-cutting Engler into power and shifted both the tone and the content of statewide policies and politics for years to come. Engler's dramatic and successful cutoff of state general assistance payments to able-bodied males in 1991 was not something Milliken would have done, out of his concern for urban populations

Northern Conscience

and the poor, and it was something Blanchard could not do for fear of alienating Detroit's Mayor Young and African Americans in general. Engler popularized business and personal tax cuts, undercut environmental protections and business regulation, and pushed public funding for charter schools, positions that Milliken never espoused.

An equally great difference was that of tone. During the Blanchard and Engler years, Lansing political discourse, like that of the nation, coarsened. Engler in particular ridiculed his opponents. Capitol correspondent Tim Skubick said in his memoir that he regretted not being present when Milliken and his wife "got in the Lincoln for the last time on Inauguration Day 1983. Guys who were there tell me there wasn't a dry eye despite the bitter cold and the even more chilling feeling that a civil era of Michigan politics was walking out the door . . . never to return in the same way."[58]

Trying to place Milliken within the history of the Michigan and national Republican Parties requires recognition that the moderate and progressive wings of the party as a whole were vibrant from the 1940s through the 1970s. Milliken was just one of a class of moderate to liberal northeastern and midwestern GOP governors that included Nelson Rockefeller of New York, whom Milliken supported for president in 1964; William Scranton and Richard Thornburgh of Pennsylvania; Robert Ray of Iowa; and Richard Ogilvie and James Thompson of Illinois. These men combined the traditional Republican friendliness to business with the championing of an activist government as an instrument of economic opportunity, civil rights, and conservation. But when they passed from the political scene increasingly conservative Republicans replaced them.

In her book *It's My Party Too,* former New Jersey Republican governor and U.S. Environmental Protection Agency chief Christine Todd Whitman said:

> When I came of age as a Republican [she was born in 1946], the party was much more accommodating to a range of opinions within its ranks from the far right to the moderate middle. It's hard to believe today, but there were even those who proudly called themselves liberal Republicans. The various wings of the party certainly had their irritations with each other, but they nevertheless made room for one another. I was taught by my parents—staunch

Republicans both—that this expansive, encompassing reach was one of the GOP's great strengths. My father referred to the party as "the big umbrella."[59]

In 2005, few would characterize the Michigan or national Republican Party as a big umbrella, let alone a big tent. Instead party leaders have either intuited or claimed a mandate from an increasingly conservative populace that they believe wants reduced taxes and a smaller government in the economic sphere but favors an expansive government in the policing of domestic security and the promotion of morality. The emphasis on eliminating abortion is often linked by conservatives to the party's moral origins more than 150 years ago in seeking to abolish slavery. That position indeed seems to command an increasing share of public support, but abortion is a more complex issue that involves balancing rights and personal beliefs. And many of the moral realms within which today's Republicans seek an expansive government role lend themselves even less to black-and-white judgments. Some—such as domestic surveillance of dissidents, whom conservatives consider disloyal in the age of terrorism—are deeply at odds with the party's professed goal of defending individual freedom.

Perhaps most damaging to the state and nation in the long run is the bitter division that has resulted from the party's admittedly successful exploitation of racial, gender, and security fears. A similar division resulted in the nation's only large-scale civil war and cost more than 500,000 lives in a fundamental test of the Founders' ideals. It was, of course, the first Republican president, Lincoln, who presided over that war but sought a reunified nation whose wounds would be quickly healed. "Moderates have an indispensable role to play: We must bring the Republican Party, and American politics generally, back toward the productive center," Whitman said in her book. She exhorted her moderate cohort to articulate "a position that is true to the historic principles of our party and our nation, not one that is tied to an extremist agenda."[60]

During his 22 years in elective office, William Milliken shunned extremes and sought to govern from the center. In his final State of the Stage message to the legislature on January 14, 1982, he quoted Judge Learned Hand: "The temper which does not press a partisan advantage to its bitter end, which can understand and respect the other side, which feels a unity between all citizens . . . which recognizes their common fate and their common aspirations; in a word, which has faith in the sacredness of the individual . . . this is what we have striven for." Of all these qualities, perhaps the one that ran deepest in Milliken was the ability to "understand and respect the other side." He saw adversaries and opponents but no enemies. Too many politicians of both major parties, but especially of the Republican, see enemies in abundance.

To this, Milliken never could or would adapt. Even in the 2004 campaign season, one of the most poisonous in American history, he offered a perspective that coming from another politician might have sounded naive or disingenuous—and not credible. In an interview for the magazine *Michigan History,* he said, "I've always felt that good government is good politics. It certainly has resulted in progress in this state . . . not only in my time but in other administrations as well. When people realize a public official is trying to do an honest and open job, they tend to remember that at election time. Good government is a precursor to a successful political career . . . And it's just as valid today. It's a key to maintaining the public's trust and respect for public officials. When that is lost, the strength of our democracy is weakened. Right now there is widespread feeling that too many politicians are pandering to special interests and are self-serving. The net effect of that is disengagement on the part of citizens. That's borne out by the fact that voter turnout is appallingly low."[61]

In a time of deep political polarization, even liberals found themselves hoping for the resurgence of a special breed of Republican exemplified by Milliken: the moderate. "In a very real sense, the health of our democracy may hinge on the conscience of Republican moderates," wrote Theodore Roszak in October 2004.[62] "Only they can keep their party from being hijacked by crony capitalists and gay-and-feminist-bashing evangelicals . . . When polarization becomes as severe as it is in our country today, politics becomes pathological. Unprincipled campaign managers (and they exist in both parties) and slick spin doctors become the arbiters of elections. Obfuscation is honed to a high art, moderation becomes 'girlie-man' cowardice, war becomes the touchstone of patriotism. Worst of all, people not only lose sight of the common good but of their own obvious interests."

Mel Larsen, a former state representative who also served as chair of the Michigan Republican Party during Milliken's last term in office, evaluated the former governor's singular stance from a historical perspective in 2005. "During my tenure as State Party chair . . . I learned how conservative the grassroots Republican Party was and is in Michigan. It was true then and is still today almost impossible for a moderate Republican to survive a statewide primary. This has held true for over 50 years with the exception of Governor Milliken and had he run for governor without the incumbency would he have been so successful? The Republican Party in Michigan has never been moderate—more conservative or less conservative, but never moderate."[63]

Two-time gubernatorial campaign foe Sander Levin, with whom the Millikens developed a friendship beginning in the late 1990s, described his view and the possible verdict of history on Milliken this way:

> I think Bill Milliken has always been a thoroughgoing pluralist. He cherishes diversity and differences of opinion, and he shuns extremism. That is very basic as to how one approaches public issues and public life.
>
> He's a Republican. There are some differences in our beliefs, his background is different from mine, but he came from a background where he genuinely cared for the "little guy." Republicans today don't have nearly the same regard for the little guy.
>
> I think the Republican Party has abandoned the Bill Millikens of the world. My hope is that history will show he was closer to the mark than the Republican Party of today.[64]

But it seemed possible early in the twenty-first century, despite the attempts of Jennifer Granholm to model herself after Milliken as governor, that his style of politics and governing would not come back in fashion for decades if ever. The progressive Michigan of the 1960s and 1970s that he had led, characterized by rising taxes and government services, by compassion for the poor and opportunity for persons of color, by environmental advancement and educational investment, and most emphatically by openness, decency, and civility, seemed largely a memory, unlikely to be renewed.

But there is always a chance that the recurrence of a fundamental Michigan character exemplified by both William and Helen Milliken will make their times relevant again. Longtime *Detroit Free Press* editor

Joe Stroud, a friend of the couple, equated them with the state itself after a visit to Traverse City early in their retirement in 1985.

"As Gov. Milliken talked, there was such a sense of place, of the changing of the seasons, of the rituals that give life a continuity and predictability that I envied him his Northern Michigan roots . . . Other politicians might live and die by the airport, and they might lust for the Potomac, but Bill Milliken knew he was first, last and always a creature of Michigan, and specifically of northern Michigan, and that was important. It still is . . . One of the reasons a lot of Michiganians . . . felt comfortable with Bill Milliken as governor was that he had some-how held onto [the sense of place]. He might have let that budget deficit get out of hand, and he might not have moved early enough on PBB, but he knew who he was, and he knew who we were, and it surely felt right."[65]

As Stroud and his wife sat with the Millikens in their home over-looking Grand Traverse Bay on one of the first warm days of late win-ter, Stroud could see the ice beginning to break free from the shore. Milliken, who had observed the bay all his life—including on many weekends when he was governor and insisted on returning home—said a moment would come soon when the wind would shift. The ice would break loose from the shore with a loud noise, and within a few hours the bay would become ice free.

So too, might the winds of Michigan politics shift again and clear its surface of obstructions, opening up the power of the people regardless of partisan loyalties to build a more just and civil state.

NOTES

PROLOGUE

1. Pat Fitzgerald, "Jobless Rate No News: Second Year of Double-Digit Unemployment," *Lansing State Journal,* December 6, 1981, 2B.

2. Ibid.

3. David Hoffman, "Job Outlook Bleak: Nine Million Jobless, First Time since '39," *Detroit Free Press,* December 5, 1981, 1A.

4. Chris Andrews, "MSU Leads in Program Cuts," *Lansing State Journal,* December 4, 1981, 1B.

5. David Kushma and Hugh McDiarmid, "Ten Workers' Comp Bills on Way to Milliken's Desk," *Detroit Free Press,* December 16, 1981, 3A.

6. Lorraine Anderson, "Milliken Sure Can Keep a Good Secret," *Traverse City Record-Eagle,* December 21, 1981, 1.

7. Associated Press, "Milliken to End Suspense This Week," *Traverse City Record-Eagle,* December 21, 1981, 4.

8. Ibid.

9. Joanna Firestone, "Milliken Has 'Made Decision' on Future—Wife," *Detroit News,* December 4, 1981.

10. "Michigan Gov. Milliken Rips the Veil from His Plans This Week," *Washington Post,* December 21, 1981, A6.

11. Associated Press, "Suspense to End: Gov. Milliken's 'D-Day' at Hand," *Grand Rapids Press,* December 20, 1981, 2E.

12. Personal communication, November 17, 2003.

13. Statement of Governor William G. Milliken, Press Conference, December 22, 1981.

14. Interview with author, September 5, 2003.

15. Interview with author, October 7, 2003.

16. Robert E. Roach, "Milliken Gives Young an Early Call," *Detroit News,* December 23, 1981, 1.

17. "Governor Milliken: A True Friend to Detroit," *Michigan Chronicle,* January 9, 1982, A5.

18. "The Milliken Years," *Detroit News,* December 23, 1981.

19. "Milliken Made Right Decision," *Marquette Mining Journal,* December 23, 1981.

20. "William Milliken, A Worthy Leader," *Grand Rapids Press,* December 23, 1981, 10A.

21. "Milliken: His Decision Not to Run May Alter the Future of Michigan Politics," *Detroit Free Press,* December 23, 1981.

22. Loraine Anderson, "Milliken Uncertain until Walk in TC," *Traverse City Record-Eagle,* December 23, 1981, 1.

23. Deborah D. Wyatt, "Milliken Settles In: Out of the Limelight, Not Out of the Issues," *Traverse, the Magazine,* August 1983, 30.

24. Ed Hoogterp, "Statewide Reactions Vary as Milliken 'Runs for Cover,'" *Grand Rapids Press,* December 23, 1981.

CHAPTER I

1. *Traverse City Record-Eagle,* March 22, 24, April 7, 9, 1922.

2. "Attempt to Kill Wiedoft Fails," *Traverse City Record-Eagle,* March 29, 1922, 1.

3. "Boil Bay Water," *Traverse City Record-Eagle,* April 7, 1922, 1.

4. "The Water Situation," *Traverse City Record-Eagle,* April 8, 1922, 4.

5. "'Timber' Salvation of Cut-Over Lands," *Traverse City Record-Eagle,* April 10, 1922, 1.

6. Joyce Braithwaite and George Weeks, *The Milliken Years: A Pictorial Reflection,* ed. Robert D. Kirk (Traverse City: *Traverse City Record-Eagle* and Village Press, 1988), 15.

7. First Congregational Church of Traverse City, Michigan, "Tribute to James W. Milliken," *Church Visitor* 2, no 5 (July 1908): 1.

8. "Gone Beyond: Death of Hon. J. W. Milliken, of Traverse City," *Michigan Tradesman,* 1908, 10.

9. William G. Milliken, introduction to *Michigan: Photography of Balthazar Korab* (Charlottesville, VA: Howell Press, 1987).

10. Lawrence Wakefield, *Queen City of the North: An Illustrated History of Traverse City from Its Beginnings to the 1980s* (Traverse City: Village Press, 1988), 13.

11. Ibid., 12.

12. "Gone Beyond."

13. Ibid.

14. First Congregational Church of Traverse City, Michigan, "Tribute to James W. Milliken," 3.

15. Robert D. Wilhelm and Theodore C. Wright, *Heritage for the Future: Commemorating the 125th Anniversary of the First Congregational United Church of Christ, Traverse City, Michigan, 1863–1988* (Traverse City: Village Press, 1988), 19.

16. First Congregational Church of Traverse City, Michigan, "Tribute to James W. Milliken," 2.

17. Ibid.

18. Ibid., 1.

19. Quoted in ibid., 7.

20. Ibid., 16.

21. William G. Milliken, interview with author, July 10, 2003.

22. William G. Milliken, interview with author, September 24, 2003.

23. Ruth Milliken, interview with author, November 21, 2003.

24. Ibid.

25. However, a portion of the site of the family cottage is now protected as a township park.

26. William G. Milliken, interview with author, September 24, 2003.

27. Ibid.

28. Ibid.

29. Frank Ochberg, interview with author, January 29, 2004.

30. Traverse City High School, "Report of Bill Milliken," Class 9–2, 1937, copy in author's possession.

31. Marcy Murningham, "Milliken Politician as Teen: Governor of Traverse City High," *Lansing State Journal,* undated clipping in author's possession.

32. John Milliken, interview with author, June 18, 2004.

33. Braithwaite and Weeks, *The Milliken Years,* 21.

34. Dan Angel, *William G. Milliken: A Touch of Steel,* introduction by Robert P. Griffin (Warren, MI: Public Affairs Press, 1970).

35. Ibid.

36. Ruth Milliken, interview with author, November 21, 2003.

37. William G. Milliken, interview with author, July 10, 2003.

38. Ibid.

39. Ibid.

40. Angel, *William G. Milliken.*

41. Ibid.

42. John Milliken, interview with author, June 18, 2004.

43. An undated news article from the *Traverse City Record-Eagle* credited the elder Milliken with carrying the day. "The voters rallied to the municipal ownership standard and the decisive defeat of the [private] franchise was to a great extent an appreciation of their confidence in his advice . . . [for] without the former mayor's opposition the franchise might have carried."

44. Hillel Levin, "Milliken: The Man You Never Knew," *Monthly Detroit,* February 1982, 49.

45. Braithwaite and Weeks, *The Milliken Years,* 22.

46. Yale University application for admission to the freshman class in 1940, February 21, 1940, copy in author's possession.

CHAPTER 2

1. Conley Brooks, personal communication, July 8, 2004.

2. "Making Sacrifices: William G. Milliken," *Michigan History,* November–December 1991, 53.

3. Ibid.

4. William G. Milliken, interview with author, September 24, 2003.

5. Braithwaite and Weeks, *The Milliken Years,* 24.

6. Helen W. Milliken, interview with author, September 24, 2003.

7. Ibid.

8. Ibid.

9. Helen W. Milliken, interview with author, September 24, 2003.

10. "Making Sacrifices," 54.

11. Ibid.

12. Angel, *William G. Milliken.*

13. Office of the Squadron Surgeon, 721st Bomb Squadron, 450th Bomb Group, March 25, 1945.

14. "Making Sacrifices," 55.

15. William G. Milliken, personal communication, February 9, 2005.

16. Ibid.

17. "Making Sacrifices," 56.

18. William G. Milliken, interview with author, September 24, 2003.

19. Ibid.

20. Angel, *William G. Milliken.*

21. "Making Sacrifices," 56.

22. Ibid.

23. Ibid.

24. Braithwaite and Weeks, *The Milliken Years,* 23.

25. Ibid.

26. William G. Milliken, interview with author, September 24, 2003.

27. Ibid.

28. Helen W. Milliken, interview with author, September 24, 2003.

29. Ibid.

CHAPTER 3

1. Interview with author, July 10, 2003.

2. Interview with author, February 9, 2005.

3. Ibid.

4. Ibid.

5. Appointment letter from Governor Kim Sigler, August 25, 1947, in author's possession.

6. United Press International, "Waterways Post Goes to Milliken," *Traverse City Record-Eagle,* August 26, 1947.

7. Interview with author, July 9, 2003.

8. Ibid.

9. Interview with author, September 24, 2003.

10. Personal communication, November 8, 2004.

11. Ibid.

12. Undated newspaper clipping in author's possession.

13. Undated newspaper clipping in author's possession.

14. Interview with author, November 26, 2003.

15. Angel, *William G. Milliken.*

16. Ibid.

17. Interview with author, February 9, 2005.

18. Interview with author, August 20, 2003.

19. Braithwaite and Weeks, *The Milliken Years,* 27.

20. "Great Banquet Launches New C. of C. Year," *Traverse City Record-Eagle,* January 21, 1955, 1.

21. Braithwaite and Weeks, *The Milliken Years,* 27.

22. Interview with author, September 24, 2003.

23. Interview with author, February 9, 2005.

24. Interview with author, February 18, 2004.

25. Interview with author, February 9, 2005.

26. Interview with author, July 9, 2003.

27. Lewis L. Gould, *Grand Old Party: A History of the Republicans* (New York: Random House, 2003), 14.

28. Tom George, "Leading the Way: Michigan and the Birth of the Republican Party," *Michigan History,* October–November 2004, 10.

29. Ibid., 16.

30. Ripon, Wisconsin, also claims the title of Republican Party birthplace by virtue of a meeting held there on February 28, 1854, at which a coalition of dissidents vowed to create a new party if the Nebraska-Kansas bill became law.

31. Sister Mary Karl George, R.S.M., *Zachariah Chandler: A Political Biography,* (East Lansing: Michigan State University Press, 1969), 222.

32. Gould, *Grand Old Party,* 311–12.

33. Ibid.

34. Ibid.

35. "W.G. Milliken Candidate for State Senate: Will Seek GOP Nomination for This District," *Traverse City Record-Eagle,* March 24, 1960, 1.

36. "Sen. Minnema Candidate for Re-Election," *Traverse City Record-Eagle,* March 25, 1960, 1.

37. Interview with author, September 24, 2003.

38. Personal communication, November 8, 2004.

39. Ibid.

40. "Bill Milliken for State Senator," advertisement, *Traverse City Record-Eagle,* July 30, 1960, 2.

41. Braithwaite and Weeks, *The Milliken Years,* 29.

42. United Press International, "Conservative Senate Bloc Overthrown; Liberal Group Stages Coup," *Traverse City Record-Eagle,* January 18, 1961.

43. Quoted in Angel, *William G. Milliken,* 53.

44. Interview with author, July 9, 2003.

45. The other moderate senators were Stanley Thayer of Ann Arbor, Fred Hilbert of Wayland, Harry Litowich of Benton Harbor, John Stahlin of Belding, Farrell Roberts of Pontiac, John Fitzgerald of Grand Ledge, and Tom Schweigert of Petoskey.

46. Braithwaite and Weeks, *The Milliken Years,* 29.

47. "GOP State Senators Map 12-Point Program," *Traverse City Record-Eagle,* August 19, 1961, 1.

48. Ibid.

49. Ray Courage, "'Moderates' Map Plan to Sway GOP," *Detroit Free Press,* August 19, 1961, 3.

50. Ray Courage, "GOP Moderates Warn Lobbyists Not to Meddle," *Detroit Free Press,* August 27, 1961, 4.

51. Angel, *William G. Milliken,* 54.

52. Interview with author, July 9, 2003.

53. Quoted in Angel, *William G. Milliken,* 57.

54. Ibid., 58.

55. Interview with author, August 20, 2003.

CHAPTER 4

1. Angel, *William G. Milliken,* 65.

2. John T. Dempsey, "Romney for Governor: The 1962 Michigan Election Campaign," unpublished manuscript in author's possession, 63.

3. Angel, *William G. Milliken,* 58–60.

4. Tim Robison, "Milliken to Offer Scenic Beauty Bill," *Traverse City Record-Eagle,* February 14, 1964.

5. Interview with author, July 9, 2003.

6. Ibid.

7. Ibid.

8. This ended a system in which the governor and lieutenant governor were elected separately, sometimes belonged to different political parties, and occasionally clashed over decision making, particularly when the governor was out of the state and Michigan's executive power devolved to the lieutenant governor.

9. Angel, *William G. Milliken,* 65.

10. Charles Harmon, "Governor's Draft Talk Shocks Some," *Bay City Times,* January 8, 1964.

11. Glenn Engle, "Michigan Politics: Romney Upsets Campaign Applecarts," *Detroit News,* January 12, 1964.

12. "Sen. Milliken Candidate for Lt. Governor," *Traverse City Record-Eagle,* March 10, 1964.

13. James S. Brooks, "GOP Ticket Taking Shape, Milliken, Peterson in Ring," *Coldwater Daily Reporter,* March 10, 1964.

14. Interview with author, March 10, 2004.

15. Ibid.

16. Interview with author, March 4, 2004.

17. Interview with author, July 9, 2003.

18. Interview with author, July 10, 2003.

19. Interview with author, February 18, 2004.

20. Martha Mongeau, "Michigan Public Personalities: Milliken Sees New Era for Non-public Schools," *Catholic Weekly,* February 21, 1964, 10.

21. Allison Green to William G. Milliken, April 30, 1998, letter in author's possession.

22. Glenn Engle, "Griffin, Milliken Set for State or National GOP Race in '64," *Detroit News,* July 7, 1963.

23. Angel, *William G. Milliken,* 71–72.

24. William F. McLaughlin, "Politician: Remembrances of 20 Years at the Political Grass Roots," undated manuscript in author's possession.

25. "The Essential Quality," *Traverse City Record-Eagle,* September 22, 1964.

26. Angel, *William G. Milliken,* 76.

27. Interview with author, July 9, 2003.

28. Personal communication, November 11, 2004.

29. Personal communication, January 10, 2005.

30. United Press International, "Romney Wins Despite State Dem Landslide," undated clipping in author's possession.

31. "Milliken Becomes Lt. Governor Friday," *Traverse City Record-Eagle,* December 31, 1964, 10–11.

32. Charles Harmon, "Milliken Sits in 'Hot Seat' In Presiding over Senate," *Grand Rapids Press,* November 8, 1964, 11.

33. Ibid.

34. *Grand Rapids Press,* January 3, 1965, 42.

35. Associated Press, "Milliken off Unit: Senate Democrats See Authority Conflict," undated clipping in author's possession.

36. Angel, *William G. Milliken,* 80.

37. Bill Sudomier, "Lt. Gov William Milliken, Easy Grin, Hard Battler," *Detroit Free Press,* undated clipping in author's possession.

38. Ibid.

39. Willard Baird, "Milliken Faces Fast-Paced Timetable," *Lansing State Journal,* January 10, 1965.

40. Robert A. Popa, "Milliken Is Touring Hinterlands, Takes Office 'to the People,'" *Detroit News,* July 11, 1965.

41. Angel, *William G. Milliken,* 81.

42. Ibid., 82.

43. Interview with author, July 9, 2003.

44. Sam Martino, "Milliken Embarrassed: Misses LBJ Plane," United Press International, undated clipping in author's possession.

45. Don Hoenshell, "State to Butter Up Mayor—or Vice Versa," *Detroit News,* undated clipping in author's possession.

46. Interview with author, July 9, 2003.

47. Ibid.

48. Ibid.

49. Personal communication, November 11, 2004.

50. Angel, *William G. Milliken,* 84–87.

51. Mary Ann Weston, "Milliken Tells Schools to Seek Court Action: Teachers Quit in One Suburb," *Detroit Free Press,* undated 1965 clipping in author's possession.

52. Interview with author, July 9, 2003.

53. Angel, *William G. Milliken,* 86–87.

54. Interview with author, November 26, 2003.

55. Interview with author, June 30, 2004.

56. Roger Lane, "Milliken Looks Like Governor Candidate," *Detroit Free Press,* November 2, 1966, 3A.

57. "The Detroit Riot of 1967," http://www.67riots.rutgers.edu/d_index.htm.

58. University of Phoenix, "12th Street Riot," Free Dictionary.com, http://encyclopedia.thefreedictionary.com/12th%20Street%20Riot.

59. David Crumm, "Untold Stories of '67 Region Divide Our Region, Our Lives," *Detroit Free Press,* October 14, 2004, http://www.freep.com/news/nw/anger14e_20041014.htm.

60. Ibid.

61. Interview with author, July 9, 2003.

62. McLaughlin, "Politician," 59.

63. Bud Vestal, "Milliken Champions Housing Fight," *Muskegon Chronicle,* December 14, 1967.

64. Ibid.

65. William E. Cote, "Milliken Vows Open Housing Battle Will Continue," *Flint Journal,* December 22, 1967, 26.

66. Bill Langley, "Milliken's Muskegon Speech Shocks Conservatives," undated press clipping in author's possession.

67. Ibid.

68. Bud Vestal, "Few Noticed, but Milliken Became 'Governor,'" *Grand Rapids Press,* November 26, 1967, 42.

69. Interview with author, July 10, 2003.

70. Ibid.

71. Ibid.

72. Interview with author, October 17, 2003.

73. "Michigan on the Move: A Progress Report of the First Romney Administration," 1964, undated political advertising newspaper insert in author's possession.

74. Braithwaite and Weeks, *The Milliken Years,* 33.

CHAPTER 5

1. "Romney's Farewell to People of Michigan: Governor Calls Milliken Able, Experienced," *Michigan Republican Plain Talk,* January 1969.

2. Roger Lane, "Milliken Splits with Romney by Supporting Parochiaid," *Detroit Free Press,* January 10, 1969, 1.

3. United Press International, "Milliken Urges Prudent State Spending," *Traverse City Record-Eagle,* January 9, 1969.

4. Ibid.

5. Lt. Governor's Message to the 75th Michigan Legislature, January 9, 1969, in *Addresses and Special Messages of Governor William G. Milliken, 1969–1982* (Lansing: State of Michigan, 1983), 1–4.

6. Ibid., 2.

7. Ibid., 3.

8. Ibid., 4.

9. Ibid., 6–9.

10. Interview with author, June 30, 2004.

11. Dempsey was the author's father.

12. Glen Engle, "Milliken Defends Selection of Aide," *Detroit News,* January 29, 1969.

13. Curt Hanes, "Reaction to Milliken Generally Favorable," *Lansing State Journal,* January 10, 1969, A3.

14. William G. Milliken, personal communication, November 11, 2004.

15. "The State of the State Offers Hope to Detroit," *Detroit Free Press,* January 10, 1969, 6A.

16. Elmer E. White, "Milliken: Businessman Who Turned Politician," *The Eccentric* (Birmingham, MI), December 27, 1968, A13.

17. Clark Hoyt, "Milliken's 'Nice Guy' Image—and the Governor's Office," *Detroit Free Press,* November 24, 1968, B1.

18. W. Gardner Weber, "Traverse City's Bill Milliken Now Michigan's 44th Governor," *Traverse City Record-Eagle,* January 23, 1969.

19. Ibid.

20. Associated Press, "Milliken's Inauguration Will Outclass His First," *Flint Journal,* December 20, 1970.

21. Braithwaite and Weeks, *The Milliken Years,* 37.

22. Interview with author, June 26, 2004.

23. Interview with author, March 5, 2004.

24. Hugh McDiarmid, "Braithwaite: A Little Life in the Party," *Detroit Free Press,* August 22, 1978.

25. Interview with author, July 10, 2003.

26. Interview with author, March 5, 2004.

27. Interview with author, October 23, 2003.

28. Interview with author, October 7, 2003.

29. Interview with author, July 9, 2003.

30. Ibid.

31. Personal communication, May 25, 2005.

32. James Phillips, "Governor Milliken's Day Is Packed with Work, Duties," *Battle Creek Enquirer and News,* February 21, 1969, A3.

33. Ibid.

34. Interview with author, September 24, 2003.

35. Ibid.

36. Interview with author, June 30, 2004.

37. Ibid.

38. William G. Milliken, Jr., "An Analysis," November 30, 1970, copy in author's possession.

39. McLaughlin, "Politician," 113.

40. Ibid., 120.

41. Clark Hoyt, "Angry Romney Retakes GOP from Milliken," *Detroit Free Press,* February 25, 1970, 3A.

42. Ibid.

43. Robert L. Pisor, "Romney Puts Lenore Back in Race; Milliken Bows to Power Play," *Detroit News,* undated 1970 clipping in author's possession.

44. Quoted in McLaughlin, "Politician," 120.

45. Ibid., 122.

46. Ibid., 126.

47. Ibid., 125–27.

48. Willard Baird, "Milliken Makes It Official," *Lansing State Journal,* June 9, 1970, A1.

49. McLaughlin, "Politician," 138.

50. William G. Milliken Jr. "An Analysis," 3.

51. Robert Longstaff, "Economic Woes Hit Michigan," Booth Newspapers, undated 1970 clipping in author's possession.

52. "A Vote for Milliken," *Detroit News,* October 11, 1970, C3.

53. "Milliken's Quality Tells amid Adverse Campaign," *Detroit Free Press,* November 1, 1970, B2.

54. Robert L. Pisor, "Milliken Scores Victory in Debate, Levin Left Speechless," *Detroit News,* October 6, 1970, A12.

55. Clark Hoyt, "Milliken Shakes Lethargic GOP, Won't Forget Who Didn't Help," *Detroit Free Press,* October 16, 1970, A3.

56. Interview with author, March 4, 2004.

57. "Milliken Has Both Talent, Assets to Build Mandate," *Detroit Free Press,* November 7, 1970, A8.

58. Interview with author, May 18, 2005.

59. Revised schedule, Mrs. William G. Milliken, Monday, September 21, through Sunday, September 27, 1970, copy in author's possession.

60. Helen Fogel, "Helen Milliken Says, 'We Must Understand Each Other's Needs,'" *Detroit Free Press,* November 5, 1970, D1.

61. Lee Winfrey and Roger Lane, "Milliken Victory Conceded after 42-Hour Cliff Hanger," *Detroit Free Press,* November 6, 1970, A1.

CHAPTER 6

1. Interview with author, October 7, 2003.

2. Interview with author, January 9, 2004.

3. Interview with author, July 10, 2003.

4. Ibid.

5. Robert Longstaff, "Governor Roughs It at U.P. Park," Booth News Service, undated 1980 news clipping in author's possession.

6. Ibid.

7. Frank Mainville, "Progress Hurts Environment, Mrs. Milliken Tells Youths," *Lansing State Journal,* undated 1970 clipping in author's possession.

8. Mrs. William G. Milliken, "Michigan's First Lady and the Quality of Environment," *Michigan Republican Plain Talk,* February 1970, 3.

9. Dr. George J. Wallace, "Insecticides and Birds," *Audubon Magazine,* January–February 1959. Originally a paper presented at Fifty-fourth Annual Convention of the National Audubon Society.

10. Rachel Carson, *Silent Spring* (rpt.; New York: Houghton Mifflin, 1994), 2.

11. John Carew, "As It Looks to Me," *American Vegetable Grower,* November 1963.

12. "State Moves to Ban Sale of DDT," *Detroit Free Press,* April 17, 1969.

13. William G. Milliken, "Special Message to the Legislature on the Environment," January 22, 1970, in *Addresses and Special Messages of Governor William G. Milliken,* 44.

14. Ibid.

15. Ibid., 48.

16. Tom Opre, "Our Hats Go off to Gov. Milliken," *Detroit Free Press,* February 8, 1970, D6.

17. Interview with author, January 9, 2004.

18. Interview with author, April 13, 2004.

19. Ibid.

20. United Press International, "Mercury Poison Brings St. Clair Fishing Ban," *Traverse City Record-Eagle,* April 11, 1970, 1.

21. Ladd Neuman, "Milliken Urges 'Truth in Pollution,'" *Detroit Free Press,* April 16, 1970, A1.

22. Helen Clegg, "Officials Push Pollution Fight," *Lansing State Journal,* April 23, 1970, A3.

23. Ibid.

24. Interview with author, July 10, 2003.

25. Bill O'Brien, "Milliken Keeps Watch on Ruling; Court to Decide Who Can Sue under MEPA," *Traverse City Record-Eagle,* undated 2004 news clipping in author's possession.

26. "Remarks by Gov. William G. Milliken," Michigan United Conservation Clubs Annual Convention, Traverse City, June 21, 1970, copy in author's possession.

27. "Qualified, Competent—Female," *Detroit Free Press,* undated August 1973 news clipping in author's possession.

28. David Johnston, "Milliken Names Two to DNR Board," *Detroit Free Press,* August 15, 1973, B9.

29. Howard Tanner, interview with author, February 10, 2004.

30. Interview with author, October 15, 1999.

31. Snell resigned from the commission in October 1983 after James J. Blanchard became governor.

32. Interview with author, March 10, 2004.

33. Ibid.

34. Gordon Charles, *Pigeon River Country: The Big Wild* (Grand Rapids: Eerdmans, 1985), ix.

35. Ford Kellum to Helen Milliken, January 22, 1975, Helen Milliken Papers, Box 7, Bentley Historical Library, University of Michigan.

36. Interview with author, September 24, 2003.

37. Personal communication, December 18, 2003.

38. Helen Milliken to Joan Wolfe, January 31, 1975, Helen Milliken Papers, Box 7, Bentley Historical Library, University of Michigan.

39. Ibid.

40. Martin Hirschman, "Michigan Could Become Nuclear Dumping Site," *Lansing State Journal,* May 27, 1976, B6.

41. Kirk Cheyfitz, "State Favored for A-Dumps," *Detroit Free Press,* August 23, 1976, A1.

42. Louis M. Heldman, "State Gets Veto over A-Dump," *Detroit Free Press,* September 24, 1976, A3.

43. "Michigan Won't Be A-Waste Site—Milliken," *Detroit News,* June 15, 1977.

44. Tom Dammann, "Navy to Brief Wary U.P. on 'Sanguine' Plan," *Detroit News,* undated news clipping in author's possession.

45. Paul Branzburg, "Navy Eyes UP for Installing Underground Antenna Net," *Detroit Free Press,* March 26, 1973.

46. Paul Branzburg, "A Doomsday Grid in the UP? The Navy's Project Sanguine," *Detroit Free Press,* February 10, 1974, B1.

47. George Weeks to Governor William G. Milliken, February 12, 1974, memorandum in author's possession.

48. "Verdict Should Be Clear with All Seafarer Facts," *Detroit Free Press,* April 9, 1976.

49. George Weeks, "Michigan Loses Military System," *Detroit News,* October 10, 2004, http://www.detnews.com/2004/editorial/0410/10/a20–298632.htm.

50. U.S. Representative Phil Ruppe to Governor William G. Milliken, August 9, 1976, memorandum in author's possession.

51. United Press International, "Ford Pledge Gives State Final Say on Seafarer," November 1, 1976, news clipping in author's possession.

52. Governor William G. Milliken to Secretary of Defense Harold Brown, March 18, 1977, memorandum in author's possession.

53. Weeks, "Michigan Loses Military System."

54. "Political Cowardice," *Marquette Mining Journal,* March 21, 1977.

55. "The Contamination Crisis in Michigan: Polybrominated Biphenyls, a Report from the Special Senate Investigating Committee," Senator John A. Welborn, Chair, Michigan State Senate, July 1975.

56. David Everett, "PBB Crisis 10 Years Later: The Accident Still Haunts us," *Detroit Free Press,* May 29, 1983.

57. "Final PBB Report from the Michigan Department of Agriculture," November 9, 1982.

58. Interview with author, July 9, 2003.

59. Michigan Department of Public Health, Department of Communication Services, news release, December 30, 1981.

60. Interview with author, February 5, 2004.

61. Alden K. Henderson, Daniel Rosen, Gayle L. Miller, et al., "Breast Cancer among Women Exposed to Polybrominated Biphenyls," *Epidemiology* 6, no. 5 (September 1995): 544–46.

62. Ashraful Hoque, "Cancer among a Michigan Cohort Exposed to Polybrominated Biphenyls in 1973," *Epidemiology* 9 (July 1998): 373–77.

63. Michigan Department of Community Health, Division of Environmental and Occupational Epidemiology, "PBB News Update," fall 2003.

64. Everett, "PBB Crisis 10 Years Later."

65. Interview with author, July 10, 2003.

66. "State Suppressed PBB Finding," *Lansing State Journal,* February 5, 1977.

67. Kathy Stariha to Governor William G. Milliken, memorandum, February 7, 1977, William G. Milliken Papers, Box 815, Bentley Historical Library, University of Michigan.

68. Ibid.

69. Joanna Firestone, "Pbb Issue Sparks Milliken, Crim Feud," *Traverse City Record-Eagle,* August 18, 1977.

70. Executive office, news release, October 20, 1978.

71. Great Lakes Water Quality Agreement of 1978, Agreement with Annexes and Terms of Reference between the United States of America and Canada, signed at Ottawa, November 22, 1978, http://www.ijc.org/php/publications/pdf/ID609.pdf.

72. William G. Milliken, remarks at Great Lakes Water Resources Conference, Mackinac Island, Michigan, June 11, 1982, in *Addresses and Special Messages of Governor William G. Milliken,* 308–11.

73. Personal communication, November 18, 2004.

74. Joe Stroud, "Milliken Embodies the Best of this Great State," *Detroit Free Press,* November 12, 1997, A10.

75. Governor John Engler to William G. Milliken, November 6, 1997, memorandum in author's possession.

76. William G. Milliken, "Michigan's Soul Is in its Land," reprinted in *Detroit Free Press,* November 12, 1997, A11.

77. "Michigan's Land, Michigan's Future," Michigan Land Use Leadership Council, http://www.michiganlanduse.org.

78. Besides those mentioned in this chapter, the laws include the Wetland Protection Act, the Sand Dune Protection and Management Act, and the Kammer Land Trust Fund Act (later the Natural Resources Trust Fund).

79. Interview with author, February 10, 2004.

80. Personal communication, January 7, 2005.

CHAPTER 7

1. William G. Milliken, "School Finance Reform in Michigan," in "A Revolution in School Finance?" *Theory into Practice,* Ohio State University, 11, no. 2 (April 1972): 97.

2. William G. Milliken, Lieutenant Governor's Message to the 75th Michigan Legislature, January 9, 1969, in *Addresses and Special Messages of Governor William G. Milliken,* 1.

3. "Gov. Milliken Must Lead School Financing Reform," *Detroit Free Press,* March 30, 1969, B2.

4. "Milliken Warns State Is in School Crisis," *Traverse City Record-Eagle,* April 3, 1969, 1.

5. Interview with author, May 17, 2004.

6. Interview with author, November 26, 2004.

7. Ibid.

8. Interview with author, May 17, 2004.

9. William Grant, "Ex-Harvard Chief Attempts to Speed State School Plan," *Detroit Free Press,* February 19, 1970, C1.

10. *The Governor's Commission on Educational Reform,* Governor William G. Milliken, chairman, 1. Copy in author's possession.

11. Ibid., 2.

12. Ibid., 11.

13. Ibid., 14.

14. The first assessment measured fourth- and seventh-grade math and reading skills and was the result of work by State Superintendent of Public Instruction Ira Polley, Dr. C. Philip Kearney, and Milliken. Charles Greenleaf, personal communication, January 24, 2005.

15. Roger Lane, "Pass School Plan Now—Milliken," *Detroit Free Press,* November 13, 1969, A3.

16. William Grant, "Scrap School Millage—Milliken," *Detroit Free Press,* April 13, 1971, A1.

17. Tim Skubick, *Off the Record* (Ann Arbor: University of Michigan Press; Traverse City: Petoskey Publishing, 2003), 215.

18. Quoted in ibid., 218.

19. "Milliken's Decision an Appeal to Reason," *Lansing State Journal,* November 7, 1971, C2.

20. Skubick, *Off the Record,* 217.

21. "We Need a Better Way to Pay for Schools," *Detroit Free Press* editorial, October 11, 1972, A6.

22. "Proposal C Foe Explains Stand," *Lansing State Journal,* October 28, 1972, A3.

23. Ibid.

24. "New School Financing 'Won't be Cheaper': Taxpayers Being Lied to, DeMaso Charges," *Lansing State Journal,* October 23, 1972, B4.

25. William Grant, "Milliken Pushes Hard for Proposal C," *Detroit Free Press,* November 5, 1972.

26. William Grant, "School Tax Revision Rejected," *Detroit Free Press,* November 8, 1972, A1.

27. "What Now for the Schools?" *Detroit Free Press* editorial, November 9, 1972, A5.

28. Less than a year later, the court revoked its ruling for unspecified reasons, saying only that the initial opinion had been "improvidently given."

29. Governor William G. Milliken, "Special Message to the Legislature on Education," February 7, 1973, 1. Copy in author's possession.

30. Gene Caesar, Robert N. McKerr, and James Phelps, *New Equity in School Finance: The Story of the Bursley Act* (Lansing: Senate Committee on Education, Senator Gilbert E. Bursley, Chairman, June 1, 1974), 4.

31. Ibid., 25.

32. Personal communication, February 9, 2005.

33. Ibid., 26.

34. Interview with author, November 26, 2004.

35. Skubick, *Off the Record,* 214–28.

36. Reprinted in Braithwaite and Weeks, *The Milliken Years,* 18.

37. Craig Ruff, interview with author, January 7, 2004.

38. Governor William G. Milliken, "Special Report to the Legislature," March 9, 1978. Copy in author's possession.

39. Interview with author, July 10, 2003.

40. "Workfare, Staff Cuts in Budget," *Outreach* (Michigan Department of Social Services) 6, no. 10 (May 1981): 3.

41. "From the Director," *Outreach* (Michigan Department of Social Services) 6, no. 7 (January–February 1981): 3.

42. "Caseworkers' Pressure Challenges Rhino Hide," *Saginaw News* editorial, April 7, 1982.

43. Gus Harrison, interview with author, April 7, 2004.

44. Ibid.

45. C. Patrick Babcock, interview with author, December 16, 2003.

46. Charlie Greenleaf, interview with author, June 26, 2004.

CHAPTER 8

1. Keith Schneider, "Michigan Apartheid: Reforming Land Use Policy Can Help Most Segregated State," Great Lakes Bulletin News Service, April 17, 2003, http://www.mlui.org/reportarticle.asp?fileid=16480.

2. McLaughlin, "Politician," 58–59.

3. Interview with author, September 24, 2003.

4. "Freedom Rally Hears Call for Nonviolence," *Detroit News,* undated 1965 newspaper clipping in author's possession.

5. Robert L. Pisor, "Milliken Makes Bid for Racial Harmony," *Detroit News,* May 18, 1969, B4.

6. Ibid.

7. Personal communication, January 25, 2005.

8. See, for example, Roy Levy Williams to Governor Milliken, memorandum, August 6, 1973, William G. Milliken Papers, Box 599, Bentley Historical Library, University of Michigan.

9. Bill McGraw, "Young Shaped Detroit, Confronted Critics, and Fought for Racial Justice," *Detroit Free Press,* November 30, 1997, http://www.freep.com/news/young/.

10. Coleman Young with Lonnie Wheeler, *Hard Stuff: The Autobiography of Mayor Coleman Young* (New York: Viking, 1994), 120.

11. Michigan's lieutenant governor has the constitutional prerogative to preside over state Senate sessions and can cast a tiebreaking vote.

12. Interview with author, August 12, 2004.

13. Ibid.

14. Young and Wheeler, *Hard Stuff,* 219.

15. Jerry Kabel, personal communication, July 9, 2004.

16. Interview with author, March 4, 2004.

17. Ibid.

18. Young and Wheeler, *Hard Stuff,* 218.

19. Nancy Dunn, "'Marriage' Could Pay Off for Milliken and Young," *Grand Rapids Press,* September 11, 1977.

20. Hugh McDiarmid, "Guides and Guards Gear for Governors," *Detroit Free Press,* September 4, 1977, A1.

21. Hugh McDiarmid, "'Urban Lab Is Getting Posh Start,'" *Detroit Free Press,* September 8, 1977, A3.

22. Susan Watson, "Governors Find Our Warts Are à La Mode," *Detroit Free Press,* September 9, 1977.

23. Associated Press, "Crime Area Tour Disappointing, Only Two Governors Interested," *Lansing State Journal,* September 10, 1977.

24. Bob Campbell, "Renaissance Not Citywide: Visiting Governors See the Real Detroit," *Macomb Daily,* September 8, 1977.

25. "For the Governors, a New Detroit," *Detroit News,* undated newspaper clipping in author's possession.

26. Hugh McDiarmid, "Milliken Raps GOP on Blacks," *Detroit Free Press,* September 12, 1977, B13.

27. Associated Press, "Save the Cities, Milliken Urges," *Benton Harbor Herald-Palladium,* September 8, 1977, 8.

28. Young and Wheeler, *Hard Stuff,* 239.

29. Ibid., 244.

30. Hugh McDiarmid, "Budget Seeks 'Distressed Cities' Program," *Detroit Free Press,* January 27, 1981, A3.

31. Nancy Dunn, "Milliken Sets Sights on Bailout of Detroit," *Grand Rapids Press,* February 12, 1981.

32. "Coleman Young Will Be Hard Act to Follow," *Detroit Free Press,* December 1, 1980, A16.

33. "Popularity Poll: How Leaders Rate," *Detroit Free Press,* December 1, 1980, A16.

34. Paul Hillegonds, interview with author, January 6, 2004.

35. Marisol Bello, "Detroit's Budget Crisis Could Force Massive Cuts, Kilpatrick Warns," *Detroit Free Press,* January 5, 2005, http://www.freep.com/news/locway/finances5e_20050105.htm.

36. Interview with author, July 9, 2003.

37. Interview with author, February 20, 2004.

CHAPTER 9

1. Fred L. Dixon, "Stanley T. Wallbank: Of Such Character Are Men Made—60 Years on the Purple Trail," spring 1976, 3, magazine clipping in author's possession.

2. Interview with author, September 24, 2003.

3. Ibid.

4. Ibid.

5. Mary Ann Damme, "State's No. 2 Lady Starts Classes: Settling into Her New Home," *Detroit Free Press,* January 17, 1965, C2.

6. Ibid.

7. Ibid.

8. Gail Osherenko, "The 'P' in Politics Is People to Them," *Christian Science Monitor,* September 22, 1969, 12.

9. Ibid.

10. Marcia Van Ness, "Millikens Disagree: Have Different Views on Parochiaid," *Lansing State Journal,* October 19, 1970, D1.

11. Interview with author, September 24, 2003.

12. Ibid.

13. Ibid.

14. Quoted in Skubick, *Off the Record,* 195.

15. Ibid.

16. Bill Barringer, "Helen Milliken Ready to Fight Political Wars," *Detroit Free Press,* undated clipping in author's possession.

17. Helen Fogel, "A Down-to-Earth Look at the Governor's Wife," *Detroit Free Press,* September 24, 1970, C1.

18. Noreen Murphy, "Michigan's First Lady Visits with Shiawassee Republican Club," *Owosso Argus-Press,* undated clipping in author's possession.

19. "Michigan's First Lady Comes to Davison," *Davison Index,* May 19, 1971, 9.

20. Interview with author, September 24, 2003.

21. *Detroit News,* September 22, 1971, A1.

22. Mary Lou Butcher, "Art: The Train Comes In," *Detroit News,* September 22, 1971, C2.

23. Mary Perpich, "National Chairman for Arts Visits Mrs. Milliken, Artrain," *Lansing State Journal,* October 1971 clipping in author's possession.

24. The Artrain has visited more than 800 communities in Michigan and other states since 1971.

25. Joanna Firestone, United Press International, interview with Helen W. Milliken, filed March 21, 1974, copy in author's possession.

26. Ibid.

27. Michigan for Milliken Committee, "Meet Mrs. Milliken: Michigan's First Lady," 1974 campaign brochure in author's possession.

28. Personal communication, December 5, 2004.

29. Interview with author, September 24, 2003.

30. Barbara Hoover, "The Little Voice That Grew: Helen Milliken Found a Cause and She's Not about to Fade Away," *Michigan: The Sunday Magazine of the Detroit News,* December 5, 1982, 53.

31. Ibid.

32. Interview with author, February 18, 2004.

33. Associated Press, "Milliken's Daughter Makes a Case for Legal Aid to Indigent Women," *Grand Rapids Press,* August 27, 1975.

34. Interview with author, September 24, 2003.

35. Ibid.

36. Roberta W. Francis, Chair, ERA Task Force, National Council of Women's Organizations, "The History Behind the Equal Rights Amendment," available at http://www.equalrightsamendment.org/era.htm (accessed September 25, 2005).

37. The proposed amendment read in its entirety: "*Section 1.* Equality of rights under the law shall not be denied or abridged by the United States or by any state on account of sex. *Section 2.* The Congress shall have the power to enforce, by appropriate legislation, the provisions of this article. *Section 3.* This amendment shall take effect two years after the date of ratification."

38. Francis, "History Behind the Equal Rights Amendment."

39. Helen Milliken to U.S. Representative Elford Cederberg, December 18, 1974, Helen Milliken Papers, Box 7, Bentley Historical Library, University of Michigan.

40. Interview with author, February 9, 2005.

41. Martha Hindes, "Helen Milliken Urges More ERA Support," *Detroit News,* June 17, 1979, B2.

42. George Bullard, "Mormons Refuse to Meet ERAmerica," *Detroit News,* December 22, 1979.

43. Nancy E. Dunn, "Helen Milliken Finds Her Own Role," *Ann Arbor News,* July 14, 1980, A9.

44. Nancy E. Dunn, "Reagan Unconvinced by State ERA Backers," *Ann Arbor News,* July 16, 1980, A5.

45. Correspondence dated May 1, 1981, and May 11, 1981, Helen Milliken Papers, Box 1, Bentley Historical Library, University of Michigan.

46. Ibid.

47. Letter dated May 7, 1981, Helen Milliken Papers, Box 1, Bentley Historical Library, University of Michigan.

48. Correspondence dated November 4 and November 6, 1981, Helen Milliken Papers, Box 5, Bentley Historical Library, University of Michigan.

49. Correspondence dated March 26, 1979, Helen Milliken papers, Box 5, Bentley Historical Library, University of Michigan.

50. Michigan Catholic Conference, *Public Affairs Communicator,* September 13, 1978.

51. "Milliken's Abortion Veto Upheld," *Michigan Report,* February 10, 1982.

52. Jacqueline Teare, "Reproductive Rights Milliken's Campaign," *Ann Arbor News,* November 21, 1987, A5.

53. United Press International, "Loss of Women's Rights Feared: Warning by Mrs. Milliken," *Detroit News,* November 8, 1981, B3.

54. Helen W. Milliken, "ERA Guards Rights of All," *Detroit News,* November 26, 1981, A19.

55. Hoover, "The Little Voice That Grew," 52.

56. Ibid.

57. Marie Averill, "Fashion Is Fun but Low Priority in Life of Michigan's First Lady," *Traverse City Record-Eagle,* August 12, 1981.

58. Interview with author, February 9, 2005.

59. Lucille DeView, transcript of interview with Helen Milliken for the *Detroit News,* Helen Milliken Papers, Box 7, Bentley Historical Library, University of Michigan.

60. Personal communication, May 16, 2005.

61. Hoover, "The Little Voice That Grew," 52.

62. Ibid., 51–53.

63. Betty J. Blair, "Governors' Wives Are Doing More Than Pouring Tea," *Detroit News,* September 9, 1977, D1.

64. Ibid.

65. Interview with author, September 24, 2003.

66. Personal communication, February 23, 2005.

67. Program for 1995 Women of Courage banquets, document in author's possession.

CHAPTER 10

1. Levin, "Milliken," 44.

2. Ibid., 45.

3. Interview with author, November 10, 2003.

4. Ibid.

5. Interview with author, April 15, 2004.

6. Harry H. Whiteley, personal communication, May 6, 2004.

7. Richard Bearup, personal communication, December 1, 2003.

8. Ibid.

9. Lani Jordan, personal communication, November 9, 2004.

10. David Cooper, "Milliken Got Tough on Transit Bill," *Detroit Free Press,* undated clipping in author's possession.

11. Ibid.

12. James Phillips, Associated Press, "Rebels Feeling Milliken's Ire: Underlings Can't Disagree with Governor," undated 1969 clipping in author's possession.

13. Interview with George Weeks, circa 1983, transcript in author's possession.

14. Marcia Van Ness, "Petite Secretary Has Big Job: Mrs. Dell Finds Her Rapport with Governor an Important Asset," *Lansing State Journal,* January 18, 1970, A14.

15. Interview with author, November 19, 2003.

16. Interview with author, April 5, 2004.

17. Joyce Braithwaite Brickley, personal communication, November 20, 2003.

18. Van Ness, "Petite Secretary Has Big Job."

19. Interview with author, November 19, 2003.

20. Michael D. Moore, personal communication, January 4, 2004.

21. Nancy Dockter, interview with author, November 19, 2003.

22. Jody Trock, "Kindness from Governor Touches Romanian Visitor," *The Eccentric,* November 4, 1971, 1.

23. Interview with author, March 25, 2004.

24. Ibid.

25. Associated Press, "Man Faces 2nd Trial in Killing of Teen," *Lansing State Journal,* November 30, 2004, http://www.lsj.com/apps/pbcs.dll/article?AID=/ 20041130/NEWS01/411300325/1001/news.

26. Interview with author, January 29, 2004.

27. Ibid.

28. Interview with author, November 26, 2004.

29. Governor William G. Milliken, "Special Message to the Legislature on Ethics and Election Reform," October 25, 1973, in *Addresses and Special Messages of Governor William G. Milliken,* 93–97.

30. Ibid.

31. Interview with author, January 7, 2004.

32. Jim Neubacher, "Del Rio Girl Friend Is Paid $18,462 Salary for Chats," *Detroit Free Press,* April 8, 1973, A1.

33. Remer Tyson and Hugh McDiarmid, "Milliken's Palace Guard," *Detroit Free Press,* February 20, 1977.

34. Interview with author, October 7, 2003.

35. Interview with author, April 5, 2004.

36. Joyce Braithwaite-Brickley, personal communication, January 5, 2005.

37. Ibid.

38. Interview with author, April 5, 2004.

39. Ibid.

40. Interview with author, January 9, 2004.

41. Hugh McDiarmid, "Milliken Defends Aide, Calls Senator's Attacks 'Crude,'" *Detroit Free Press,* December 24, 1976, A5.

42. Joyce M. Braithwaite to Senator Joseph Mack, December 20, 1976, copy in author's possession.

43. McDiarmid, "Milliken Defends Aide."

44. Willah Weddon, "Strong Women Work," *Lansing State Journal,* February 28, 1974, D1.

45. Robert H. Longstaff, "Key Milliken Aide's Rise like Female Horatio Alger," *Flint Journal,* January 16, 1977, D2.

46. "Thorns or Laurels," *Jackson Citizen Patriot* editorial, May 26, 1980.

47. Interview with author, December 4, 2003.

48. Braithwaite remembers the appointment differently, saying she recommended Fletcher to Milliken, who instantly seized on it.

49. Interview with author, October 17, 2003.

50. Personal communication, November 17, 2003.

51. Tyson and McDiarmid, "Milliken's Palace Guard."

52. Ibid.

53. Milliken did not know about the loan until he was told of it in 2004, saying then that he was "touched by this." Personal communication, December 14, 2004.

54. Interview with author, December 16, 2003.

55. Ibid.

56. Interview with author, January 20, 2004.

57. Ibid.

58. Personal communication, December 14, 2004.

59. Roger Lane, "Milliken's Dollar-a-Year Man a Political Crusader," *Detroit Free Press,* May 13, 1970, A8.

60. Personal communication, January 29, 2004.

61. Personal communication, November 14, 2003.

62. Interview with author, June 30, 2004.

63. Ibid.

64. Interview with author, March 15, 2004.

65. William G. Milliken to William Ryan, July 12, 1999, letter in author's possession.

66. Interview with author, March 25, 2004.

67. Interview with author, February 18, 2004.

68. Michael D. Moore, personal communication, January 5, 2004.

CHAPTER 11

1. William Ballenger, personal communication, January 8, 2005.

2. First Congregational Church of Traverse City, Michigan, "Tribute to James W. Milliken," 2.

3. Bob Voges, Associated Press, "Another Milliken: Old Timers Recall Late Senator with Respect and Affection," *Lansing State Journal,* April 15, 1971, H2.

4. Ibid.

5. Family scrapbook in author's possession.

6. Ibid.

7. Neil Staebler, *Out of the Smoke-Filled Room: A Story of Michigan Politics* (Ann Arbor: George Wahr, 1991), 29.

8. Jim Nichols, Associated Press, "Bill Milliken Isn't Likely to Change Much," *Flint Journal,* December 25, 1968, 21.

9. Clark Mollenhoff, *George Romney: Mormon in Politics* (New York: Meredith, 1968), 203.

10. Carolyn Stieber, *The Politics of Change in Michigan* (East Lansing: Michigan State University Press, 1970), 72.

11. Interview with author, May 7, 2004.

12. Robert Longstaff, "Conservatives Threaten to Split GOP," *Grand Rapids Press,* August 30, 1970, A16.

13. Ibid.

14. Bill Kulsea, "GOP Governors Listen to What Milliken Has to Say," *Grand Rapids Press,* June 26, 1971, A11.

15. Interview with author, July 10, 2003.

16. "Milliken on the Rise," *Detroit Free Press* editorial, December 16, 1970.

17. Hugh McDonald, "Milliken Wins Nixon Pledge of 'Millions' for Jobs in State," *Detroit News,* undated 1970 clipping in author's possession.

18. James Phelps interview with author, November 26, 2004. The recollection is borne out by a letter Milliken received from Nixon dated August 1, 1972, in which Nixon said that Ehrlichman would arrange the U.S. Justice Department's help in "obtaining a stay as you requested. Hopefully, in the long pull, we will achieve more permanent relief from these excessive busing orders." President Richard M. Nixon to Governor William G. Milliken, August 1, 1972, letter in author's possession.

19. Remer Tyson, "Agnew, Rebel Governors to Meet," *Detroit Free Press,* undated 1970 clipping in author's possession.

20. Ibid.

21. Interview with author, July 10, 2003.

22. Remer Tyson, "Cheering GOP Governors Back Agnew for Veep in '72," *Detroit Free Press,* November 19, 1971, A10.

23. Governor William G. Milliken to Vice President Spiro T. Agnew, June 9, 1972, copy in author's possession.

24. Vice President Spiro T. Agnew to Governor William G. Milliken, July 7, 1972, original in author's possession.

25. George Weeks, notes of Milliken and Republican governors' meeting with President Nixon, November 20, 1973, in author's possession.

26. McLaughlin, "Politician," 222.

27. Ibid., 223.

28. Ibid., 232.

29. Jack W. Germond, *Fat Man in a Middle Seat: Forty Years of Covering Politics* (New York: Random House, 2002), 116–17. Milliken aide George Weeks said the governor's office requested the meeting with the premier of Ontario in order to distance Milliken from Nixon.

30. Rowland Evans and Robert Novak, "Alienating the GOP Governors," *Washington Post,* December 5, 1974, A27.

31. "The Plight of the GOP," *Time,* August 23, 1976, 18–19.

32. Keith Dysart, quoted in Jon Bowermaster, *Governor: An Oral Biography of Robert D. Ray* (Ames: Iowa State University Press), 1987, 164.

33. McLaughlin, "Politician," 279.

34. Quoted in ibid., 284.

35. Original speech text in author's possession.

36. "Milliken's Historic Footnote," *Flint Journal* editorial, August 20, 1976.

37. William Kulsea, "Milliken Was at Odds with Dole in '71," *Kalamazoo Gazette,* August 20, 1976.

38. Governor William G. Milliken to Senator Robert Dole, June 4, 1971, copy in author's possession.

39. William G. Milliken, Executive Office news release, August 19, 1976, copy in author's possession.

40. See, for example, a Public Broadcasting Service transcript of a discussion of the 1976 presidential and vice presidential debates. http://www.pbs.org/newshour/debatingourdestiny/dod/1976-broadcast.html.

41. Jack W. Germond and Jules Witcover, ". . . But It's Moderately Unwell," *Detroit Free Press,* September 12, 1977, A7.

42. George H. W. Bush to William G. Milliken, September 15, 1973, copy in author's possession.

43. Interview with author, July 9, 2003.

44. Pat Shellenbarger, "Maverick in His Own Right," *Grand Rapids Press,* December 12, 2004, J4.

45. Gary F. Schuster, "Reagan Urges Milliken to Try for Senate Seat," *Detroit News,* October 11, 1981, A3.

46. Mike Norton, "Cabinet-Level Post for Milliken? Columnist Says 'Real Bond' Exists between Bush, Ex-governor," *Traverse City Record-Eagle,* undated 1988 clipping in author's possession.

47. Interview with author, August 20, 2003.

48. Interview with author, July 9, 2003.

49. Ibid.

50. Ibid.

51. Susan Taylor Martin, "Moderateman: Democrats to the Left of Him, Republicans to the Right of Him, Straight down the Middle Runs Our Governor," *Detroit News Sunday Magazine,* July 6, 1980.

52. Personal communication, January 14, 2005.

53. Joanna Firestone, "GOP Right Takes Aim at Milliken," *Detroit News,* November 15, 1981, B1.

54. Interview with author, July 10, 2003.

55. Bill O'Brien, "Milliken to GOP: I'm Embarrassed—Former GOP Governor Critical of Party's Campaign against Jennifer Granholm," *Traverse City Record-Eagle,* http://www.record-eagle.com/2002/oct/24millik.htm.

56. William G. Milliken, endorsement statement for presidential candidate John F. Kerry, October 17, 2004, copy in author's possession.

57. Eric Sharp, "This Republican Votes for Environment," *Detroit Free Press,* October 21, 2004.

58. Charlie Cain, "Milliken Endorses Kerry," *Detroit News,* October 19, 2004.

59. David Broder, "GOP Governors: Sane, Serene, Sincere," *Pensacola Journal,* December 4, 1978.

60. William G. Milliken, executive office statement issued August 11, 1971, in author's possession.

61. Personal communication, December 14, 2004.

62. Elly Peterson, personal communication, February 24, 2004.

63. Interview with author, November 26, 2003.

64. Interview with author, August 20, 2003.

65. Colleen F. Keyes, "Where Are the New Millikens?" *Detroit Free Press,* letter to the editor, undated clipping in author's possession.

CHAPTER 12

1. McLaughlin, "Politician," 220.

2. Governor William G. Milliken to Stanley T. Wallbank, January 30, 1974, copy in author's possession.

3. A. James Barnes, personal communication, January 5, 2004.

4. Ibid.

5. Executive office news release, March 7, 1974, in author's possession.

6. Remarks by Lieutenant Governor James H. Brickley, Ionia County Lincoln Day Dinner, April 16, 1974.

7. Interview with author, July 9, 2003.

8. A. James Barnes, personal communication, January 5, 2004.

9. Remarks by Governor William G. Milliken, Michigan Municipal League Annual Meeting, September 11, 1974.

10. Ibid.

11. Interview with author, May 18, 2005.

12. Interview with author, November 26, 2004.

13. McLaughlin, "Politician," 257.

14. Ibid.

15. Cited in Alvin P. Sanoff, "Double Reverse at the *Free Press,*" *Columbia Journalism Review* 14 (January–February 1975): 47.

16. McLaughlin, "Politician," 259.

17. William K. Stevens, "Detroit Paper Staff in Turmoil over Disputed Article," *New York Times,* November 27, 1974, C16.

18. McLaughlin, "Politician," 259.

19. Ibid., 260.

20. Sanoff, "Double Reverse at the *Free Press,*" 48.

21. Ibid.

22. Ibid., 49.

23. Stevens, "Detroit Paper Staff in Turmoil over Disputed Article."

24. Sanoff, "Double Reverse at the *Free Press,*" 50.

25. Ibid.

26. Ibid., 51.

27. Interview with author, May 18, 2005.

28. Robert Pisor, "For Milliken, a Personal Triumph: Victory Propels Him onto National GOP Scene," *Detroit News,* November 6, 1974, A1.

29. "A Tough Job Lies beyond Milliken's Impressive Win," *Detroit Free Press,* undated clipping in author's possession.

30. Pisor, "For Milliken, a Personal Triumph."

31. Stevens, "Detroit Paper Staff in Turmoil over Disputed Article."

32. Personal communication, March 3, 2004.

33. Skubick, *Off the Record,* 231.

34. Interview with author, July 9, 2003.

CHAPTER 13

1. Robert Longstaff, "Milliken Is Considering 1978 Bid for Reelection," *Grand Rapids Press,* March 7, 1976, B11.

2. Ibid.

3. Frank Angelo, "Milliken: Ready for New Ventures?" *Detroit Free Press,* December 28, 1977, A7.

4. Larry McDermott, "Gov. Milliken's '78 Campaign Underway?" *Benton Harbor Herald-Palladium,* September 9, 1977.

5. Ibid.

6. Personal communication, March 8, 2004.

7. McLaughlin, "Politician," 318.

8. Remer Tyson and Hugh McDiarmid, "The Making of a GOP 'Dream Ticket,'" *Detroit Free Press,* February 20, 1978, 1A.

9. Ibid., A11. Although the quote cited refers to Milliken's lack of desire to appear as a vice presidential candidate on the national Republican ticket, it could well be said of his overall outlook on holding federal office.

10. "The Notch Manifesto," memorandum to Governor William G. Milliken from Joyce Braithwaite and George Weeks, Oct. 10, 1977, copy in author's possession.

11. Remer Tyson and Hugh McDiarmid, "GOP Chiefs Say Milliken Needed Here," *Detroit Free Press,* September 19, 1977.

12. Tyson and McDiarmid, "The Making of a GOP 'Dream Ticket.'"

13. Joyce Braithwaite to Governor William G. Milliken, January 12, 1978, copy in author's possession.

14. Ibid.

15. Steven Thomas, personal communication, May 8, 2004.

16. Damman launched a bid for the U.S. Senate seat held by Griffin but pulled out after Griffin reversed his retirement plans.

17. Keith Molin, personal communication, March 7, 2004.

18. Skubick, *Off the Record,* 231.

19. Interview with author, July 9, 2003.

20. Interview with author, January 6, 2004.

21. The first was Helen Berthelot, who managed the 1954 gubernatorial campaign of Democrat G. Mennen Williams.

22. McDiarmid, "Braithwaite."

23. Hugh McDiarmid, "Milliken's Pitch for the Regular Guys," *Detroit Free Press,* April 11, 1978.

24. Richard Willing, "Milliken Swipes at Foe: Unfit to Lead, He Taunts," *Detroit News,* August 27, 1978.

25. Susan Taylor Martin, "Milliken, Fitzgerald Swap Jabs in Debate," *Detroit News,* September 26, 1978, A1, 7.

26. Keith Molin, personal communication, March 7, 2004.

27. William C. Kulsea, "Labor Leaders Like Milliken, Won't Campaign against Him," *Grand Rapids Press,* April 2, 1970, B7.

28. Hugh McDiarmid, "Blunt Bill Marshall vs. Hatchet Lady," *Detroit Free Press,* April 10, 1979.

29. Skubick, *Off the Record,* 369.

30. Hugh McDiarmid and Remer Tyson, "Blue Collars Called Cure for the GOP Blues," *Detroit Free Press,* September 18, 1977.

31. Personal communication, January 5, 2005. Braithwaite-Brickley spoke at Marshall's memorial service after the labor leader's death in 2000.

32. Skubick, *Off the Record,* 237.

33. McDiarmid, "Blunt Bill Marshall vs. Hatchet Lady."

34. Susan Fleming, "Women's Groups Fight Fitzgerald," *Detroit News,* September 21, 1978, A1.

35. Hugh McDiarmid, "Milliken Accused of Ducking Debates, Charge Denied," *Detroit Free Press,* October 17, 1978.

36. Susan Taylor Martin, "Milliken Blisters Fitzgerald's Ads," *Detroit News*, October 6, 1978, B1.

37. Personal communication, January 5, 2005.

38. Martin, "Milliken Blisters Fitzgerald's Ads."

39. Ibid.

40. "Governor Milliken: The Choice Is Overwhelming," sampling of 1978 newspaper endorsements of Milliken produced by the Milliken campaign, copy in author's possession.

41. "His Own Worst Enemy?" *Detroit News* editorial, October 8, 1978, A22.

42. Frederick P. Currier, "Fitzgerald Gains on Milliken, Race Becomes Neck and Neck," *Detroit News*, October 15, 1978, 1.

43. McLaughlin, "Politician," 338.

44. Interview with author, January 6, 2004.

45. Personal communication, February 26, 2005.

46. Karl Payne, "Ruppe Hits Milliken as Selfish," *Detroit News*, November 9, 1978, A1.

47. David Ashenfelter, "Milliken's Quiet Style Wins the Day," *Detroit News*, November 8, 1978, B1.

48. J. F. terHorst, "GOP Can Learn a Lot from Milliken's Style," *Detroit News*, November 12, 1978, A23.

49. Joyce Braithwaite-Brickley, personal communication, March 8, 2004.

50. William Dunn, "Yes, He's Nice, but . . .: Some Opinions from the Three Men Who Ran against Him," *Michigan: The Sunday Magazine of the Detroit News*, December 5, 1982, 56–57.

51. John E. Peterson, "Voters Call for Thriftier Government," *Detroit News*, November 9, 1978, A1.

CHAPTER 14

1. Hugh McDiarmid, "Governor Sees New Age of Limits: Inaugural Speech," *Detroit Free Press*, January 2, 1979, A1.

2. Ibid.

3. Ibid.

4. Roger Lane, "State Cash Bind May Force New Tax Increases," *Detroit Free Press*, undated 1971 clipping in author's possession.

5. Pat McCarthy, "State Must Chop $180 Million: Milliken Takes Cut," *Lansing State Journal*, February 14, 1975, A1.

6. James Phelps, interview with author, May 17, 2004.

7. Senate Fiscal Agency, "Michigan State Government Expenditures (millions of dollars)," chart, February 24, 2004, copy in author's possession.

8. California Budget Project, "Proposition 13: Its Impact on California and Implications for State and Local Finances," April 1997, http://www.cbp.org/1997/9704pr13.htm.

9. Skubick, *Off the Record*, 222.

10. The Headlee amendment specifically requires that from all of its taxes, fees, and other sources, the state's total revenue cannot exceed 9.49 percent of personal income in Michigan. If the state mandates that local governments provide any new or expanded programs, it must provide full funding. Local governments cannot add new

taxes or increase existing ones, or increase certain bonded indebtedness, without securing approval of the voters. Finally, the state cannot reduce the portion of its outlays that goes to local governments below 41.61 percent, its level when the amendment was passed. Mackinac Center for Public Policy, http://www.mackinac.org/article.asp?ID=5574.

11. Hugh McDiarmid and Julie Morris, "Milliken Endorses Tax-Limit Proposal," *Detroit Free Press,* August 5, 1978.

12. Ibid.

13. Skubick, *Off the Record,* 222.

14. Patrick L. Anderson, "Remembering Headlee: A Champion of the Taxpayer," *Detroit Free Press,* November 11, 2004.

15. Dawson Bell, "Tax Crusader Richard Headlee Dies at 74," *Detroit Free Press,* November 11, 2004.

16. Interview with author, July 9, 2003.

17. Skubick, *Off the Record,* 222.

18. "Executive Budget of the Governor for Fiscal Year 1980–1981," January 21, 1980, 1–2.

19. "Executive Budget of the Governor for Fiscal Year 1981–1982," January 26, 1981, 1.

20. "Executive Budget of the Governor for Fiscal Year 1982–1983," January 25, 1982, 1, emphasis in original.

21. Lucia Mouat, "Michigan Governor Sees Rays of Hope Piercing State's Economic Gloom," *Christian Science Monitor,* December 11, 1981, 14.

22. Ibid.

23. Stephen Monsma, personal communication, January 10, 2005.

24. George Weeks, notes of interview with Governor William G. Milliken, undated manuscript in author's possession.

25. "Televised Special Message on Economy and Budget," March 10, 1982, in *Addresses and Special Messages of Governor William G. Milliken,* 294–99.

26. "Milliken Must Swim Upstream," *Grand Rapids Press* editorial, March 14, 1982, E4.

27. "The Choice: Painful as It May Seem, a State Tax Increase Is the Best Alternative," *Detroit Free Press* editorial, March 11, 1982, 8A.

28. Senator Gilbert R. DiNello, "Lansing is Taking Taxpayers for a Ride," *Detroit Free Press,* April 22, 1982, A8.

29. David Kushma, "GOP Unveils a 'Wish List' of Cuts," *Detroit Free Press,* March 12, 1982, A3.

30. James N. Crutchfield and David Kushma, "Milliken, Others Will Give up One Week's Pay," *Detroit Free Press,* March 25, 1982, A3.

31. David Hoffman, "Mich. Jobless Rate Tops 16%, Nation at 9%," *Detroit Free Press,* April 3, 1982.

32. In the Michigan House, 56 votes are ordinarily required for passage of legislation, but due to vacancies in April 1982 the necessary margin for passage was just 54 votes.

33. Interview with author, January 6, 2004.

34. Ibid.

35. Ibid.

36. Jim Frisinger, "Geerlings the Subject of Capital Manhunt," *Muskegon Chronicle,* April 9, 1982, A2.

37. Interview with author, July 10, 2003.

38. Frisinger, "Geerlings the Subject of Capital Manhunt."

39. David Kushma, "Tax Hike Defeated," *Detroit Free Press,* April 29, 1982, A1.

40. Luther Keith and Pat Shellenbarger, "Milliken Gives up on Tax Increase," *Detroit News,* May 7, 1982, A3.

41. John Broder, "Milliken Fires Final Tax Salvo," *Detroit News,* May 10, 1982, A3.

42. "Tax Increase Fails to Stop Credit Crash," *Grand Rapids Press,* May 12, 1982, A2.

43. Ibid., 1A.

44. Bob Law to William G. Milliken, memorandum, May 18, 1982, William G. Milliken Papers, Box 621, Bentley Historical Library, University of Michigan.

45. "Deficit Doubles in New State Budget," *Detroit News,* December 2, 1982, C10.

46. Dinah Eng, "Milliken Gets Plea for Homeless," *Detroit News,* December 2, 1982, A3.

47. Ken Fireman, "'Human Emergency' Declared: Food, Shelter Program Announced by Milliken," *Detroit Free Press,* December 17, 1982, A1.

48. Robert Longstaff, "Republicans Fight over Milliken Record," *Grand Rapids Press,* undated 1982 clipping in author's possession.

49. Kenneth VerBurg and Charles Press, "He Was a Man of the Pros, Not the Pols," *Michigan: The Sunday Magazine of the Detroit News,* December 5, 1982, 48.

50. Ibid., 39.

51. Senate Fiscal Agency to State Senator Liz Brater, memorandum, February 23, 2005, copy in author's possession.

CHAPTER 15

1. Hugh McDiarmid, "Milliken Attacked in Candidate's Ad," *Detroit Free Press,* March 30, 1982, A5.

2. John Castine, "GOP Foes Gang up to Debate Brickley," *Detroit Free Press,* April 21, 1982, A3.

3. "For the Republicans—Brickley," *Detroit News* editorial, August 1, 1982, A10.

4. Joanna Firestone and Susan R. Pollack, "The Longest Campaign: Undecided Could Upset Leaders Blanchard, Brickley," *Detroit News,* August 8, 1982, A1.

5. "Blanchard vs. Headlee," *Detroit News* editorial, August 12, 1982, A18.

6. Susan R. Pollack, "Organization Key to Headlee Success," *Detroit News,* August 11, 1982, A2.

7. Skubick, *Off the Record,* 137.

8. "Sex Fires up State Politics," *Grand Rapids Press* editorial, September 5, 1982.

9. Sharon McGrayne, "State GOP Women in Bind," *Lansing State Journal,* undated clipping in author's possession.

10. Harry Cook, "Marchers at Capitol Urge Defeat of Bills to Curb Abortions," *Detroit Free Press,* March 26, 1982, A3.

11. James N. Crutchfield, "Headlee's Pitch to Women Misses Some," *Detroit Free Press,* September 15, 1982.

12. Hugh McDiarmid, "It's Time Feminists Spoke Out on Headlee," *Detroit Free Press,* September 19, 1982, A3.

13. Ibid.

14. Matt Beer and Kay Richards, "Yours Truly," *Detroit News,* September 23, 1982.

15. Sharon McGrayne, "Women's Issues Positions Divide Governor Camps," *Lansing State Journal,* September 26, 1982.

16. Susan R. Pollack, "'You're Right,' Headlee Tells Foes of Abortion," *Detroit News,* September 26, 1982, A10.

17. Barbara Walters, "Headlee Lashes Out at Brown during Campaign Stop Here," *Kalamazoo Gazette,* September 27, 1982.

18. Crutchfield, "Headlee's Pitch to Women Misses Some."

19. Hugh McDiarmid, "See Elly Back Jim—See Dick Go Nuts," *Detroit Free Press,* October 7, 1982.

20. Ibid.

21. James N. Crutchfield, "Women's Survey Rates Blanchard over Headlee," *Detroit Free Press,* October 20, 1982.

22. Sharon McGrayne, "Headlee 'Never Heard of Them,'" *Lansing State Journal,* October 20, 1982.

23. James N. Crutchfield, "Headlee: Pro-ERA Means Pro-Gay," *Detroit Free Press,* October 22, 1982, A1.

24. James N. Crutchfield, "Headlee Assailed for ERA Remark," *Detroit Free Press,* October 23, 1982.

25. Marvin R. Stempien, "ERA Sponsor Wants Apology," letter to the editor, *Ann Arbor News,* October 27, 1982.

26. Ibid.

27. Ken Fireman, "Headlee Hurting, Milliken Asserts," *Detroit Free Press,* October 28, 1982.

28. Joe Stroud, "Headlee Takes Governor's Race to New Low," *Detroit Free Press,* October 24, 1982.

29. Jane Myers, "Headlee's Foot-in-Mouth Fetish Is Getting Silly," *Ann Arbor News,* October 25, 1982.

30. Glen Macnow, "Ruppe, Headlee Trade Barbs at GOP Unity rally," *Detroit Free Press,* October 27, 1982.

31. James N. Crutchfield, "Headlee Claims Young Wants to Be the State's Mayor," *Detroit Free Press,* October 28, 1982.

32. Associated Press, "Brennan Says Milliken Era Was Too Long," *Detroit Free Press,* Saturday, October 29, 1982.

33. Hugh McDiarmid, "Michigan's GOP: How Sweet It Isn't," *Detroit Free Press,* October 31, 1982, A3.

34. Susan R. Pollack, "Contrasts Collide in Governor's Campaign," *Detroit News,* November 1, 1982, A3.

35. "Blanchard Defeats Headlee," *Grand Rapids Press,* November 3, 1982, A2.

36. Charlie Cain, "Appalling: From the Sidelines, Milliken Puts All the Blame on Headlee," *Detroit News,* November 3, 1982, A1.

37. "The GOP Disaster in Michigan," *Detroit News* editorial, November 4, 1982, A14.

38. Susan R. Pollack, "Battered State GOP Must Find a New Leader," *Detroit News,* November 4, 1982, A3.

39. David Waymire and Pamela Klein, "Headlee's Defeat Is Attributed to Social Issues," *Grand Rapids Press,* November 7, 1982, A12.

40. Robert Longstaff, "Headlee's Error: A Narrow View of Voter Issues," *Grand Rapids Press,* November 7, 1982, D4.

41. Hugh McDiarmid, "Milliken Comment: In a Word, 'Gross,'" *Detroit Free Press,* December 16, 1982, A3.

42. Ibid.

43. Hugh McDiarmid: "Milliken: Headlee Is Not a Carpenter," *Detroit Free Press,* August 18, 1983, A3.

44. Interview with author, July 9, 2003.

45. Skubick, *Off the Record,* 135.

46. After an appointment by Milliken to the state Supreme Court, Brickley later became chief justice.

47. Hugh McDiarmid, "The Lame Duck That Roared in Lansing," *Detroit Free Press,* December 12, 1982, A3.

48. "Brickley Sworn in as Supreme Court Justice," *Detroit News,* December 28, 1962, B6.

49. "Milliken 'Reappoints' 18 to Posts," *Detroit News,* December 21, 1982, A3.

50. Pat Shellenbarger, "Changeover: Milliken's Last Day Busy One," *Detroit News,* December 30, 1982, A1.

51. Ibid.

CHAPTER 16

1. William G. Milliken, interview with author, July 9, 2003.

2. Andrew H. Malcolm, "Ex-Gov. Milliken Finds Basic Changes Are Needed in Midwest," *New York Times,* January 19, 1983.

3. Ibid.

4. Deborah D. Wyatt, "Milliken Settles In: Out of the Limelight, Not out of the Issues," *Traverse: The Magazine,* August 1983, 34.

5. Carol Althouse, "Conversations: William Milliken after the Governorship," *Detroit* (magazine of the *Detroit Free Press*), November 22, 1987, 6.

6. Ibid., 33.

7. Ted Roelofs, "William Milliken, at Ease," *Grand Rapids Press* Sunday magazine, March 17, 1985, 3.

8. "Milliken Staff Reunion, November 7, 1987," invitation in author's possession.

9. Dale Arnold, interview with author, February 11, 2004.

10. Jack Lessenberry, "Milliken Never Afraid of a 'Principled Stand,'" *Traverse City Record-Eagle,* September 6, 2002, F9.

11. Bill Thomas, "Too Bad There Aren't More Like Milliken," *Traverse City Record-Eagle,* February 2, 2003.

12. Associated Press, "Milliken Steps up to Back Proposal," *Traverse City Record-Eagle,* October 15, 1987.

13. "Michigan: Anti-assisted Suicide Campaign Begins," http://www.euthana sia.com/propb2.html.

14. Michigan Department of State, 1998 Official Election Results, http://miboecfr .nicusa.com/election/results/98gen/90000002.html.

15. William G. Milliken, "Milliken: State Proposal Goes Too Far," *Detroit Free Press,* October 21, 2000.

16. Michigan Department of State, 2000 Official Election Results, http://mibo ecfr.nicusa.com/election/results/00gen/90000002.html.

17. "Milliken Assails GOP Tactics: Ex-Governor Labels Court Ads 'Shocking,'" *Detroit Free Press,* October 30, 2000.

18. "Supreme Shame," *Detroit Free Press* editorial, October 30, 2000.

19. "Lawsuit Limits? Two Rulings Signal Trouble for Environmental Law," *Detroit Free Press* editorial, August 17, 2004, http://www.freep.com/voices/editori-als/emepa17_20040817.htm.

20. James Prichard, Associated Press, "ACLU Fights Crime Database," *Detroit Free Press,* August 4, 2004.

21. "Privacy Intruder: Michigan Correctly Drops out of Matrix System," *Detroit Free Press,* March 15, 2005, http://www.freep.com/voices/editorials/ematrix15e_ 20050315.htm.

22. Interview with author, July 9, 2003.

23. Ibid.

24. William G. Milliken, "Mandatory Minimum Drug Bills Need Reform," *Traverse City Record-Eagle,* September 13, 2002.

25. Gary Heinlein, "Milliken: Drug Lifer Law Wrong," *Detroit News,* February 18, 1998, A1.

26. William G. Milliken, "It's Time to Repeal Michigan's Drug Lifer Law," *Detroit Free Press,* undated newspaper clipping in author's possession.

27. Hugh McDiarmid, "It's Time to Right the Wrong Done by Michigan's Drug-lifer Law," *Detroit Free Press,* February 19, 1998.

28. Pat Shellenbarger, "Maverick in His Own Right," *Grand Rapids Press,* December 12, 2004, J4; "Celebrating Success in Michigan," FAMMGRAM (newsletter of Families against Mandatory Minimums), winter 2003, 1.

29. "Honoring Justice, Building the Future," remarks by William G. Milliken, FAMM dinner, October 10, 2003, copy in author's possession.

30. Shellenbarger, "Maverick in His Own Right."

31. Ibid.

32. Letter from Governor and Mrs. Milliken in support of the Battered Women's Clemency Project, http://www.umich.edu/~clemency/milliken.html.

33. George Weeks, "GOP Meeting Hears Echo of Milliken Years," *Detroit News,* May 1, 1990, F3.

34. Ibid.

35. Hugh McDiarmid, "Young's Tongue Back in Top Form," *Detroit Free Press,* May 18, 1986, page A3.

36. Thomas BeVier, "On the Millikens' Day, There's Only One Party," *Detroit News,* August 28, 1988, B1.

37. Remarks of William G. Milliken, December 5, 1997, copy in author's possession.

38. George Weeks, "Elaine Milliken," obituary, *Detroit News,* October 7, 1993.

39. Interview with author, July 9, 2003.

40. Interview with author, August 20, 2003.

41. Interview with author, September 23, 2003.

42. Interview with author, May 26, 2005.

43. Interview with author, September 18, 2005.

44. William G. Milliken, note to file; note from Governor James J. Blanchard, in author's possession.

45. Interview with author, July 10, 2003.

46. Tim Skubick, "Milliken Was a Master of Compromise," *Lansing State Journal,* November 26, 1993, A4.

47. Interview with author, February 9, 2005.

48. Hugh McDiarmid, "GOP Considers Life after Engler," *Detroit Free Press,* April 24, 1990.

49. Chris Andrews, "Moderate Republican to Help Granholm," *Lansing State Journal,* January 15, 2003, B2.

50. Interview with author, June 30, 2004.

51. Ibid.

52. Ibid.

53. John Stewart, interview with author, March 18, 2004.

54. William G. Milliken to State Representative John Stewart, November 17, 2003, copy in author's possession.

55. John Stewart, interview with author, March 18, 2004.

56. Peter Kobrak, "Michigan," in *The Political Life of the American States,* edited by Alan Rosenthal and Maureen Moakley (New York: Praeger, 1984), 115.

57. Ibid., 112.

58. Skubick, *Off the Record,* 134.

59. Christine Todd Whitman, *It's My Party, Too: The Battle for the Heart of the GOP and the Future of America* (New York: Penguin, 2005), 30.

60. Ibid., 12.

61. Interview with author, August 19, 2004.

62. Theodore Roszak, "Where Did the Middle Go? How Polarized Politics and a Radical GOP Have Put a Chill on Measured Debate," originally published in the *San Francisco Chronicle,* October 10, 2004, accessed at http://www.commondreams.org/views04/1012–22.htm.

63. Personal communication, January 31, 2005.

64. Interview with author, May 18, 2005.

65. Joe H. Stroud, "A Ritual of Ice in Michigan's North," *Detroit Free Press,* March 10, 1985, B2.

INDEX

Milliken, William G. (*continued*)
  integrity in office of, 153–54
  lieutenant governor
    candidacy for in 1964, 49–54
    election as in 1964, 55
    performance as, 56–60
  meeting and courtship of Helen Wall-
    bank by, 24, 30
  mental health policies of, 114–15
  "nice-guy" image of, 69, 228
  relations of with African-Americans,
    6, 45, 61, 109–10, 119–21, 154, 205
  relations of with Engler, John, 246–47
  relations of with Headlee, Richard,
    225, 229–30
  relations of with news media, 72–73
  relations of with Republican Party,
    42–44, 164–80, 237, 239, 243,
    248–49
  relations of with Romney, George,
    47, 54, 57–59, 75
  relations of with Young, Coleman A.,
    6, 121–28, 198
  religious (private) schools, legislation
    of, 48, 51, 66–67
  religious views of, 26
  retirement from office of, 2–8
  retirement years of, 234–54
  sense of humor of, 154–55
  and state business climate, 2
  temper of, 147–49
  urban policies of, 68–69
  views on lobbyists of, 49
  Washington, D.C., ambitions of,
    49
  wedding of, 30
  and women's rights, 140, 201–2
  World War II service of, 23–30, 130
Milliken, William Jr., son of William G.
  and Helen Milliken, 5, 36, 37, 51,
  55–56, 136, 162, 244
Minnema, John, state senator and opponent of William Milliken in 1960,
  39–40
Molin, Keith, 51, 80, 195, 198–99
Monsma, Stephen, 211
Moore, Michael D., 151

Moskal, Jerry, 3
Murphy, Frank, governor of Michigan,
  14

Natural Resources, Michigan Department of, 87, 91–92, 102
Nixon, Richard M., 62, 63, 64, 152, 167,
  168, 171, 172, 183, 185
nuclear waste storage proposal for
  Michigan, 94–95

Ochberg, Frank, 17

Parks, Chris, 4
Patterson, L. Brooks, Oakland County
  Executive, prosecutor, 2, 220
PBB contamination of Michigan,
  97–101, 201–2
Peterson, Elly, 50, 62, 71, 119, 139, 179,
  224, 225
Phelps, James, 106, 107, 111–14, 153, 170,
  207
phosphorus laundry detergent limita-
  tion, 90–91
Pigeon River Country State Forest,
  92–94
Pollack, Lana, state senator, 143, 203
Pratt, Stanley, 160–61
Project Sanguine (also known as Project
  Seafarer and ELF), 95–97

Reagan, Ronald, U.S. president and
  governor of California, 6, 139, 168,
  173, 174, 175, 179, 236
Reizen, Maurice, 160
Republican party
  of Grand Traverse County, 13, 36
  history of in Michigan, 38–39
Riegle, Donald, U.S. senator and member of U.S. House of Representatives, 2, 76, 179
Riley, Dorothy Comstock, Michigan
  supreme court justice, 232
Roe, Jerry, 179
Romney, George, governor of Michigan,
  50, 54–55, 64–65, 166, 226, 230
  appointment of as U.S. secretary of